DOING YOUR OWN RESEARCH

South Essex College
Further & Higher Education, Thurrock Campus
Woodview Grays Essex RM16 2YR
Tel: 01375 391199 Fax: 01375 373356
Minicom: 01375 362740

Doing Your Own Research

Basic Descriptive Research
in the Social Sciences and Humanities

Eileen Kane

Marion Boyars
London & New York

First published in Great Britain and the United States in 1985 by
Marion Boyars Publishers
24 Lacy Road, London SW15 1NL
237 East 39th Street, New York, N.Y. 10016

Reprinted in 1987, 1990, 1991, 1993, 1995

Distributed in Australia and New Zealand by Peribo Pty Ltd
58 Beaumont Road, Mount Kuring-gai, NSW 2080

British Library Cataloguing in Publication Data
Kane, Eileen
   Doing your own research: basic descriptive research in the social sciences and
   humanities.
   1. Social sciences—Methodology.   I. Title.
   300'.72   H61

Library of Congress Cataloging in Publication Data
Kane, Eileen
   Doing your own research
   Bibliography: p.
   Includes index.
   1. Social sciences—Research—Methodology
   2. Humanities—Research—Methodology.   I. Title.
   H62.K275   1985   300'72   84–28582

ISB N 0–7145–2843–9 Paperback

First published in 1984. Turoe Press, Dublin, Ireland

Printed and bound in Great Britain by Itchen Printers Ltd, Southampton

Contents

PART THREE: PREPARING THE RESULTS

FIGURES

Preface and Acknowledgments

THIS IS a book for people with little or no experience of social research. It will take you through all the stages of a descriptive research project, step-by-step, from developing the basic idea to collecting the material and producing the final paper. It can be used not only by university and secondary-level students, but also by the average adult in the community who would like to explore a situation or subject and produce a respectable piece of research. It covers both 'field' research and library sources. I emphasise the importance of descriptive research because while computer technology has revolutionised the analysis of social research, the collection of meaningful, accurate data is still the foundation of good research.

My aim is to demystify the basic research process. Knowing how to get information is a source of power in modern society. The satisfaction of finding out for oneself and making a contribution to knowledge is a right and responsibility which should be enjoyed by everyone who is prepared to take it.

The Research Outline approach presented in Chapters II and III is the result of twenty years of classroom experimentation and community experience, and has been used successfully by Ph.D. students and fourteen-year-olds. It helps to overcome a common problem which is neglected by most books on research: 'What information do I need to collect?' The Research Outline can be applied to research in most fields of study. The research techniques presented here for gathering information reflect the author's and contributors' backgrounds in anthropology and sociology, but can be applied to a wide range of research projects in the social sciences and humanities.

Many people have helped me in the preparation of this book, especially my students over the years, whose research interests have presented so many challenges; Professor Conor K. Ward of University College, Dublin, who gave me invaluable comments and encouragement; Ellen Murphy of the Library of Congress, for her work on Chapter IX; Catherine Rose of Turoe Press for her support and confidence; Hester Nettles and Patrice Kane for their careful typing, and Janet Martin of Turoe Press for her editing and Emer O'Neill for her proofreading. I am particularly grateful to St Patrick's College, Maynooth and to Professor Liam Ryan for arranging the leave of absence which enabled me to complete the book.

Finally, I would like to thank my husband, Everett Nathan, for all the practical help and encouragement which he gave me. Because of him, I shall always remember with pleasure the time I spent writing this book.

Eileen Kane
Dublin, 1983

To Edward A. Kennard,
Teacher, scholar and friend.

And to my mother
Margaret Kane.

Introduction

A. Why Learn to Do Research?

MANY people are almost as reluctant to undertake a piece of real research as they might be to do brain surgery. Yet doing research involves steps and skills which are no more complicated than many of the things which the average person can do easily, such as navigating from one side of the city to another, keeping a household budget, playing bridge or gardening.

Why should you know how to do research? One reason is that you are just interested in something, and want to find out more about it. But you may have more practical reasons. You may be doing a course or studying for a degree which requires a paper or thesis. Perhaps the group or association to which you belong needs more information on a subject so that it can make its services more useful, or so it can present a good case to the public or the government. Your business may need to reorganise a department or find out what people think about one of its products. Can you do the research yourself?

Often, you can. In the case where you cannot, you will save time, and probably money, and maintain more control over the research by discovering what kinds of things you need to know and *what kind of help you need.*

A final reason for knowing how to do research is that you will be better able to weigh the value of other people's research. We are all 'consumers' of research, and in almost no other area of consumerism are we less able to distinguish good quality from poor quality. We are bombarded daily with newspaper headlines such as —

Working mothers more satisfied, claims researcher
Dog lovers more emotionally balanced, study says
Research shows drinkers more prone to heart trouble

Rarely do we ask what the researcher means by 'working mothers', 'satisfied', 'dog lovers', 'emotionally balanced', 'drinkers', 'heart trouble'. What questions was he or she asking? Are the conclusions really based on research, or has the 'research' just been used as stuffing for a hobbyhorse?

Most people are terrified by the idea of doing research. 'You have to go to university to do research'; or, 'only academics and professional researchers can do research', they think. Many academics, however, will admit that although they were exposed to a lot of research, they were never really taught how to do a piece of research starting with the original idea and finishing with the final paper; they had to learn the process themselves.

Many first-time researchers run into all kinds of problems. They do not know where to begin; they do not know how long it will take; they use a particular research technique not because it is the best one for their problem, but because it is the one they know best, or the only one they know. They do not know how to record the information, unless they are using simple questionnaire forms. They do not know when they are finished – all they know is that they allowed themselves, or were allowed, two months to do the research and since the two months are up, they must be done. They are unable to analyse their material properly because they have it on hundreds of dog-eared bits of paper spread all over the floor, in which case they cram it all in a box and avoid the room containing the box.

Even if they escape these problems first timers can find that what they collect does not match the title. Then they have to figure out what they do have, and find a title to justify it. They may have had to invent a whole new field of human knowledge to correspond to their meanderings through a range of topics which had no logical connection except for the fact that they accidentally happened to study them.

Most people who have already done a study or a thesis will recognise these problems – many, in fact, live in the guilty secret belief that they are the only people to whom this has ever happened.

This book is about these problems. It will help you to answer the questions 'How do I begin? What do I collect? How? What do I do with it after I've collected it? How do I write it up?'

B. What is Research?

You do research every day. If you are trying to get from one place in the city to another by bus and have never made the trip before, what do you do? You ask someone who has made the trip, or you get a route and timetable booklet, or you telephone the bus company. If you are very cautious, you may do all three. Suppose you then go to the bus stop and find that the Number 44 never seems to pass there, despite what everyone says. You re-check to make sure you got it right. That is just horse sense, you say. It is also research.

So the basic elements and procedures of research are already there in your everyday activities. Of course, you may say, but arranging to catch a bus isn't scientific. That is the first point to get clear; science is not a thing, a laboratory, a piece of equipment, or a field of study. Science is a *way of doing things*, a *way of looking at things*. There is a scientific way of finding the Number 44 bus and a non-scientific way. The non-scientific way is to telephone the gas company or to run after every bus on the road until you find a 44. Science is (a) the getting of systematic and reliable knowledge about any aspect of the universe, carried out by means of observations, and (b) the development of means for interrelating and explaining your observations (Pelto 1970:29). You were doing (a) when you were tracking down the Number 44 bus. If, after getting all the information, you then concluded 'The Number 44 doesn't run on time' and after finding this true of all buses, said 'Buses are an unreliable means of transport' you were on your way to doing (b). We will look at this again later on.

You already have the beginnings of basic scientific research approaches and skills. What you need to do is to organise them and put them to work on what you want to know.

C. Descriptive research and explanatory research

The first step in any research is to find out what is happening or what has happened. This involves describing attitudes, behaviours, or conditions, and is called *descriptive research*. A second step, analysing why these attitudes, behaviours or conditions occur is called *explanatory research*. It can be no better than the descriptive data upon which it is based. In recent decades, explanatory research has been greatly aided by the use of computers and increasingly sophisticated computer packages, but we are still left with the first step – how do we get good descriptive information, either to use for its own sake, or as a basis for explanatory research? This book concentrates on improving the quality of descriptive research.

The following chart illustrates the order for developing your research, from the initial rough idea to the final paper. The chapters in the book follow this line of development.

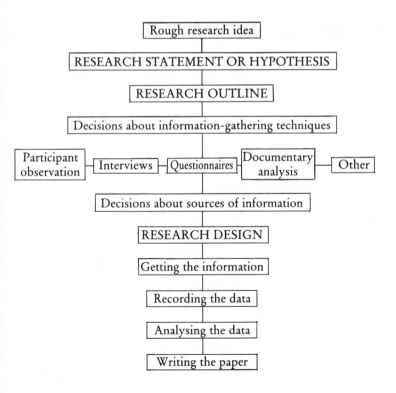

A word of warning about Chapter Two, *The Research Statement,* and Chapter Three, *The Research Outline and the Research Design.* The process presented in these is not difficult but it is tedious and time-consuming when you apply it for the first time. Halfway through, you may wonder why you ever bothered. However, when this phase of the research process is completed in an actual project, you can usually cheer yourself up with the thought that you are probably about one-third of the way finished with your research.

PART ONE

What Do You Want to Know?

I. The Research Statement

THE most difficult hurdle to overcome in doing research is not in learning the techniques or doing the actual work or even writing the report. The biggest obstacle, surprisingly, lies in figuring out what you want to know. Two problems are very common —

• Choosing a topic which is too broad. Most people start with an idea which is much too big. I have had the following type of conversation with university students dozens of times.

> Student: I've come about my research problem. I know what I want to study.
> Me: What is it?
> Student: Drugs.
> Me: What is it about drugs that you want to study?
> Student: Oh, just drugs, like. I've always been sort of interested in drugs, you know what I mean?

The topic 'drugs', of course, includes medicinal drugs; it can also include the various types of drugs, their characteristics, the medical, pyschological, social and economic effects of each type of drug on the user, his family and society; the causes of drug-taking, the characteristics of drug-takers, the legal aspects of drug control, the distribution of drugs, the methods of drug-taking, to mention but a few aspects, for all people taking any drug anywhere in the world. That is what you let yourself in for if you decide to study something as big as 'drugs'.

By questioning the would-be researcher, one can usually discover that he has no intention of covering all these topics; what he really wants to know is why some teenagers in his own neighbourhood take drugs illegally and some do not. That topic is not the same as 'drugs'.

• 'Dressing up' a topic. People often feel they have to 'dress' their subject to make it sound more scientific. Recently, a student told me that she wanted to study 'The Viability of the Nuclear Versus the Extended Family'.

'What exactly do you mean by that?' I asked.

'Well, I can't put it in so many words, but I can show you. I've got about twenty pages written on it already.'

She had twenty pages written on a subject she could not put into so many words.

Rule one. If you cannot put it into so many words (or other symbols, in some cases), you cannot study it.

So we begin again. 'What do you mean, "versus"'? In what sense?

'I don't know. I guess I want to study role failure in the nuclear family.'

After about ten minutes of probing, we got through the fancy dressing, and found out that she did indeed have a basic idea: her father had died recently, and she wanted to know what happened to families like hers, psychologically, when one parent died. She was so impressed by pseudo-science that she was actually calling a parent's death 'role failure'.

If I asked you right now what you wanted to study, you would probably give me a whopper of a topic: juvenile deliquency, mental illness, road safety, unmarried mothers, poverty, television violence, alcoholism, community development, pollution, advertising, sub-standard housing, your local area, industrialisation, Silken Thomas, company performance, the Montessori method. On the other hand, if you have the idea that research, to be research, must be festooned with impressive 'academic'-sounding words, you may have come up with something like 'The Semantic Viability of Empathy in the Gestalt of Social Interaction'. By the time you have worked up a title like that, it is probably closer to you than your own child, but wrench it from your heart.

The first thing to do is take a running jump at it and write the following single sentence: I want to study (or find out about) .... (Finish the sentence).

Now look at it. Supposing you wrote 'juvenile delinquency' even after I warned you. There are a lot of aspects of juvenile delinquency.

- What is juvenile delinquency? Is, for example, a thirteen-year-old murderer a juvenile delinquent? What do you mean by juvenile delinquency?
- Who are juvenile delinquents? Will you cover only those who have been caught? Only those convicted? Only those sentenced? Both sexes? Everyone between seven and the legal age? Are you interested in their characteristics, such as family, residence, social class, ethnic group, education? Who interacts with them – 'processing' them through the legal system? Who treats them?
- Where are they? Will you cover all juvenile delinquents, everywhere? Where are they treated? Where do they commit their crimes?
- Are you going to study how they become juvenile delinquents? How are they dealt with once they are apprehended? How do they respond to treatment?

Obviously you cannot study all of this. Even if you have a team of 100, and twenty-five years to do the study, you would miss at least one Siberian or Aborigine teenager. There is, in fact, little point in, and no possibility of, covering everything listed above. But if you stick to the topic 'juvenile delinquency' you will have to.

As you answered the questions above, you probably began to sort out what you had in the back of your mind when you said 'juvenile delinquency'. You can probably now say to yourself 'I only mean those young people who have been convicted' or 'I only want to know if certain circumstances are related to delinquency'.

So we begin again. Perhaps you have a theory that juvenile delinquents are not what they used to be — that is, that the characteristics of juvenile delinquents are changing. You may wonder whether more children from higher income homes are committing crimes today, and whether more girls are becoming involved. It is possible that the average age of juvenile delinquents has declined, as well.

Your first job is to get all of this into one sentence, if possible: *Changing Characteristics of Juvenile Delinquents* is a good description. However, it is still too big. First of all, you are not going to study all the juvenile delinquents in the world. You can cut down your numbers in several ways:

1. You can concentrate on a certain age range, such as teenagers 13-18 years old: *Changing Characteristics of Juvenile Delinquents Aged 13-18 Years.*

2. You can be more specific about what you mean by 'juvenile delinquents'. Taken at its broadest, a juvenile delinquent could be an eight-year old boy who throws a rock through a neighbour's window. So first you have to decide what you mean by juvenile delinquency.

You can take a professional definition from the literature of sociology, psychology, criminology, etc, or a legal definition, or you can settle on one of your own. If you are a student of sociology, for example, you may want to take a sociological perspective into account when framing your definition: for example, 'social acts of juveniles that are deemed legally or socially deviant' and then try to phrase it more specifically. This definition would allow you to include people who are thought by 'society' to be delinquent, but who have never been officially charged. In most places, juvenile offenders who are charged usually fall into one of two categories: 'status offenders' which means the juvenile has committed an act which, if committed by an adult, would not be an offence – such as constant refusal to obey parents, or running away from home. The second category consists of 'delinquents', that is, juveniles who have committed acts which are considered criminal, regardless of the age of the offender – such as murder or theft. You may wish to omit status offenders and restrict your definition to a legal one – any person under eighteen who has committed a crime – but then you have the problem of including people who were never caught or charged. So you may end up with 'any person under eighteen who has been officially convicted of having committed a crime'. Now we have *Changing Characteristics of Convicted Juvenile Delinquents Aged 13-18 Years.*

However you reach a definition, you must get one which is clear and which can be studied. *Failure to define major research words is probably the most important mistake made by researchers.* If you do not settle on a clear definition, you will be cheating both yourself and anyone who reads your

study. You will also find that as your work progresses, you will be changing the definition so gradually that you will not even notice it happening.
People and objects will begin to wander in and out of your study, and you
will lose sight of what you set out to do. The ragbag you finally assemble at
the end of your research will have little bearing on your supposed subject.

When you do settle on a definition, think for a moment about the following points:

- Are the kinds of people (or objects or processes) which you originally
  wanted to study still in the study, according to your definition? Who is
  left out? According to our definition of juvenile delinquency, boys who
  constantly harass old ladies by breaking their windows, but who are
  never caught, are left out. If that does not suit you, broaden the definition.
- Are there people (objects, processes) now covered in the study in whom
  you are not particularly interested? Defining juvenile delinquency as
  'social acts that are deemed legally or socially deviant' could involve the
  inclusion of the boy down the street who eats his goldfish, or who
  teaches 'bad' words to all the younger children in the neighbourhood. If
  you do not want them in the study, narrow the definition.
- Will your definition involve you in looking for material which you may
  not be able to find? Defining a juvenile delinquent as 'anyone under
  eighteen who has committed a crime' may require you to go around
  detecting crimes, if some of the delinquents have never been caught.
- Have you now broadened/narrowed your definition to the point where
  it is ridiculous, includes everyone/no one, or has no interest for you or
  anyone else?

3. You can cut down numbers when you decide where you want to do this
study – perhaps in your home town, or perhaps you might restrict it even
more to juvenile delinquents who have passed through one particular
institution: *Changing Characteristics of Juvenile Delinquents Aged 13-18
Years in* ....

If you choose one particular institution, of course, the problem of a
definition of juvenile delinquency may be solved for you; you can decide, if
it is appropriate, that all the young people who are committed to the centre
are, for purposes of your study 'juvenile delinquents'. Of course, if the
young people who pass through St Michael's are a mixed bag, some convicted, some there because they are homeless or abused, then you will still
need a definition of juvenile delinquency in order to decide which of the
youths to study and which to leave out. The same is true if you use your
home town instead of a juvenile delinquent centre – you need a definition
which allows you to single out some youths for study while ignoring
others.[1] Anyway, if all goes well, you now have *Changing Characteristics*

---

[1] This may sound as if you are defining juvenile delinquency in order to cut down your
numbers. Certainly, a definition does allow you to do that, and is essential, in fact, for
doing so. However, you also develop a definition for many other reasons: to test its

of Convicted Juvenile Delinquents Aged 13-18 Years in St Michael's Correctional Institution.

There are a number of other ways in which you can restrict your study of juvenile delinquents – by studying only one sex, or those who have committed particular crimes, or by length of sentence. A choice based on any of these would depend on the way you look at delinquency and what you hope to find out.

For purposes of our hypothesis, that the characteristics of juvenile delinquents are changing, we need both sexes, and we want to include all crimes and lengths of sentences in order to see if these have changed over time.

We now have to look at the other major words in the Research Statement, to see if we want to make them more scientific. Remember, if you use a very broad, general word, you are responsible for studying all of its aspects.

So let us see if we want to make 'characteristics' more specific. If we leave it as it is, we will be expected to study all characteristics of juvenile delinquents – physical, social, emotional, economic, attitudinal, etc. Are we really interested in the heights or dental characteristics of juvenile delinquents? It depends on what your original theory or hypothesis was – ask yourself if, in the back of your mind, one of the changing characteristics which you had a hunch about was improvement in the health of juvenile delinquents? Assuming we are only interested in changes in class, types of crime committed, education, age and sex, if those were all social characteristics, we could redefine our topic to 'Changes in Selected Social Characteristics of Convicted Juvenile Delinquents aged 13-18 Years in St Michael's Correctional Institution' – 'selected' since we are not studying all social characteristics – but since the characteristics we have selected are not all social, we will simply call it *Changes in Selected Characteristics of Convicted Juvenile Delinquents Aged 13-18 Years in St Michael's Correctional Institution'.*

'Changes' is the last major word left in our original research statement. There are many ways to study changes. You may want to plot the changes over time, degree by degree, or you may want to do a sort of 'before and after' look. Suppose your original theory was based on a notion that the characteristics of juvenile delinquents have changed since you were young. The simplest thing to do then is to compare the characteristics of juvenile delinquents in St Michael's this year with those in the centre in, say, the year 1950, or whenever you were young. If St Michael's did not exist then, you may want to choose another institution or group of juvenile delinquents which allows you to make as close a comparison as possible. We now have *Changes (1950/1980) in Selected Characteristics of Convicted Juvenile Delinquents aged 13-18 years in St Michael's Correctional Institution'.*

---

usefulness or validity, or to compare your findings with others who have used the same definition, for example.

Please bear in mind that this statement is not the title of your study, although you may use it as your title if you like. (On the other hand, you may give your study any title that strikes your fancy – 'Social Dynamite', 'Delinquents Old and New' or whatever.) What we have been working on in this section is your *Research Statement*. This is the core of your research, and the basis for the next step in your work, the Research Outline.

To summarise, these are the steps:

1. Choose your topic and decide what aspect of it you wish to study. Do this through any method which works for you. One method is to do what I did on page 16 and ask 'Who?', 'What?' 'Where?', 'When?', 'Why?', 'How?' in relation to your topic. The answers reflect aspects of the topic. (Not all of these questions are appropriate to every topic. Don't force it. It is only a simplified method to help you.)

2. State what you want to study in one sentence.[2]

3. Look at every word. Define each noun, verb, adjective and adverb, if necessary. (Depressed prisoners fight more frequently – 'depressed', 'prisoners', 'fight', and 'more frequently' each have to be defined.) Restrict the scope of each word as much as possible without interfering with what you hope to study. Be particularly careful about words which people assume have common meanings. 'Successful', 'frequent', 'roadworthy', 'elderly', 'satisfaction' are examples. You can define these any way you think useful, but do define them, and then keep to the definition all through your research, unless something happens part way through your research which indicates that your definition is so irrelevant or off-base that you have to redefine it and start again. In some cases, it is not so much a question of a formal definition as a decision as to what you will take as items or people qualifying for inclusion in your study. For example, you may say 'I will define a refrigerator as "satisfactory" if the purchaser has not replaced it or sought repairs to it within one year after purchase'. Not everyone will agree with you, but as long as you make it very clear what your criteria for being 'satisfactory' are, you can select any that you think appropriate.

4. Rewrite your sentence, taking into account all the decisions you made in step three. *This is your Research Statement.*

---

[2] Most people tend to believe that *their* research is too complex to be expressed in a single sentence. Obviously not all research can be encapsulated in one sentence, but the discipline of trying to do so is useful for clarifying one's aims and thinking, and will probably work. If it takes more than one sentence, you may have a multi-phase problem which is going to require a more extensive research effort than you may have intended; on the other hand, you may not have thought your problem out clearly enough.

II. The Research Outline and the Research Design: Your 'Map'

A. The Research Outline

THE NEXT step in the research process is to take the Research Statement, which we developed in the last chapter, and use it to make a *Research Outline*. This tells you what information you need to collect. Failing to prepare a Research Outline is like going on a scavenger hunt without a list. It is a part of the research process about which you rarely hear anything, but it is essential. This and the preceding chapter, therefore, are the most important in this book. You should carefully work out both the Research Outline examples which I give below.

The simplest way to make the Research Outline is to take each major word or phrase in your Research Statement, and list it under all the sub-points which that word could logically contain. For instance —

- *Group Recreational Facilities* (I) for *Children* (II) in *Monkstown* (III).
- *Problems* (I) of *Children* (II) in *Single-Parent Families* (III).
- *Work Productivity* (I) by *Selected Factors* (II) in *Youngstown Factories* (III).
- *Relationships* (I) between *Immigrant Families* (II) and *Native Families* (III) in a *British Suburb* (IV).
- *Attitudes* (I) of *Doctors* (II) towards *Midwives* (III) and *Home Births* (IV).

The major words and phrases which I have numbered are, in fact, *variables*. A variable is an attribute or characteristic which can vary. When referring to people, it is a value which can take different forms in different people. Age, for example, is a variable, as are sex, religious beliefs, location, ethnicity, class, education, height, marital status, work productivity, occupation, migration intentions and so forth.

In this chapter, we will make a Research Outline from the Research Statement, *Changes (1950/1980) in Selected Characteristics of Convicted Juvenile Delinquents aged 13-18 Years in St Michael's Correctional Institution*, which we developed in the first chapter. But first, here is a practice example.

A major problem in many communities in the west of Ireland has been a declining population owing to migration of young people. Recent development and industrial programmes may be encouraging them to remain at home. A research project which examined the migration intentions of secondary school students in the west, or, more modestly, in a particular local area, might be useful.

- *Migration Intentions* (I) of *Secondary School Students* (II) in *Ballyglass* (III).

This Research Statement has three major words or phrases. We can begin with any one of them. The order does not matter. Two are particularly easy; (II) is a 'people' point, and (III) is a 'place' point. Almost every Research Statement has a 'people' or 'place' point, or both, and the practice you get here will be widely applicable.

Let us begin, then with point II, 'Secondary School Students'. To make an outline for this or any other point, simply list all the components or characteristics which the word or phrase could have; in other words, break it down into all its possible parts. People, as people, automatically have certain features and characteristics; age, sex, height, weight, marital status, residence, education, occupation, health, and so on. Secondary school students, as people, have all those characteristics, plus some special ones peculiar to them as students; for instance, year in school, major subjects of study, performance or record, extracurricular interests. Make a list of all the attributes you can think of for people:

> age, sex, race or ethnic group, socioeconomic group, height, weight, hair colour, marital status, education, residence, occupation, number of children, political affiliation.

Some of these are probably irrelevant, but do not be too quick to decide that at this stage. Write each of the words from the list above, or each of your own words, on a separate index card. Now see if you can sort them into related categories and give each category a name. Some cannot go into categories with others, and must be left as they are.

Bear in mind that there are many possible ways to sort these words. A simple one is to sort them all into two piles, 'physical characteristics' and 'social characteristics':

> Physical characteristics: age, sex, race or ethnic group, height, weight, hair colour
>
> Social characteristics: marital status, socieconomic group, residence, education, occupation, number of children, religion, political affiliation.

These groupings are not ideal. For one thing, some of the 'physical characteristics' are also the basis for social groupings; age, sex, race, etc. But, for the moment, we will keep them.

Make a similar rough list of the characteristics which these people will also have because they are secondary school students. Let us assume that there are several second-level schools in Ballyglass, one 'traditional' secondary, one comprehensive, and one vocational.

So we can add —

school, type of education, major subject, performance, extracurricular activities.

If you can group related points together in a way that suits you, do so. Now put all the points together. Discard any that you are pretty sure are irrelevant. (Be ready to put them back if your early research indicates that they may be relevant.) Notice that I have moved 'education' out of one list and made it the heading for another list.

II. *Secondary School Students*
   A. Physical characteristics
      1. age
      2. sex
   B. Social characteristics
      1. socioeconomic group
      2. residence
      3. education
         a. school
         b. type of education
         c. class year

I am omitting some of the points which I originally listed, such as 'major subjects' because, although they may have a bearing on the decision to migrate, I am simply trying to provide a basic description of the student's characteristics before moving on to their intentions. Using that argument, I could omit several other points as well, but until I am sure they are irrelevant, I will leave them in.

You may ask why you bothered to list all the points you could think of to begin with. It is a good exercise to include all the points you can think of, and then cross out the ones that are irrelevant to your particular study. That way, you have *chosen* to omit them, and you know what you have omitted. You get an opportunity to consider and reject points, and have greater control over the content of your research. At the close of your study, if someone asks 'But why didn't you include such-and-such a point in your study?' you will *know* why, not because you did not think of it, but because you considered it and decided not to include it.

The next word I want to make an outline for is 'Ballyglass', which is a 'place' word. All places have certain characteristics: history, location, area, topography, size; inhabited ones have population, an economy, government, major religions, and so on. The list goes thus —

history, location, area, topography, size, layout, population, economy, government, major religions.

Can you re-group these into a smaller number of categories?

Physical characteristics: location, topography, size, area, population, layout.

Social characteristics: economy, government, major religions.

Notice here that, as always, you are writing logical points, not questions, and not answers. I did not write 'What is the population?' nor 'Population: 6000'. So why not write questions? The reason is simply that it is tempting to run up a fully-developed questionnaire or interview schedule or something that looks like one. In fact, questionnaire development and wording is a separate job, requiring additional skills. So make the Outline first; later on in the research, use the Outline points to develop the questions for your questionnaire, if you are using one. Nor should you attempt answers in the Outline. Remember the Outline is a guide to what you need to collect, not a recording form for answers. Besides, if you start jotting down answers at this stage, you are probably rushing to conclusions and not being as objective as you should be.

Do not think, because of the way I broke down 'Secondary School Students' and 'Ballyglass', that everything can or should be divided into 'physical characterstics' and 'social characteristics'. Here is the final breakdown of 'Ballyglass':

III. *Ballyglass*
    A. Physical characteristics
        1. location
        2. topography
        3. size
            a. area
            b. population
                (1) numbers
                (2) composition
                    (a) ages
                    (b) sexes
        4. layout

Notice, in the final breakdown here, that I have worked out sub-points for some of the points. I could do this for the others, if necessary. For example, if I were doing an economic study of Ballyglass, I might want many sub-points under 'topography' – rivers, soil composition, mineral resources, etc.

Under 'layout' I could look at streets, buildings, major services and utilities. I probably do not need these for this study.

    B. Social characteristics
        1. economy
            a. tourist economy
            b. agricultural economy
            c. industrial economy
            d. other

Note: these sub-points are not answers: they are points to study, based on your knowledge of the local economy.

Under 'Social characteristics', I have decided not to list 'Government' or

'Major religions' which might normally feature, because I do not think they are necessary here. After all, what I am trying to do is simply to get enough information on Ballyglass to describe it in the opening of my final paper, not do an exhaustive study of Ballyglass. Perhaps I could omit some points under 'A' as well, such as 'topography'.

Since I now have just one point under the heading 'Social characteristics' *that* point should become the heading. So now I have —

B. Economy (not 'Social characteristics')
    1. tourist economy
    2. agricultural economy
    3. industrial economy
    4. other

The last major point to break down is 'Migration Intentions'. The first thing I should do is define what I mean by 'migration'. It can mean leaving one's home area but remaining in the country; and it can mean leaving the country, or emigration. I will assume that I want to know about three categories; those who intend to stay at home, those who intend to leave home but remain in Ireland, and those who intend to emigrate. The simplest breakdown under 'Migration Intentions' would, therefore, be a list of these three categories. If that is all I want to know, fine. However, I might explore some other facets of migration to see if they might usefully be studied.

To do this, think of all the possible points which could occur under 'Migration Intentions'. For example, *where* will they migrate? One way to help yourself think of possible points is to ask yourself the questions 'Who? What? Where? When? Why? How?' in relation to migration:

- Who?   Who is migrating?
- What?   What are they going to do? – Migrate or stay at home?
- Where?   Where will they go if they migrate?
- When?   When will they go?
- Why?   Why are they leaving or staying?
- How?   How will they manage the process of migration?
                    Will they go to relatives abroad?
                    Will they try to get a job before going?

You can probably think of a lot more points arising out of these questions.

I. *Migration Intentions*
    A. Choice
        1. remaining at home
        2. leaving home, remaining in Ireland
        3. emigrating

   B. Destination
     1. Ireland
        a. nearest market town
        b. national city
        c. other
     2. Abroad
        a. U.S.A.
        b. Britain
        c. Scotland
        d. Europe
        e. Australia
        f. Other

Note: some preliminary knowledge of current destinations will help you to fill in the sub-points here.

   C. Time of Migration
     1. before completion of secondary school
     2. upon completion of secondary school
     3. within three years of completion of secondary school
     4. within five years of completion of secondary school

You can break down these periods in any way that is appropriate. Knowing something of the history of migration in the area will help you to fix realistic time periods. You might also decide to use age groups rather than periods in relation to leaving school.

   D. Reasons
     1. remaining at home
        a. better quality of life
        b. proxmimity to relatives and friends
        c. interest in local occupations
        d. other

Here, a preliminary survey would help you to establish possible reasons. Let us assume that I did such a survey and the results indicated that these were the most common reasons.

     2. leaving home, remaining in Ireland
        a. better job opportunities
        b. better wages
        c. better working conditions
        d. other

Do not list categories if you have not got this preliminary information. Do not hazard guesses, no matter how plausible they might seem. Wait until you know enough to fill in such points.

    3. emigrating
      a. better job opportunities
      b. better wages
      c. better working conditions
      d. travel and adventure
      e. other
  E. Method of Emigration
    1. go to relatives abroad for help in accommodation and job-hunting
    2. go abroad and live on savings while job-hunting
    3. get job offer first before going
    4. other

Once again, it helps to know something of local patterns before filling in possible points. Otherwise, do a preliminary survey to get categories.

The preliminary Outline which follows is now complete. Your Outline, however, is not meant to be like the Ten Commandments carved in stone. You will have to change it if you discover that some points are irrelevant, others must be added, and new sub-points filled in as you learn enough to develop your categories. This flexible attitude allows you to make enough of an Outline to begin your work, but not such a rigid structure that you have pre-judged what you will find.

There are two real dangers to avoid:

- sticking to an Outline that is obviously irrelevant as your research progresses, thus forcing what you find into inappropriate categories; and
- allowing the research project to change subtly without altering the Outline at the same time. The project thus takes on a life of its own, drifting without a real Outline as a guide. Usually, you will not know this is happening, and will write up your final results as though they actually fit into the various Outline categories. Another possibility here is that if you do you see the gap between the Outline and the actual research, you might abandon the Outline and neglect to create a new one.

Here is the complete Research Outline:

MIGRATION INTENTIONS OF SECONDARY SCHOOL STUDENTS IN BALLYGLASS

II. *Secondary School Students*
  A. Physical characteristics
    1. age
    2. sex
  B. Social characteristics
    1. socio-economic group
    2. residence
    3. education
      a. school
      b. type of education
      c. class year

III. *Ballyglass*
  A. Physical characteristics
    1. location
    2. size
      a. area
      b. population
        (1) numbers
        (2) composition
          (a) ages
          (b) sexes
    3. layout
  B. Economy
    1. tourist economy
    2. agricultural economy
    3. industrial economy
    4. other
    I. *Migration Intentions*
      A. Choice
    1. remaining at home
    2. leaving home, remaining in Ireland
    3. emigrating
  B. Destination
    1. Ireland
      a. nearest market town
      b. national city
      c. other
    2. Abroad
      a. U.S.A.
      b. Britain
      c. Scotland
      d. Europe
      e. Australia
      f. other
  C. Time of Migration
    1. before completion of secondary school
    2. upon completion of secondary school
    3. within three years of completion of secondary school
    4. within five years of completion of secondary school
  D. Reasons
    1. remaining at home
      a. better quality of life
      b. proxmity to relatives and friends
      c. interest in local occupations
      d. other
    2. leaving home, remaining in Ireland
      a. better job opportunities
      b. better wages
      c. better working conditions
      d. other

    3. emigrating
       a. better job opportunities
       b. better wages
       c. better working conditions
       d. travel and adventure
       e. other
E. Method of emigrating
    1. go to relatives abroad for help in accommodation and job hunting
    2. go abroad and live on savings while job hunting
    3. get job offer first before going
    4. other

The process of making a Research Outline is difficult at first, and takes a lot of time. It becomes much easier, almost like a game or puzzle, after a while. Do not be dismayed if it takes you a long time to follow the practice exercises in this chapter, or if it takes you a long time to do the first Outline you tackle on your own. Even people who have found the process almost impossible at the beginning have, after a few tries, produced excellent Outlines of their own, and used them as the bases for very good pieces of research.

Not every research topic can be dealt with in this way, but most can. If you are having trouble with yours, it is possible that your sentence is not as clear as it might be. For example, 'Women in the Army and What men Think About Them' is unwieldy. Try: '*Attitudes* (I) of *Men at Fort Brown* (II) towards *Women* (III) in *Selected Army Positions* (IV)'.

There are a few situations in which you do not use this kind of Research Outline. One is when you are doing emic research (see page 65). In a second type of research project, the Community Study, you can develop a Research Outline from scratch, or you can use someone else's as a base upon which to build. I developed such an Outline for my own research in the west of Ireland by taking a brief Community Study outline from an article by Conrad Arensberg (1954) and expanding it (Kane 1977). You, in turn, could take mine or anyone else's and refine or change it to meet the needs of your own community study.

Now, let us work on a second example, based on the Research Statement developed in Chapter I: '*Changes (1950/1980) in Selected Characteristics of Convicted Juvenile Delinquents Aged 13-18 Years in St Michael's Correctional Institution.*'

It breaks down like this:

Changes (1950/1980) (I) in *Selected Characteristics* (II) of *Convicted Juvenile Delinquents Aged 13-18 Years* (III) in *St Michael's Correctional Institution* (IV).

This Research Statement has four major words or phrases. We can begin with any one of them. The order in which you deal with them does not matter. Let us begin then with what will probably be the easiest one, number IV 'St Michael's Correctional Institution'.

To make an outline for this or any other point, list all the aspects or characteristics which this phrase could possibly have; in other words, break it down into its component parts. 'St Michael's Institution' is a 'place' phrase. Once again, all places have certain characteristics — a location, a history, a size, a function, and so forth — and a correctional institution, in addition has certain characteristics peculiar to it — inmates, rules, etc. We begin the job of making an outline by listing as many characteristics as we can think of. Some may have to be discarded later, but do not worry about that now.

IV. *St Michael's Correctional Institution:*
      location, physical layout, history, functions, number of inmates, types of inmates, staff.

When you run out of ideas, you may find that working in a group is helpful. When I am teaching this method in a classroom, someone always suggests a point I had not thought of. But you probably will not have people around you who are familiar with the method, so just ask anyone — your children or your fellow workers: 'If you were studying a correctional institution (juvenile detention centre, etc.) what things would you need to know?' Since they do not know your entire Research Statement, they may suggest things that, while interesting, are not that useful in this particular study, such as 'what the people in the neighbourhood think of the place' but that may also suggest something you would have overlooked, for example, the types of inmates it keeps. List everything. You can throw out irrelevant points later. When you run out of ideas, ask yourself 'Who? What? Where? When? Why? and How?' in relation to the point.

- Who? Who is in it?
  inmates, staff
- What? What is it? What does it do? What does it hope to do?
  nature of the institution, function, aims
- Where? Where is it?
  location
- When? When was it founded?
  history
- Why?
  purpose
- How? How does it do what it is supposed to do?
  method of treatment

Now we have a lot of points. We want to group them together in some sensible way. Some of them overlap; others are duplicates or near-duplicates. One way of grouping them is to write each point on a separate card and then sort the related cards into the same pile. Write down each point, one to a card and sort them in any way that you think appropriate. Throw out duplicates.

IV. *St Michael's Correctional Institution*
A. History
B. Physical characteristics
    1. location
    2. facilities
  C. Nature
  D. Functions
  E. Aim
  F. Population
    1. staff
    2. inmates
  G. Methods of treatment

You might find that you have grouped the words according to a different plan, or may have done it more efficiently with fewer main categories and more sub-points. You may have used a different order. Can you think of anything you have left out? I can, for my Outline. How is the place organised and run? None of my points covers that. I will call it 'Structure' or 'Organisation'.

Also, look to see if you need to know more about any of the particular points.

IV. *St Michael's Correctional Institution*
  A. History

What do I need to know about the history of the place? In this case, probably not too much; just enough to give a brief background of the centre in the opening paragraphs of my final paper. To get the sub-points to list under 'History' simply take the points you need to know about the place *today* and list them under 'History' too.
  B. Current
    1. Physical characteristics
      a. location
      b. size
      c. buildings
      d. layout
      e. facilities

Every place has physical characteristics: location, placement, area, layout; some have buildings, facilities. Think of all possible characteristics a place can have and then choose the ones relevant to your topic.
    2. Nature

This point addresses the question, 'What is it?'
    3. Organisation or structure

How is it organised? Is it a local unit of a larger institution? Is it under national jurisdiction, county jurisdiction. Who runs it?
    4. Functions

Here, you want to know 'What does it do?' You may want to distinguish between its formal functions and its informal functions — or its official functions and its unofficial functions. For example, a place can have as its formal function the sale of hamburgers and ice cream. Its informal function may be to act as a hangout for young people, or even a place where drugs are traded.

5. Aims or purpose

This point asks what the centre is supposed to do, or what it hopes to do. Remember, write points to study, not answers. The outline is not the place for answers, even if you know them. What is worse is when you do not, and jump to conclusions, such as —

E. Aim
    1. To protect society
    2. to encourage good future citizenship
    3. to rehabilitate offenders
    Next,
    6. Population
        a. staff
            (1) number
            (2) types
            (3) ages
            (4) sexes
            (5) occupations
        b. inmates
            (1) numbers
            (2) ages
            (3) sexes
            (4) offenses committed
            (5) average length of sentence

This is a 'people' word and could have many sub-points: height, weight, marital status, education, residence, and special characteristics peculiar to certain groups, such as type of training, length of service, previous occupation, etc. Write down all the characteristics which you can think of and then discard the ones which are irrelevant or which will give you more information than you need.

    7. Methods of treatment
        a, b, etc.

Once again, do not guess at possible methods of treatment. Leave the points blank until you do enough research, either before or during the project, to fill in relevant types. Suppose we have done this, and they are:

- incarceration
- rehabilitation programmes
- educational programmes
- work programmes

These are not answers. They are the types of treatment about which you must now get information.

At this point, it is a good idea to take stock and remember our priorities. We do not want to do an exhaustive study of every aspect of St Michael's Correctional Institution. We just need to know enough about it to be able to see our main point – changes in selected characteristics of juvenile delinquents – in perspective. We simply want to be able to describe the centre at the beginning of our paper. So we do not have to go into all possible details (whether the staff have a pension fund, for example). We *do* want to know a lot more about the inmates or juvenile delinquents but we will list those points under 'Selected Characteristics' or 'Convicted Juvenile Delinquents Aged 13-18 Years Old'.

Let us take 'Selected Characteristics' as our next point. We already know what the main points are going to be, since we settled on them when we worked out the Research Statement.

II. *Selected Characteristics*
    A. Age
    B. Sex
    C. Socio-economic class
    D. Education
    E. Type of offence committed

All we have to do now is ask what we need to know, specifically, about each of these points:

II. *Selected Characteristics*
    A. Age
        1. current
          a, b, (age groupings go here if used)
        2. age at each offence
          a, b, (age groupings go here if used)

For 'Age' we will probably want to know not only the person's age now but also the age at which he or she committed the offence; or, if he has a history of offences, the age he was on each occasion. Sometimes, it is more useful to use *age groups*, rather than individual ages: 30-34, 35-39, etc. Grouping makes the data more compact. Also if you wish to compare your material to that of a national census, for example, or other official records, or the results of another study which uses groupings, you may find that you gain more than you lose by grouping. In our example here, if the juvenile records are kept according to groups, such as 13-15, 16-18, you might do the same. Otherwise, we are dealing with such a small range of years that we might as well record individual ages.

C. Socio-economic class

Use any kind of groupings which are appropriate. You will probably find that the traditional class groupings, lower, middle and upper, are rather meaningless. You may wish to do emic research (find out how the people categorise themselves and others in their group – see page 65) to determine appropriate class categories. If you do, you cannot fill in the sub-points under 'socio-economic class' or simply 'class' until you complete the emic research.

On the other hand, you may use 'established' categories of some sort, especially if you wish to compare your findings with those of someone else. In Ireland one might use the eleven socio-economic categories found in the Irish census, which are based upon occupation. These occupation-based classes roughly reflect social groupings, at least in urban areas. On the other hand, the USA census lists seven major occupational categories which are not very useful for socio-economic research. In the 1960 U.S. presidential election, for example, voters were categorised instead into 480 social types in order to make computer projections of voting patterns [de Sola Pool and Popkin 1965].

D. Education
    1. level completed
    2. type
    3. performance

We may want to know not only what level of education the person completed, but also the type of education (technical, classical academic, etc.) and perhaps even performance at school.

    1. level completed
        a. primary school
            (1) part
            (2) all
        b. secondary school
            (1) part
            (2) all
        b. third level education
            (1) part
            (2) all

We can break these points down into great detail. For example, we can list the possible levels completed, in any kind of detail we like. Since the oldest of our juvenile delinquents is eighteen, it is hardly likely that anyone has completed third level education.

    2. type (of last level)

One can also consider all the possible types of education. There is a large number, especially at third level. Once again, our upper limit age of eighteen helps to cut out some of these. Some types could be:

formal standard academic, formal vocational, formal mixed academic/vocational, apprenticeship, other.

These vary from one place and one situation to another; preliminary research can give the categories most appropriate to your study. On the other hand, if you want to compare your research with a national census or someone else's research, you will have to use already-established categories.

3. performance

We will have to decide what we mean by the word and what we will take as a measure of performance. School marks? Exam performance? Assessment of teachers? Whatever you take, you will have to make sure that the records are available for the juvenile delinquents in the 1950's as well as the juvenile delinquents of 1980.)

E. Offence committed

Note the change in this heading from 'Type of Offence Committed'. Let us say that we have decided that we want to know more than the type of offence alone.

1. number

Perhaps we also want to know if more than one offence was committed; we may also want to know the circumstances, if, for example, it was under the influence of alcohol, or with a group of older youths.

2. type
a. murder and manslaughter
b. forcible rape
c. robbery
d. aggravated assault
e. burglary
f. larceny/theft
g. motor vehicle theft
h. arson

For the type of offence, we might use the categories which the institution or the state uses. In some studies, it would be appropriate to use emic categories – the offences as categorised by the inmates themselves – but since one of our groups, the inmates of 1950, might not be available for interview, we probably have to use formal categories.

3. circumstances

Next, we have 'Convicted Juvenile Delinquents Aged 13-18 Years'. The most important thing which we have done with this word is define what we mean by 'juvenile delinquents'. Since we have already broken down 'Selected Characteristics', thereby selecting the characteristics of juvenile delinquents which we wish to study, we need only to ask if there is anything else about the juvenile delinquents which we wish to know. Probably just how many there are, and a name or indentifying number for each.

III. *Convicted Juvenile Delinquents Aged 13-18 Years*
    A. Number in institution
    B. Name or identifying number of each

This, once again, is a 'people' phrase. Normally, you would think of all the characteristics which people can have and any special ones that this particular group of people or type of person can have. In our example, however, we already decided on the characteristics we wanted to study when working on 'Selected Characteristics' in our Research Statement.

    Finally, we have 'Changes (1950/1980)' as the last remaining major word in our Research Statement.

I. *Changes (1950/1980)*

When we worked out the Research Statement, we decided to study change simply by comparing two years, 1950 and 1980. You may wish to expand this to two periods rather than two single years, for example, the periods 1945-50 and 1975-80.

    So we might have —

I. *Changes (1945/1980)*
    A. 1945-1950
    B. 1975-1980

You can leave it at this, remembering that you have to study all the 'Selected Characteristics' of 'Convicted Juvenile Delinquents Aged 13-18 Years Old' in 'St Michael's Correctional Institution', for both 1945-50 and 1975-80.

    An easier way of dealing with this point, however, is to drop it as a major point on its own, and instead, insert it as a reminder under all the other main points. Here is a brief example of what I mean:

III. *St Michael's Correctional Institution*
    A. 1945-1950
        1. physical characteristics
           a. location
           b. size
           c. buildings
           d. layout
           e. facilities
and continue with all points, through to '7. Methods of treatment'.

    B. 1975-1980
        1. physical characteristics
and continue with all points, through to '7. Methods of treatment'.

I. *Selected Characteristics*
    A. 1945-50
        1. Age
           a. current (meaning in 1945-50 period)
           b. age at each offence

2. Sex
   a. male
   b. female

and continue on with all the points we worked out for 'Selected Characteristics'. Then —

B. 1975-1980
   1. Age
      a. current
      b. age at each offence

and so on. Finally, insert the two time periods under 'Juvenile Delinquents Aged 13-18 Years'

II. *Convicted Juvenile Delinquents Aged 13-18 Years*
   A. 1945-1950
      1. number in institution
      2. name or identifying number of each
   B. 1975-1980
      1. number in institution
      2. name or identifying number of each

You can now refine your entire Outline, inserting more sub-points as you become more familiar with the process, and as you learn more about the subject you are studying. If you are stuck for points for your Outline, you might consult professional taxonomies or guides. For the social sciences, there is Murdock's *Outline of Cultural Materials* (1950) (above), *Notes and Queries on Anthropology* (1950) and folklore handbooks. Murdock's work actually contains points in an outline form; the latter two sources list questions on a range of topics. The questions must be converted into points, as explained in this chapter; otherwise you might be deluded into thinking you have a questionnaire.

B. The Research Design

WE ARE now at the final stage of preparing our research 'map'. Here is a chart showing the points we have worked out. The first column of each page is the Research Outline itself. Not all the subpoints are filled in yet since we need more information before committing the points to paper. This Outline, in fact will probably go through several revisions before it is finally ready for use, and items may be changed during the course of the research. We may learn, for example, that point I. A. 4. c, 'educational performance' for inmates during the 1945-50 period may be nearly impossible to get without great effort and expenditure. We might decide that it will be all right to drop 'performance' altogether. There are two more columns on the charts 'Techniques' and 'Sources'. When you have all the points in your draft Research Outline completed, do two things:

1. Look at each point and decide what techniques would be appropriate for getting information on it. List them in the second column of the chart.

As you will see in the next chapter, the greater the number of appropriate techniques you can use for each point, the more likely you are to get a better picture. The question you should ask yourself, therefore, is not 'Which technique shall I use for this point?' but rather 'Which techniques *can't* I use for the point?', and then use all the rest. Never decide on the technique before you have broken down the problem into a Research Outline. People sometimes say 'What we need is a survey (usually meaning a questionnaire or interviews) on such and such.' You will not know if you need a survey until you know what the points to be studied are. *The problem determines the techniques.*

When you examine the following charts it might appear that for some of the points we are using a lot of techniques to get simple, straightforward information. Part of that, of course, is because I am trying to illustrate the principle – use as many techniques as are reasonably possible. But even in a straightforward project like this, it is quite possible that there are gaps in St Michael's records, that the inmates will not cooperate on certain inform-ation, that some of the staff have a vested interest in presenting a certain point of view, or that the documents you read have important flaws. Then, it is essential that you use every technique available to you.

2.   Look at each point and decide from what source you will get the information. List them in the third column of the chart. If the technique is 'documentary analysis' and the documents you need are public records, list the types of records; if the technique is interviewing, figure out the category of people, or which individual person you have to interview; for example, all mothers of children under three years old, or local councillors, or all the nursing staff of City Hospital.

When you have all three – (1) the Research Outline containing your research points, (2) the techniques to be used on each point, and (3) the sources from which you will get the information on each point – you have a *Research Design.* A major part of your work is done.

Your next steps are to draw up a research schedule and budget, design interviews and questionnaires, if you are using them, and train interview-ers, if necessary. Then, at last, you are ready to begin your research.

C. Sample Research Design

Changes (1945/1980) in *Selected Characteristics* of *Convicted Juvenile Delinquents Aged 13-18 Years* in *St Michael's Correctional Institution*

OUTLINE	TECHNIQUES	SOURCE
III. St Michael's Correctional Institution		photographs: *Greenville News* archives
A. History		
1. physical characteristics	documentary	maps: University School of
a. locations	analysis	Architecture Library
b. size		maps: St Michael's Institution
c. buildings		archives
d. layout		Harry, B. *The History of Juvenile Correction Institutions in the County.* Anytown: Bray Publishing Co., 1944
e. facilities	documentary	Bryce, Annie, *The Story of*
(1) correctional	analysis	*Greenville*, Greenville: Jones &
(2) educational		Co., 1948 (contains chapter on
(a) academic		St Michael's.)
(b) vocational		Department of Justice. *Juvenile*
(c) moral or civic		*Correction Centres*, 1910-1940.
(3) recreational		Capital City: Government Pub-
(4) residential	and	lication Office, 1943
	interviews	former staff / former inmates
2. nature of institution	documentary analysis and interviews	Barry, B. *The History of Juvenile Correction Institutions...* former staff former inmates
3. organisation or structure	documentary	Department of Justice. *Juvenile*
a. external (part of larger	analysis	*Correction Centres...*
institution)		St Michael's Institution *Annual*
b. internal (organisation		*Report(s)* Capital City, Govern-
within the institution		ment Publication Office.
c. administration	and	1919-1945
d. jurisdiction, or area it serves	interviews	former staff / former inmates
4. functions	interviews	former staff
a. official	and	former inmates
(1) punitive	documentary	Barry, B. *The History of Juvenile*
(2) rehabilitative	analysis	*Correction Institutions...*
(3) educational		Department of Justice. *Juvenile Correction Centres...*
b. unofficial	interviews	former staff
(1) production of recidivism		former inmates
(2) educational		older residents of the
(a) criminal professionalism		community

OUTLINE	TECHNIQUES	SOURCE
(b) expertise in law	and	
(3) venue for illegal activities	documentary	court records
(a) homosexuality	analysis	
(b) drug circulation		
(c) assault, theft		
(d) other		
5. aims	interviews	former staff
a.	and	former inmates
b.	documentary	Department of Justice. *Juvenile*
c.	analysis	*Correction Centres...*
6. population		St Michael's Institution. *Annual*
a. staff		*Reports...*
(1) number	documentary	St Michael's Institution, personnel
(2) types	analysis	records
(a) administrative	and	former staff
(b) corrective	interviews	former inmates
(c) educational		older residents of the community
(d) domestic		
(e) other		St Michael's Institution, personnel
(3) ages		records
(4) sexes		
(male)		
(female)		
(5) occupations		
(a)		
(b)		
(c) etc		
b. inmates		
(1) numbers	documentary	St Michael's Institution, records
(2) ages	analysis	
(a) under 15	documentary	St Michael's Institution, records
(b) 15-18	analysis	
(3) sexes	documentary	St Michael's Institution, records
(a) male	analysis	
(b) female		
(4) general offences	documentary	St Michael's Institution, records
(dealt with more specifically under 'Selected Characteristics')	analysis	
(5) average length of sentence	doc. analysis	St Michael's Institution, records
7. methods of treatment	interviews	former staff /former inmates
a. incarceration	and	older residents of the community
b. rehabilitation programmes	documentary	St Michael's Institution, *Annual*
c. educational programmes	analysis	*Report(s)*. 1919-1950.
d. work programmes		archives: Greenville Hist. Soc.
		Dept. of Justice. Juv. Corr. Cen...

(We end our 'History' here with this description of the institution. We are not going to do a hisory of 'Selected Characteristics' or 'Convicted Juvenile Delinquents' since we do not need it.)

OUTLINE	TECHNIQUES	SOURCE
B. 1945-1950		photographs: *Greenville News*
1. physical characteristics	documentary	maps: University School of
a. location	analysis	Architecture Library
b. size		blueprints: Horizon Engineering
c. buildings		Co., Greenville
d. layout		
e. facilities	documentary	Stanton, John, *Inside our Prisons*
(1) correctional	analysis	West City: Middletown Press,
(2) educational	and	1953
(a) academic	interviews	former staff
(b) vocational	and	former inmates
(c) moral or civic	questionnaires	community residents
(3) recreational		
(4) residential		former staff
2. nature of institution	interviews	former staff / former inmates
3. organisation or structure	documentary	St Michael's Institution, *Annual*
a. external (part of larger	analysis	*Report(s)*. 1945-1950
institution)		
b. internal (organisation	questionnaire	former staff
within the institution	and	
c. administration	interviews	former staff
d. jurisdiction, or area it serves		former inmates
4. functions	questionnaire	former staff
a. official	and	
(1) punitive	interviews and	former staff / former inmates
(2) rehabilitative	documentary	
(3) educational	analysis	any sources?
b. unofficial		former staff
(1) production of recidivism	interviews	former inmates
(2) educational		community residents
(a) criminal professionalism		
(b) expertise in law	and	
(3) venue for illegal activities	documentary	court records
(a) homosexuality	analysis	
(b) drug circulation		
(c) assault, theft		
(d) other		
5. aims	questionnaire	former staff
a.	and interviews	former staff / former inmates
b.	and	
c.	documentary	St Michael's Institution. *Annual*
	analysis	*Report(s)*. Capital City: Govern-
		ment Public. Office, 1945-1950.
6. population		
a. staff	questionnaire	former staff
(1) number	and	St Michael's Institution, *Annual*
(2) types	documentary	*Report(s)*... 1945-1950.

OUTLINE	TECHNIQUES	SOURCE
(a) administrative	analysis	St Michael's Institution, personnel records.
(b) corrective		
(c) educational		
(d) domestic		
(e) other		
(3) ages		
(4) sexes		
(male)		
(female)		
(5) occupations		
(a), (b) etc.		
b. inmates		
(1) numbers	documentary analysis	St Michael's Institution, records
(2) ages		
(a) under 15	documentary analysis	St Michael's Institution, records
(b) 15-18		
(3) sexes	documentary analysis	St Michael's Institution, records
(a) male		
(b) female		
(4) general offences	documentary	St Michael's Institution, records
(dealt with more specifically under 'Selected Characteristics')	analysis	
(5) average length of sentence	documentary analysis	St Michael's Institution, records
7. methods of treatment	questionnaire	former staff
a. incarceration	and interviews	former staff / former inmates
b. rehabilitation programmes	and	community residents
c. educational programmes	documentary	St Michael's Institution, *Annual*
d. work programmes	analysis	*Report(s)*... 1945-1950
C. 1975-1980		
1. physical characteristics	documentary	City of Greenville: city maps
a. location	analysis	blueprints: Horizon Engineering
b. size	and	Co., Greenville
c. buildings	participant	grounds, buildings of
d. layout	observation	St Michael's Institution
e. facilities	questionnaire	staff
(1) correctional	and interviews	staff / inmates
(2) educational	and	
(a) academic	participant	St Michael's Institution
(b) vocational	observation	
(c) moral or civic	and	
(3) recreational	documentary	any sources?
(4) residential	analysis?	
2. nature of institution	interviews and	staff
	participant	inmates
	observation	St Michael's Institution

OUTLINE	TECHNIQUES	SOURCE
3. organisation or structure	questionnaire	staff
a. external (part of larger	and	staff
institution)	interviews	St Michael's Institution, *Annual*
b. internal (organisation	documentary	*Report(s)*. 1975-1980
within the institution)	analysis	Dept. of Justice. *Review of*
c. administration		*Correctional Institutions*. Capital
d. jurisdiction, or area it serves		City: Govt Public. Off., 1979
4. functions	questionnaire	staff
a. official	and	
(1) punitive	interviews and	staff / inmates
(2) rehabilitative	documentary	Dept. of Justice. Review of
(3) educational	analysis	Correctional Institutions...
b. unofficial	interviews	staff
(1) production of recidivism		inmates
(2) educational		community residents
(a) criminal professionalism		
(b) expertise in law	and	
(3) venue for illegal activities	participant	St Michael's Institution
(a) homosexuality	observation	
(b) drug circulation	and	
(c) assault, theft	documentary	court records
(d) other	analysis	
5. aims	questionnaire	staff
a.	and interviews	staff / inmates
b.	and document.	St Michael's Institution. *Annual*
c.	analysis	*Report(s)*... 1975-1980.
6. population		
a. staff	questionnaire	staff
(1) number	and	St Michael's Institution, *Annual*
(2) types	documentary	*Report(s)*... 1975-1980.
(a) administrative	analysis	St Michael's Institution, personnel
(b) corrective	and	records.
(c) educational		
(d) domestic		
(e) other		
(3) ages	interviews	staff
(4) sexes		
(male)		
(female)		
(5) occupations		
(a)		
(b) etc.		
b. inmates		
(1) numbers	documentary	St Michael's Institution, records
(2) ages	analysis	

OUTLINE	TECHNIQUES	SOURCE
(a) under 15	documentary	St Michael's Institution, records
(b) 15-18	analysis	
(3) sexes	documentary	St Michael's Institution, records
(a) male	analysis	
(b) female		
(4) general offences (dealt with more specifically under 'Selected Characteristics')	documentary analysis	St Michael's Institution, records
(5) average length of sentence		St Michael's Institution, records
7. methods of treatment	questionnaire	staff
a. incarceration	and interviews	staff / inmates
b. rehabilitation programmes	and	community residents
c. educational programmes	participant	St Michael's Institution
d. work programmes	observation	
I. Selected Characteristics		
A. 1945-1950		
1. Age		
a. current	documentary	St Michael's Institution, records
(1)	analysis	
(2) (groupings)	and	
(3)	interviews	former inmates
b. age at each offence		former staff
(1)		(family, other sources
(2) (groupings)		where necessary)
(3)		
2. Sexes		
a. male		
b. female		
3. Socio-economic class		
a.		
b. etc.		
4. Education		
a. level completed		
(1) primary school		
(a) part	documentary	St Michael's Institution, records/
(b) all	analysis	school records, where necessary
(2) secondary school	and	
(a) part	interviews	former inmates
(b) all		former staff
(3) third-level education		(family,
(a) part		other sources where necessary)
b. type (of last level)		
(1) formal standard academic		
(2) formal vocational		
(3) formal mixed		
academic/vocational		
(4) apprenticeship		

OUTLINE	TECHNIQUES	SOURCE
(5) other		
c. performance	*(to be decided upon when definition of 'performance' is settled)*	
5. Offence committed		
a. number		
(1)	documentary	St Michael's Institution, records
(2)	analysis	court records
(3)		
b. type		
(1) murder and manslaughter	and	former inmates
(2) forcible rape	interviews	former staff
(3) robbery		
(4) aggravated assault		
(5) burglary		
(6) larceny/theft		
(7) motor vehicle theft		
(8) arson		
(9) other		
c. circumstances	documentary analysis and interviews	court records inmates / staff other participants, victims
B. 1975-1980		
1. Age		
a. current	documentary analysis	St Michael's Institution, records
(1)	and	
(2) (groupings)	interviews	
(3)		inmates
b. age at each offence		staff
(1)		(other sources, where necessary)
(2) (groupings)		
(3)		
2. Sexes		
a. male		
b. female		
3. Socio-economic class		
a., b. etc.		
4. Education		
a. level completed		
(1) primary school		
(a) part	documentary	St Michael's Institution, records
(b) all	analysis	(school records, where necessary)
(2) secondary school	and	
(a) part	interviews	inmates
(b) all		staff
(3) third-level education		
(a) part		

OUTLINE	TECHNIQUES	SOURCE
b. type (of last level) (1) formal academic (2) formal vocational (3) formal acad./vocat. (4) apprenticeship (5) other		
c. performance	*(to be decided upon when definition of 'performance' is settled)*	
5. Offence committed a. number (1) (2) (3)	documentary analysis	St Michael's Institution, records court records
b. type (1) murder and manslaughter (2) forcible rape (3) robbery (4) aggravated assault (5) burglary (6) larceny/theft (7) motor vehicle theft (8) arson (9) other	and interviews	former inmates former staff
c. circumstances	documentary analysis and interviews	court records inmates / staff (other participants, victims arresting officer, if necessary)
II. Convicted Juvenile Delinquents Aged 13-18 Years A. 1945-1950 1. Number in institution 2. Name or identifying number of each	documentary analysis	St Michael's Institution, records
B. 1975-1980 1. Number in institution 2. Name or identifying number of each	documentary analysis	St Michael's Institution, records

III. The Research Schedule and Budget

PREPARING a schedule and budget is the last step in developing a framework for your research. This will help you to decide whether you need financial assistance or staff; or whether you should limit your Research Statement more to cut time and costs. If you do apply for a research grant, you must have a schedule and budget in your application.

Begin your schedule by listing, in proper order, all the tasks involved in the research. These might be:

1. Prepare Research Statement
2. Prepare Research Outline
3. Prepare Research Design
4. Perform research
   a. questionnaires
   b. participant observation
5. Analyse research findings
6. Prepare research report.

Each of these tasks should be broken down into as many separate parts as necessary. Under 'Analyse research findings' you may have to allow time for computer analysis; for further computer runs as a result of what you have found; for analysing your written notes, and for checking some materials. Under 'Prepare research report' you must allow time for writing the first draft, typing it, circulating parts of it to people who may be giving you expert advice; making revisions; preparing any other necessary drafts; writing the final paper; having it typed; proof-reading it, preparing an index, if necessary; and if the paper is going to be published, following it through all the stages of manuscript preparation and publication. In the schedule shown here, only 'Questionnaires' is broken down into categories, but in an actual timetable, all points must be.

The second step is to estimate the calendar time span that will be required for each task. When tasks take place intermittently, a horizontal line is used. The example below is presented for illustrative purposes; it should not be taken as a guide to the time each task takes.

TABLE A
Project Schedule

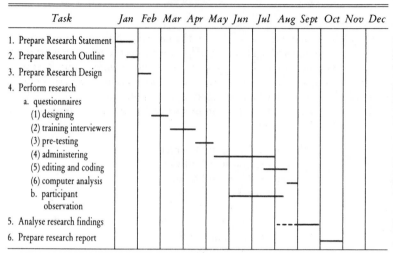

Task	Jan	Feb	Mar	Apr	May	Jun	Jul	Aug	Sept	Oct	Nov	Dec
1. Prepare Research Statement												
2. Prepare Research Outline												
3. Prepare Research Design												
4. Perform research												
a. questionnaires												
(1) designing												
(2) training interviewers												
(3) pre-testing												
(4) administering												
(5) editing and coding												
(6) computer analysis												
b. participant observation												
5. Analyse research findings												
6. Prepare research report												

There is no easy guide to estimating the amount of time each point will take. For the research techniques, the best approach is to ask researchers who are experienced in the technique to give you a rough estimate of how long it will take to apply it in a project of your type and size. Anthropologists, for example, can tell you that writing up participant observation notes takes about three hours per hour of interview or observation. Time required for each of the stages of a questionnaire will differ depending on factors like the length of the questionnaire, variety in the research population, physical distances involved, the amount of help you have, the number of open-ended questions and the skill of the interviewer.

The best rule of thumb, therefore, is to plan the time-span for each task as carefully as possible, and then increase it by one-third. If you are lucky, you will have allowed enough time.

Using the time spans in Table A as a guide, the research budget, Table B, can be prepared. The shaded areas of Table B show where monetary entries should be made, based on the time spans of Table A. The budget categories are explained in more detail in Chapter XIII, *Getting a Grant.*

TABLE B
Project Budget

Task	Budget Category	Jan	Feb	Mar	Apr	May	Jun	Jul	Aug	Sept	Oct	Nov	Dec	Total
1. Prepare Research Statement	Personnel													
	Services													
	Supplies													
	Travel													
	Miscellaneous													
	Total													
2. Prepare Research Outline	Personnel													
	Services													
	Supplies													
	Travel													
	Miscellaneous													
	Total													
3. Prepare Research Design	Personnel													
	Services													
	Supplies													
	Travel													
	Miscellaneous													
	Total													
4. Perform research a. questionnaires (1) designing	Personnel													
	Services													
	Supplies													
	Travel													
	Miscellaneous													
	Total													

This budget is based on the assumption that expenses are paid out in the same month as the activity to which they are charged is performed. This is not always the case, for instance, if you rent an office and must pay a deposit a month in advance of moving in, or you buy a piece of equipment and are billed a month later. List the expenses in the month in which they will occur. If an activity or phase of the research covers more than one month, you can divide the costs (salaries, for example) over the period.

PART TWO

How Do You Find It?

IV. The Research Techniques

RESEARCH techniques are a bit like fishing flies: you choose the right one for the fish you want to catch. No fisherman would use the same kind of fly for twenty different varieties of fish, just because it was the first kind he ever tried or even the one he felt more comfortable with. But a lot of researchers do something very similar; they learn how to design and administer questionnaires, or how to interview, and they use the same technique repeatedly for different projects, even though the technique does not yield the kind of information needed.

The major techniques explained in the next chapters are participant observation, interviews, questionnaires, and written and documentary sources. Each technique is designed to get certain types of information and does not get other types. For example, under certain circumstances, participant observation can tell you what people do or what events happen. Questionnaires and interviews tell you what people say they think and do. Sometimes you need to know only one of these; what people say they do, for example. In this situation, if you are trained in participant observation and are going to use it no matter what, the relevance of the information you collect is going to be lessened.

The diagram below shows how research techniques complement and support one another. No one technique duplicates exactly the function of the rest. Each technique yields information that only it can obtain, but it also reinforces the other techniques.

Each of these 'petals' is a research technique. At the centre they all overlap, and on the sides each overlaps its neighbours. The clear areas represent the material which this technique particularly addresses; the shaded sections are research areas which can be studied by either or preferably both techniques, and the centre is that part of the research which yields information through use of all the methods. If you had to stake your life on which of these three areas is likely to represent the most accurate, complete research information, you would choose the centre, in which you got the information through interviews and questionnaires, reinforced it by observation, and checked it through documentary analysis. In the centre section, you are getting not only what people say they do and what you see them doing, but also what they are recorded as doing. The second 'strongest' areas of information are the joint sections, where two research techniques

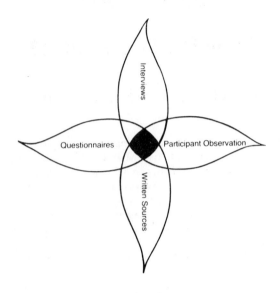

FIGURE IV. 1

can both address the same topic. Finally, in the clear areas, you are relying on only one technique, often the only one possible to use for the kind of information you need, but you are getting no verification from any of the other techniques.

Using as many techniques as possible is part of an approach known as 'triangulation' which means examining the same data through different strategies, in order to verify and strengthen the validity of the research results. *Methodological triangulation* refers not only to using different research techniques, as described above, but also to using different forms of the same technique, for example, applying two or more different questionnaires to the same data. *Theoretical triangulation* uses several theories or perspectives to examine the same material. *Researcher triangulation* requires the use of more than one researcher, for example, several people doing participant observation on the same situation. (Denzin 1978: 339-342) When designing your research, plan to use these multiple triangulation approaches for as much of your research as possible.

V. Participant Observation

OBSERVATION as a research technique covers a variety of situations and approaches. It can be done in a 'natural' setting such as a shop or a bus, or it can be done in a formal situation, such as a laboratory. The observer can be a participant, or at least visibly present; or his presence can be concealed. The observation can be 'free', that is the observer simply writes what happens; or it can be 'structured': a specific list of activities is looked for and checked off when they occur, while everything else is ignored. Observation can be direct – looking at the actors and their actions as they occur – or it can be indirect – looking at the results of actions or events. For example, instead of watching children's behaviour to see which is the most popular item of playground furniture, one looks at the wear patterns on and around the swings versus the slides or whatever.

Although this chapter deals mainly with what is probably the most common type, participant observation, that is, observation in which the observer is at least visible to the observed if not active, the necessity for rigour which is emphasised here applies to all kinds of observation.

First, forget most of what you have heard, if anything, about participant observation. It is not a magical trick that will automatically make your research more valid; on the other hand, it is not to be discounted because at first it seems so vague and subjective.

Participant observation is a technique to use when you wish to learn from people's actions what they do, as opposed to what they say they do. Both are equally important, as you will see when we come to techniques that deal with what people say they are doing.

Participant observation will tell you what people do, but only in situations where you get an opportunity to observe. And after you observe, you still have to make sense of what you saw. Often, you need to know much more than observation tells you. You may also need to know how representative your observation is, how often this kind of thing occurs, and what people say about it. You may need to know if they would behave differently if you or other observers were not present.

Participant observation simply means observing and hearing with as much attention to detail as possible. What do you observe? Any situation in your Research Outline which requires knowing what people do. If your Outline includes the point —

    1. Patient-staff interaction
      a. in canteen
      b. in wards

you will begin by going to the canteen and watching what happens: who sits where, who speaks to whom, what else is done, how it is done, and so forth.

Anthropologists frequently use participant observation and anthropological research provides a good example of participant observation in its most basic form. Most researchers are looking for answers. Most anthropologists, in working with cultures other than their own, have to start a step earlier; they do not even know the questions.

Suppose, for example, you were interested in what kinds of strains cause breakdowns in family relationships and you went to study this in a society whose culture was totally foreign to you. You could not just begin by asking questions about it; first of all, you would have to find out who they thought the members of their family were, since not all societies count their relations as we do. You would have to learn their system before you could begin to get answers to the problem you were studying. Suppose again that you wanted to know how these people resolved conflict. You would have to know what they saw as conflict, first, and this would take some observing and listening, because they could not come up with quick and easy explanations. People are not consciously aware of all the rules and principles which guide their lives. Many of the rules which they give you can sound plausible, and they might believe that this is the way life is and should be lived, but they do not actually live by such rules, for one reason or another. That is when you can often learn more by observation.

Participant observation is a good method when you are trying to learn from scratch, when superficial explanations and judgements will not work. In such cases, you can take nothing for granted. You record, to the extent that it is humanly possible, everything you see and hear in a situation. You make no value judgements; you do not toss out certain comments and actions as irrelevant or trivial. You do not *know* what is irrelevant or trivial. People who have made real contributions to labour-management relations, for example, have been successful not only because they listened to what each side said was important, or what appeared superficially important; they also assumed they knew nothing, and went in fresh with as little bias as possible, and *listened* and *looked*. The most immediately obvious is not necessarily the explanation or even an important element in the problem. The more familiar the situation is to you, the more likely you are to make premature judgements and the more effort you will have to make to avoid them.

There are two disciplines involved in this kind of participant observation:

1.   You try to make no judgements about what is significant; and
2.   You record everything that is humanly possible to record, through straightforward description.

Taken together, these mean that you try to act like a tape recorder and a camera. However, no matter how impartial you try to be, you are a human being with a particular set of orientations which influence the way you see the world. Some people argue that because of this, there is little point in trying to be 'objective', that we are 'flawed' from the start. Though there is some merit to the argument, taking it to its extreme is like saying, 'Since I don't have three-dimensional vision because I'm blind in one eye, I might as well go the whole hog and knock out the other eye.' In participant observation, as in any other research technique, improve upon the positive aspects while allowing for the distortion caused by the negative. In this case, it means becoming the best observer which you are capable of being, and checking your observation through the use of other research techniques.

Although you try to observe everything, there are obviously some things which are going to be irrelevant to your problem, such as the number of flies on the wall or the level of dust in a corner. (But remember, of course, that these things can be important in another research project.) Since the range of what you can observe is almost limitless, you have to limit it. You do this through your Research Outline. If it tells you to observe play patterns among children in a playground, you watch who plays with whom, what they play, and how fights start and end, not how many worms appear or the number of links in the chain on the playground swing. Your Research Outline helps you to focus your observation but it does not tell you what, specifically, to observe.

Participant observation has two other functions in addition to its use as a basic research technique:

1. It can be used as a generalised technique when you first get your research idea, to help you decide what aspect of the problem you really want to look at. It may also help to clarify your ideas and develop categories for later examination. You are probably doing this, anyhow; training in participant observation just makes your observation better and more systematic.

2. It can act as a 'scanner' or check on your other research techniques. If people say on questionnaires and interviews that they do a certain thing, and records and documents show they did it in the past, and yet, when an appropriate situation arises, you see people doing something else, there are certain possibilities —

    a. Your research techniques may have flaws in their design or administration; or

    b. People are not telling you the truth, or are deliberately changing their behaviour. A range of motives may be involved; they may think that the truth will be a poor reflection on them or on the group; or they may have reservations about you or your research. However, you can learn as much from people's distortions of the truth as you can from accurate statements. It is important, however, to recognise such distortions which is why you should use participant observation as part of a total method, encompassing all the appropriate research techniques and all the resources at hand. This means observing, cross-checking with other informants at other times, in different circumstances, in different historical settings through the use of documents, and checking the coherence and sense of the items in the total context of the situation. If there are inconsistencies, they are most likely to stand out when using this system.

c.   People may not be *able* to describe their own behaviour or that of others, for a number of reasons. They sometimes give inaccurate descriptions of their lives and customs because they are describing the *ideal* way. They may even wish, in fact, that the ideal way was the actual way. For instance, in many societies, the desirable and normal pattern of residence after marriage is that the bride goes to live with the groom's family. When asked, people will say that this is what is done. It may be, however, that economic circumstances force young couples to begin to live on their own or with the bride's family or any family which can take them. The researcher may find that over 60% of couples are in such a situation, yet when questioned, people will still say that the young marrieds live with the groom's family, as they used to. The fact is when the idea and reality are not the same, people often do not notice it until the change is extreme; sometimes they do not want to accept it and will continue to describe the ideal. There are other reasons why a person may not be able to describe behaviour to you. It may be too complicated for ordinary description, for instance, bodily movements in dance, facial expressions or sensations. The behaviour may differ for different groups by age, sex or status, or the person may be unaware of his/her behaviour in a particular situation, maybe have an inadequate memory; or, most elusively, the person may not be able to or think to describe things which he/she does *not* do. She never telephones men; she never listens to people when they say they are sick; she never deliberately initiates a conflict (Whiting and Whiting 1970: 284-85).

Finally, a few words on two other kinds of observation: structured observation and indirect observation. In structured observation, certain kinds of behaviour or activities are selected for observation, and when anything happens which qualifies for inclusion under these categories, it is recorded. Beatrice and John Whiting, in their study *Children of Six Cultures: A Psycho-Cultural Analysis,* looked at behaviour in different cultures to see if there are common sex, age and birth order characteristics among children, independent of culture. In order to classify the social interaction of the children whom they were observing, they developed six 'clusters' of behaviour: 'intimate dependent'; 'nurturant'; 'aggressive'; 'dominant-dependent'; 'sociable'; and 'pro-social'. If you had a number of field workers observing groups of children around the world, you could imagine the problems you would have in being sure that the kind of activity which one worker was classifying as 'nurturant' was the same as the kind of activity classified as 'nurturant' by another worker. If it was not, your project would be meaningless. To insure against this, the Whitings specified the kinds of activities which were to be included in each category: 'intimate dependent', for example, includes 'touches' and 'seeks help'. A young child asking an older child to help her dress would be classified as showing 'intimate dependent' behaviour. 'Nurturant' behaviour includes 'offers help' and 'offers support'.

This kind of approach is especially useful when you are using what are normally considered judgemental or emotive words like 'dominant', 'racist', 'aggressive' or 'withdrawn', because you specify, ahead of time, exactly what behaviours will be taken as examples of these terms. Others may disagree with how you categorise the behaviours, that a particular type of behaviour is 'racist', for example, but they will be clear about what the actual behaviour was.

Indirect observation, which falls into the category of 'unobtrusive' measures or 'non-reactive' techniques (Webb, et al., 1966) involves the study of physical traces to investigate human or other activity, much as a detective might study blood stains or fingerprints to determine the presence and activity of a suspect. Physical traces, according to Webb, et al., fall into two categories: erosion measures, in which a pattern of wear is studied; and accretion measures, in which patterns of deposit are studied. Using erosion measures, one might study wear on library books to determine use, or on museum floors to determine popularity of particular exhibits. Using accretion measures, one could determine the comparative popularity of a children's museum exhibit by the number of nose prints left on the glass over a given period; or learn something about people's lifestyles by the nature of their garbage.

In such studies, the observer does not bias the action of the observed, because observation occurs after the action has taken place. Sometimes, however, the physical traces are open to interpretation: greater wear on the pages of one book than on another may mean greater use or it may reflect a difference in paper quality or storage conditions. Obviously, as with all research methods, this one should be used in conjunction with others; Webb, et al., in fact, have helped to emphasise the need for 'triangulation' or the use of multiple research methods on the same problem or data.

Most people are poor observers when they begin, but after a few practice sessions they are usually astonished at their ability to see, remember and record. Everyone has a weakness in his or her observing abilities, and the weaknesses tend to be consistent. Try the exercises at the end of this chapter to see what yours are, and how you can improve. Before you do, remember these points:

1.   Avoid judgemental adjectives and quick leaps to abstractions. When we observe or experience something, we 'process' our observations to make judgements and reach conclusions. Thus, instead of saying 'She twisted her hands for approximately ninety seconds, paced east and west across the room for a total distance of about ten feet, and with a furrowed forehead, looked out the door four times' we give a conclusion instead: 'she was nervous' or 'she was very anxious'. That is all right in most situations when you can afford to make misinterpretations of people's behaviour, but not when you are using observation as a research tool. You can find that what appears to be 'nervous' is really 'angry'; 'calm' is 'rigidly controlled' and 'aloof' can

be 'shy'. The first time I ever visited a particular Jewish delicatessen in Pittsburgh, I was convinced that everyone was angry and fighting. Unsmiling people knelt on the seats of their booths and yelled at the people behind them, shook their fists, sent food back to the kitchen, and 'insulted' the waitress, who, in turn, slammed their orders down on the tables. A policeman came in, to break up the fight and keep down the noise, I thought, and he screamed at people and they screamed back. After many other occasions and more experiences, I realised that they had just been conversing and having a good time, and that the policeman was drawn into the fun. If I had been taking notes and had written 'everyone is angry and fighting' I would have had very little useful information because I would have 'processed' and misinterpreted the information so long ago that I would have forgotten the actual details and would have given myself no chance to re-interpret later on in the light of more experience.

Judgmental adjectives present a second problem; what you describe as 'attractive' or 'neat' or 'tall' or 'poor' may not be any of these to someone else, and, in fact, as you progress through your research, even your own standards may change. Instead of 'attractive', write 'she was wearing red chiffon harem pants, full in the leg and tight at the waist and ankle, silver kid open-toed sandals with four-inch heels, a rhinestone-studded vest, purple satin V-necked sleeveless blouse, four gold neck chains ranging in length from twenty-four to forty inches, false black eyelashes, green eye-shadow, coral lipstick, platinum blonde hair, left side-parted falling in curls to her shoulders, and a silver one-inch diameter topaz ring on the fourth finger of her right hand.'

These comments apply to judgemental verbs as well. Ignore what you learned about colourful writing in your English composition class. 'Come here,' she pouted meltingly' is not much use in participant observation notes. Do you see a distinction between 'She came forward' and 'She thrust herself forward'? If you do, use each one in the appropriate situation, but generally, the simpler verb, with careful description, if necessary, is best. You can, of course, include judgemental statements made by people you are studying. For example, you can write 'Tommy said that John is too aggressive and he didn't want to play with him any more'. You should not write 'John is too aggressive' as your own judgment.

If for any reason you think it is important to insert a judgment, give the basis of comparison. 'To me, he looked older than the other children' may be the only way to convey something difficult to describe if the child is not taller or heavier or dressed in clothing appropriate to children of an older age group. Make clear the standard of comparison: 'The house, although neat, looked dirty in comparison to the other houses on the street'. Do not use your own socio-economic background or experiences as a basis of comparison when it is irrelevant to the study.

2.   If, after all this, you feel that your own assessment of the situation may be useful to record, separate it from the body of the notes by some distin-

gushing mark. For example: /'I believe that the informant may have made this statement because his boss was present'/. The slashed lines are a constant reminder to you that you are writing an opinion, as well as being an easy way of setting off the material.

3. Do not record what people say as if it were factual truth. Do not write 'The manager had to close the canteen because the workers kept tearing it up'. It should be 'Mr Brown said that he had to close the canteen because the workers kept tearing it up', or better yet, quote Mr Brown directly. Alternatively: 'What the area needs most is a swimming pool' takes on a slightly different meaning when it is prefaced with 'The president of Ace Swimming Pools said. . .' Even if you are positive that the information is correct, record it this way.

4.   Record any questions or comments which you make in the course of an interview or observation, because they may have affected the situation. Also, unless your contribution is recorded, it may appear that the informant jumped around from one topic to the next without reason, when he was actually responding to your questions or prompting. An informant who began with his feelings about traffic congestion and then proceeded to the value of kidney machines, courtship in the old days and why a dog is man's best friend could appear to be a maniac otherwise. Use brackets for your own questions and comments: [Do you feel the community association is helpful to you?]

By following these suggestions, everything that appears outside slashed lines and brackets represents what the informant(s) said or did, or what you saw or heard happen, and that is the aim of participant observation.

Finally, here is an example of the dangers of vague notes:

This. . .

He appeared to be upset and said 'I wish I had never met you.'

could be this. . .

He paused for about thirty seconds after her comment, his face flushed and he rested his forehead on his left hand, elbow on the table. Tears flowed freely down his face during the entire observation. He said something which she appeared not to hear. I could not hear his words, either. He then said, 'I wish I had never met you.'

or it could be. . .

He took a black cast iron frying pan, about eight inches in diameter, and threw it the length of the room, approximately twelve feet, hitting the east wall and making a two-inch long dent in the plaster. Then he placed his face approximately three inches from hers, grabbed her left arm above her elbow and pinned it behind her back, saying, 'I wish I had never met you.'

Exercises for Chapter V

1.   Observe a situation containing people for two minutes (choose a setting which you can limit in terms of numbers of people and types of

action likely to occur, e.g. your room, a bus stop, a section of a pub or airport). Take notes, if you like, but you will probably find it will restrict your observation because of the short time you have.

2. Afterwards, write up everything you saw and heard in those two minutes, following the suggestions made in this chapter. You can start with 'At 10.20 a.m., the time my observation began, there were three people at the bus stop. . .' Writing up the notes will take much longer than two minutes, as you will notice.

Now answer these questions.

1. Where was the situation?
2. Where were you in relation to it?
3. What did you do during the observation?
4. What was the placement of other people?
5. What were your and their body positions? Sitting, standing, walking? If people were just passing by, include them, if possible.
6. Did you describe the movements of people?
7. What time was it? What was the temperature? Weather conditions?
8. What did the people wear? What colours, materials, lengths, styles? Do not forget accessories, shoes, hats.
9. What did people look like? Height, weight, age, hair colour and style, any distinguishing characteristics?
10. What did people say? In what order did they speak? Did anyone not speak? What gestures and body movements occurred in speech or while listening to speaking? Were there any other sounds? What about sounds in the background?
11. Did any of the above change during the observation? When? How?
12. What other physical objects were present? What was their shape, size, colour, material, texture? Where were they placed in relation to each other? If you were in a room, what were the dimensions of the room and placements of windows? Did you describe curtains or other window coverings, pictures, light fixtures, electrical outlets?

Now look to see if your notes answer those questions. What are your weaknesses? Do you notice what people say but not what they do? Are you good on people but bad on physical objects? Or do you notice colours but not materials or textures? Do you miss what other people say or do while one person is speaking or moving? List what you think are your weak points in observation.

Try a second exercise, lasting three minutes. Choose a setting which will present a good test of your weaker points, people if you are weak on gestures and conversation; a physical setting with a few people if you need to observe objects, materials, dimensions, and so forth.

Write your notes up once more and check them against the list of questions above. Then look at them against these points as well:

1. Circle all judgmental adjectives: old, slow, handsome, nervous, spacious, cozy, etc. Take each one and write what you actually saw and what led you to make the judgment to begin with?
2. Did you record everything *you* did and said during the observation?
3. To what extent do you feel your presence affected the situation? Are there some situations which should not be recorded? If people knew you were recording, what did they think about it? How would you feel if the people in your observation read your notes?

Keep trying the second exercise until you feel confident about observation. It is cheering to know that most people start out being very poor observers but become quite impressive after a few tries. Your memory and attention to detail will increase dramatically, and by monitoring your weaknesses, you will be ready to use participant observation as one of your research techniques.

For more information on participant observation, consult the following books. Friedrichs' book gives additional help on how to record and analyse the data obtained from participant observation.

Dillman, C. M. 'Ethical Problems in Social Science Research'. *Human Organisation* 36 (Winter 1977): 405-407.

Friedrichs, Jurgen and Ludtke, Harmut. *Participant Observation: Theory and Practice*. Hants, England; Lexington, Mass.: D. C. Heath & Co., 1975.

Hilbert, R. A., 'Covert Participant Observation: On Its Nature and Practice.' *Urban Life* 9 (April 1980): 51-78.

Johnson, John M. *Doing Field Research*. New York: Free Press, 1975.

Spradley, James P., *Participant Observation*. New York: Holt, Rinehart and Winston, 1980.

VI. Interviews

A. Types of Interviews

INTERVIEWS can take several forms, ranging from very informal exchanges to very structured, ordered sets of questions. The form you select depends upon your research, the subject, the kinds of information you need, the setting of your research and the characteristics of the people to whom you are talking. Parts of your research may require one kind of interview and parts may require another. One interview itself may contain various forms.

1. Standardised schedule interview

This is the most formally structured type of interview. The same information is required of each person, and each is asked exactly the same question in exactly the same order. The form from which these questions are asked is called the interview schedule and is, in fact, a type of questionnaire (see Chapter VII). Often the questions have been pre-tested on another group, to make sure that the wording and order give the best possible results. In this way, words that are confusing, phrases that seem to have different meanings for different people, and 'leading' questions that seem to bias people's answers may be removed. New questions may be inserted as a result of information gained from these 'pilot' interviews.

The standardised interview schedule is best used —

a. when you are interviewing a large number of people, because many of the answers may fall into clear-cut categories which can be coded and processed by a computer. (See Chapter X for a discussion on coding.)
b. when the people being interviewed are homogeneous and tend to share the same characteristics and outlooks. If you are interviewing people who are very different in life-style, philosophy and experience, the questions will tend to have different meanings for each sub-group, and the answers you receive, therefore, often cannot be compared.
c. When you already know enough about the subject and the kinds of interviewees that you know what is important to ask and how to ask it.

Remember that in this kind of interview, people have little opportunity to introduce serious variations on your choice of answers, and no opportunity at all to introduce a completely different orientation. This is a particularly important consideration when you are working with people whose culture is different from yours, or who represent a very different sub-group in your own society. For example, you may ask people in fictitious Oyam, which is fifty miles west of Truibui:

What do you like *least* about the train services from here to Truibui?

the expense 1
the length of time it takes 2
lack of dining facilities 3
trains not on time 4

The question and answers may seem straightforward enough, but suppose this happens to a group which believes it is dangerously foolhardy to begin any trip by going east, even if the ultimate destination is east. What they may dislike most, therefore, is the fact that they have to flout the supernatural if they ride the train, or else they have to choose other forms of transport.

Perhaps you are interested in teaching safety precautions to Paiute Indians in Nevada:

What are the *worst* things you can do in a thunderstorm?

For the oldest people who still remember and respect the old customs, the worst thing you can do is point your finger at a rainbow in the presence of a witch. Staying away from trees, avoiding sources of electricity, etc., all come second. So what you think of as 'common sense' will take you only so far once you leave your own culture.

Even in one's own society, it is easy to make invalid assumptions about respondents' points of view. The question —

Which do you thing is the most important issue in the coming national elections?

national defence 1
the economy 2
foreign relations 3
comprehensive medical insurance 4

can present second-best choices to people who think putting religion back into the fabric of society, improving women's rights or combating racism should be the basis of one's vote.

2. Standardised interview, no schedule

This type of interview is based on the assumption that it may take different kinds of questions, perhaps put in different order, to get the same information from different people. You proceed with any approach which is useful to convey to the interviewee the sense and meaning of what you want.

For example, if you want to get attitudes on drug use and abuse from illegal drug-users, doctors, law-enforcement officers, and members of the general public, you must take into account that each group may use different terms for the drugs, each may focus on a different dimension (the police, for example, focusing on the legal/illegal distinction, the doctor on the medical characteristics, the user on the methods of use and the cost). The questioning approach will be different as well; the drug-user may be reluctant and suspicious to say anything which might incriminate him; members of the public may be nervous about the whole topic; doctors may feel they are providing information which could allow even greater drug abuse. Doctors and law enforcement officers may prefer a more 'professional' approach; drug-users may be mistrustful of such an approach. Adapting the interview so that it is familiar, comfortable and meaningful to such different groups requires skill, practice and a good knowledge of the characteristics, outlooks and language of each group.

In this type of interview, the answers you get will probably cover more material and allow for group variation, but they will not fall into such neat categories as they do in the standardised schedule interview. If you are processing the information for a computer, it will take longer to code the material.

3. Unstructured interview

Here, there is no set order or wording of questions, no schedule, and you are not looking for the same information from each person. For example, if you are interested in studying the social history of a small town or village, you may approach a number of elderly people and ask them how things were in the old days. Each may remember different kinds of things; some may have been housewives, some fishermen, some farmers, some shopkeepers. You want to get from each his or her own perspective; each of the answers may lead you to develop a new question, not asked of any of the others. You may, of course, be interviewing only one person on a particular topic: the warden of a detention centre may be interviewed to find out what his day's work is; the only thatcher in the area may be interviewed to find out how thatching is done.

This form of interview is also often used at the beginning of the research project, when you know so little that you do not even know the *questions,* let alone the possible answer categories. Asking the widest, most general questions and allowing the interviewee to develop the subject the way he wishes may enable you to get a sufficiently general picture that you can then decide which specific topic of study you would like to follow.

All kinds of interviews fall into the third category; casual encounters, to take one example. Suppose you are studying, through several research techniques, the relationships between nurses and patients in a mental hospital. While you are in the canteen, a young nurse sits at your table. She mentions that she is having a hard day, that she has some of the most difficult patients in her care today. You remember that a section of your Research Outline calls for information on how the nurses categorise the types of patients. She has mentioned 'difficult' patients. What makes them difficult? What kinds are not difficult? Are there any other kinds besides difficult/

non-difficult? It is particularly important in this last type of interview that you have a clear Research Outline, and that you are familiar enough with it to carry the general points around in your head. This will allow you to make best use of chance encounters, and to keep the interview from wandering so much that it has no bearing on your research. You then, of course, have to see if these categories have meaning for other nurses, and if not, are there any that do?

A more extreme example of the third type of interview occurs when you are studying members of a group whose outlook, philosophy and customs are very different from your own. Anthropologists frequently face this problem in their study of other cultures. There are two ways to study a group: one is to find out how the group itself sees and categorises its world. This is called the 'emic' approach. A second involves imposing categories developed outside the groups: a set of questions based on standardised categories which can be used not only to study this group, but others, as well. This is the 'etic' approach. These terms, first suggested by the linguist Kenneth Pike in 1967, are borrowed from the words 'phonetic' and 'phonemic':

> Phonetics is the study of all possible sounds useable in speech production. At one time, phonetics set as a goal the accurate description of all sounds. During the early part of this century linguists shifted their attention to phonemics, the study of sound categories recognised and used by a particular language group. Emic descriptions of sound depended on discovering the native categories and perceptions. In the same way, emic descriptions of behaviour depended on discovering native categories of action. Etic descriptions, on the other hand, of sound or anything else are based on categories created by the investigator, and are usually employed to compare things cross-culturally. (Spradley: 1979: 231)

There are advantages to each approach. The emic approach allows you to see how the group perceives and organises its world; since each group is different, however, if you studied ten societies in this way, you would have no common basis on which to compare them. You would have ten pictures of the world. The etic approach allows you to compare societies, since, for all, you are using the same set of categories upon which to base questions. However, the categories may not fit each society equally well. So each approach has its advantages and disadvantages.

Try applying this, not to other societies, but to a group in your own society. If you were doing a study of St John's University students, one of the ways you might group them is by 'official' categories, that is, in the same way that the university officially categorises them: first, second, third year students; or arts students and science students, or day and evening students. Not only would you apply these categories to St John's University but they could also be applied to all other universities in the country. Thus, if you wished, you could make comparisons between universities: one university has 20 per cent science students, while another has only 9 per cent. This is an etic categorisation of students because it arose from externally-developed categories, those of officials rather than students, and since the categories are the same in other universities, it allows comparisons.

On the other hand, you might find out instead what categories the students use to group themselves: the emic categorisation. Of course they recognise the idea of first, second and third year, but do these really count very much in their day-to-day interaction? If you gave a student a pack of cards, with the name of one student written on each card, asked him 'What kind of students are here at the university?' and asked him to sort the cards into categories, would first, second and third years be an important set of groups for him? Eventually, you might discover that the students saw five categories of students: 'People who never take their noses out of books', 'Troublemakers', 'Decent People', 'Big shots', and 'Foreign students'. And you might, after further research, find that the other students generally agreed with this division and which people fell into each group. (The fact that foreign students could also be decent or troublemakers, incidentally, does not concern you; if this is the way the students group their fellows, seeing the foreigners as a group apart, so be it. Emic research is about how the group's members see things, not how you think things should be.)

This kind of research might be useful if you were looking into problems among the student body, and how to improve relations. It is not useful, however, for making comparisons; if you extend your study to St George's University it is quite possible that the students do not group their fellows in exactly the same way – they may have more or fewer categories, and entirely different divisions.

What happens if the students disagree on the categories? It may be that there is no shared picture among the group members and that in itself may be useful to know. They may, in fact, generally agree but be using different terms to cover the same categories. In this case, you will have to compare each student's categories and see whether you can find common ground. You then rephrase the categories, present them to each student, ask if he or she agrees with these, and if so, which students fall into each category.

This, then, is emic research. How do you do it? For simple categorisations, you can use the pile of cards mentioned above – on each card write a person's name, an event, an action, or a 'thing', and ask a question such as 'What types of work are done in this factory?' 'What kinds of towns are there around here?' 'What kinds of people are on these cards?' The respondent then sorts the cards into categories which mean something to him or her.

This implies that you already know enough to be able to write down the words to be sorted into piles. So the first step is to find out what there *is*, in this world you are trying to study. This is done by asking the broadest possible question: what has been called the 'grand tour question' (Spradley and McCurdy, 1972: 62): 'What happens in this factory? 'Tell me about your day as a child-minder.' 'What kinds of people come to this restaurant?'

Here is an example of how to pursue this kind of questioning. (The numbers preceding the questions are used only to clarify the explanation which follows.)

Q.1. What's here in the university?
A.1. Well, there are the buildings and the students and the faculty and the other staff and the library.
Q.2. Tell me about the buildings.
A.2. There are the historic buildings, and the modern buildings, and the Student Union.
Q.3. Tell me about the historic buildings.
A.3. There are only two – the Castle and the lodge.
Q.4. Tell me about the modern buildings.
A.4. There's the New Arts Block, the canteen and the crêche.
Q.5. Tell me about the Student Union.
A.5. The Student Union was built about three years ago and we really only use the bar.
Q.6. Tell me about the students.

Of course, you would pursue each answer further, and you can use more casual or natural wording for the questions, but I have given this example to show the pattern: except for the first question, the questioner makes up no new question of his own; he uses the replies of the interviewee to build the next question. When the student replies 'There's the New Arts Block, the canteen and the crêche', the questioner could have said 'Tell me about the New Arts Block' but decided not to pursue it. Where, then, did he get the question 'Tell me about the Student Union'? From A.2. The questioner had already asked about the first two parts of the reply, the historic buildings and the modern buildings. When every question about the buildings is exhausted, the questioner goes back to A.1., and sees what the interviewee's next point was – students. When that is exhausted, he will look at A.1. again and take the faculty as the basis for his next question. Using this method, you do not introduce questions based on your own orientation or viewpoint. Instead the interviewee provides both the answers and the basis for the questions. Notice also that you get information on the way this student categorises his environment. Why, for example, did he made a distinction between the 'modern buildings' and the Student Union, which was built only three years ago? It would be useful to know whether the other students make this same distinction. You can imagine how helpful this method would be if you were working among a people culturally different from you. Putting your own questions to them would reflect your cultural categories, not theirs.

In your questioning, in order to discover *how* people categorise things, you will find yourself asking about types and kinds, for instance, 'What kinds of students go to school here?' 'What types of juvenile delinquents are sent to this centre?' 'Tell me about all the different types of things your motorcycle club does?'

Listen carefully to the answers. People will not make your job easier by announcing categories to you. A waitress might say 'Oh, some people are big spenders on expense accounts. Others have you run off your feet all night and never leave a tip. And then there are the regulars.' So far, the waitress has given you three categories which are important for her to know about in her work. These categories are the sort of information, for example, that she might pass on to a new waitress in order to be helpful. When an interviewee says 'Mr Jones is the kind of neighbour who keeps himself to himself but Mr Smith is just a snob'; or, 'We hold motorcycle races, work on our machines, and just hang out' you are being given categories. But you have to listen for them. You might even want to find out what the difference is between a person who keeps himself to himself, and a snob.

This approach is given here simply as an aid to interviewing. More about using the complete method is available in the following —

Spradley, James P., and David W. McCurdy, *The Cultural Experience.* Chicago: Science Research Associates, 1972.
Spradley, James P., *The Ethnographic Interview.* New York, Montreal, London: Holt, Rinehart and Winston, 1979.

B. Interviewing Techniques

If you are blessed with the right personality, manner of presenting yourself and habits of interacting with others, a discussion of interviewing techniques might be largely academic. However, since the 'right' personality, manner and habits may differ, depending upon the nature and situation of the interview and the person you are interviewing, you obviously cannot rely on your natural gifts alone. A teenage girl interviewing an elderly male on the sexual needs of the elderly in institutional care is probably going to be at a disadvantage, no matter what.

Usually, the principle is that the closer the interviewer is to the respondent in class, sex, age and interests, the greater chance the interviewer has of being successful. If you have to hire interviewers, this is a safe guideline to consider, all other things being equal. Often, however, your only interviewer will be you. It will cheer you up, therefore, to consider the successful cases of Bronislaw Malinowski, the Polish-British anthropologist who worked among the people of the Trobriand Islands in the South Pacific, or Ulf Hannerz, a Swede who worked with blacks in Washington, D.C., or any number of anthropologists, most of whom are as unlike their interviewees as it is possible to be.

Since you are more likely to be interviewing members of Western society whose culture does not differ much from your own, you can use standard Western techniques of conversation: engaging in small talk to put the interviewee at ease; not leaping in immediately after a reply, thus encouraging the interviewee to comment at greater length; not showing shock or surprise at replies; looking for examples when the replies are too vague or abstract; and, more controversially, 'challenging' the interviewee who will not talk by offering viewpoints known to be different from the ones he holds. Often, a person may be encouraged to discuss a sensitive subject by letting him know that you already know something about it; for example, a local argument. Some people will not talk when others are present; others need someone present to give them support. In any kind of interview, it is important not to lead the interviewee by using words or signals which convey expectations of particular kinds of responses. Many researchers train their assistants to give standardised, non-committal comments and when more information is needed in response to a question, a standard probe is developed, to be read to the interviewee:

What do you like best about living in this neighbourhood?

Suppose this is an open-ended question and one of the respondents says 'the people'.

PROBE: What is it about the people that you like?

The word 'probe' is in uppercase letters because it is an instruction to the interviewer. Such upper-case instructions are not read aloud. Probes can be worked out in advance for potentially inadequate answers, and printed on the form itself. Interviewers can also be trained to create appropriate probes in unexpected situations. Probes expand upon an incomplete answer; they are not used to badger the respondent into giving up every smidge of information he possesses.

Many things – your tone of voice, manner, gestures, your personal characteristics and those of the interviewee, the presence of others, and interruptions – may influence the quality of the interview, so it is important to record as much as possible of the circumstances of the interview to get it in context. Later, when you read your notes and find that the whole tenor of the interview changed part way through, you may be able to discover whether it is possible to try to compare the information in this interview with that of another collected under very different circumstances.

You have got to get certain information across to the interviewee. How and when you do it depends upon the formality of the interview; in a very formal interview, you introduce yourself and follow this with

1. the name of the organisation or group you represent, if any;
2. what the study is about, presented in such a way that the interviewee sees its general relevance and, if possible, its relevance to his or her own life and experiences. If you are working in an area where your interviewees and potential interviewees have a good chance of exchanging information with each other, it is especially important that your explanation be clear, simple and that it 'travel' well, to reduce possible distortion of your purpose as the account travels from one person to another. Otherwise, future interviewees may form an attitude in advance of your arrival which biases their willingness to cooperate and their responses.
3. how he or she came to be selected for interview. If the study were about attitudes towards corporal punishment for children, a respondent might suspect that his neighbours directed you to him either as a joke or as a potential child-beater; or that some 'official' agency has mistakenly got his

name on a list of families requiring supervision. Neither of these provides the setting for a cooperative interview.

Give a brief explanation of the selection method; perhaps that people of different occupations, sexes and age groups must be included in order to get a good understanding of the situation. 'We took a random sample of all the people who ever bought Rolls Royces, and yours is one of the names in the sample.' Assure the person that his or her replies will be confidential, and that he will not be able to be identified. Not only do people usually want their replies to be anonymous, but they also fear getting their names on mysterious lists which expose them to junk mail or telephone solicitors.

In more informal interviews, such a barrage of initial information might be intimidating to a person who simply thought he was giving you a lift in his car, but once it becomes clear that you are looking for information, most people want an explanation, which can often be presented naturally as the conversation develops.

People may refuse to be interviewed. I have done so myself on several occasions when it was obvious from the general approach that so little thought or so much bias was reflected in the questions that the results would be useless or misleading. None of the standard techniques for dealing with recalcitrant interviewees would have worked on me, but since most people are not quite so pig-headed, here are some to try.

1. If a random sample (see page 000) was used to select respondents, it is necessary that the responses of *this* interviewee be included, since substitutions are not permitted. Explain that you cannot 'get someone else' as he suggests; it must be he.

2. Explain that the questionnaire will not take much time (if it will not).

3. If the respondent believes that all these studies go up in smoke, that is, that no one ever sees the results, show some published examples of similar studies, or newspaper or magazine coverage of such studies.

4. The respondent may dislike your 'type', as perceived by him on ethnic, racial, sexual or other grounds. My father would never admit a stranger with unshined shoes, since he assumed it meant that the person was up to no good. I, on the other hand, have a sneaking fondness for people with slight overbites. Since there is no accounting for tastes, you may find that it is easier to go away and send someone else who you think will be more acceptable to the interviewee.

5. You can try the 'craven grovel' approach on people who continue to refuse. Emphasise that this study is important in getting your degree or getting a good grade, or even in keeping your job as an interviewer. If the person really dislikes you, this will add to his glee. Others, however, may sympathise. Of course, on both moral and pragmatic grounds, any story you tell should be true.

6. Give the reluctant person an opening in what may be a distressing situation. A housewife with small messy children who rarely has visitors and dreams of the day when her house will be neat so she can entertain properly,

may not want to be seen as a person living in depressing squalor on one of her very infrequent 'social' occasions. An elderly couple eating their one modest meal of the day at the time of your arrival might like to preserve some vestige of dignity before a stranger. Ask if there is a convenient time for you to return, since you would really like to get their opinions. Try to get the interviewee to set a specific time.

Some sampling methods may involve you or someone else having to return several times to those who have refused, since you cannot substitute other people. This is costly to you and bothersome to all, so it is important that you do your best on the first occasion. For subsequent tries, you have to figure out what went wrong the first time and try to develop an approach which deals with it on the second visit.

After you have gone through the process of getting a research idea, refining it into a Research Statement, working out a Research Outline, selecting and learning research techniques, planning and designing a questionnaire or interview, training assistants, and perhaps applying for a research grant, it is very easy to lose sight of the fact that it is actual human beings who are going to be on the receiving end of all this. If one's preparation has taken eight months, for example, it is easy to fool oneself into imagining that the respondents have been eagerly waiting to hear from you for eight months, and that they are as fascinated by your study as you are. On the other hand, your fantasies may have produced visions of curmudgeons intent only on sabotaging your work. Thinking so dismissively of people as subjects will diminish what is, in fact, your main research aim – better human understanding. Interviewing, or any research technique, is enhanced by a proper perspective.

Since conducting an interview and administering a questionnaire involve many similar procedures and problems of question design and order, you should read Chapter Seven for further information. You may also wish to consult some of the following works:

Gordon, Raymond, L., *Interviewing*. Homewood, Ill.: Dorsey Press, 1980.

Harrison, A. A., *et al.*, 'Cues to Deception in an Interview Situation.' *Social Psychology* 41 (June 1978): 156-161.

Hyman, Herbert Hiram, *Interviewing in Social Research*. Chicago: University of Chicago Press, 1975.

Richetto, Gary M., *Fundamentals of Interviewing*. Palo Alto, Calif.: Social Research Associates, 1976.

Spradley, James P., *The Ethnographic Interview*. New York, Montreal, London: Holt, Rinehart and Winston, 1979.

Stewart, Charles J, *Interviewing*. Dubuque, Iowa: W. C. Brown Co, 1978.

VII. Questionnaires

by Ann Lavan

A. Questionnaires

THERE are several information-gathering techniques which are included in the scope of this chapter. The most general word for them is a *survey,* a technique in which a set of questions is presented to a group of respondents; either a sample, or, less commonly, an entire group. More specifically, surveys may be divided into two categories, depending upon who administers them. If they are self-administered, that is, the respondent herself writes the replies on the form, they are referred to as a *questionnaire.* Postal questionnaires are one example of this type. On the other hand, questions delivered in a face-to-face encounter by an interviewer are usually referred to as an *interview schedule.* For the purpose of this chapter, the term 'questionnaire' will be used to refer to both.

A questionnaire, like participant observation, can be used before you begin your research, to get enough preliminary information to decide how you want to limit your Research Statement, or even to decide to change the entire problem as a result of what you discover. It can also be used, after developing your Research Outline, as your only research technique, or as part of a group of techniques. This will depend upon what your problem requires.

The stages to be borne in mind in questionnaire construction are —

1. selecting the population to whom the questions will be addressed.
2. designing the questionnaire
    a. preparatory work
    b. questionnaire format
    c. question content
    d. pre-testing
3. training the interviewers
4. coding the data
5. analysing the data (discussed in Chapter XI)

1. Selecting the population

Perhaps the number in your study group is naturally restricted, all the mothers in the community association with children under five years old, and that happens to be only fifteen mothers, or all the men on a football team. But perhaps the possible number of people who could answer the questionnaire is very large: all the residents north of the river, or every nurse in Ireland. Then you have to cut the numbers, for two reasons:

- Asking everyone would take too much time and too much money.
- Once you get above a certain proportion, your chances of accuracy are not improved much.

You can cut the population in several ways. First, you can reduce it to only one area, for instance, four streets in one neighbourhood, or to just the nurses of St Vincent's Hospital. However, you cannot then claim that your study represents all of the northern part of the city, or all of the nurses in the country, because it does not.

A second way of cutting the population is to take a *sample*. Many people who have not been exposed to research think that a sample is just a helter-skelter collection of people or items. In fact, there is nothing less helter-skelter than a sample, and there are rules for sampling. You are not entitled to call your group a sample unless you have followed those rules. To learn more about sampling, see pages 90-97.

2. Designing the questionnaire

a. Preparatory Work

You get your questions from your Research Outline. Go through it noting those points marked 'questionnaire' under the column headed 'Techniques'. List the points and try to formulate a clear idea of what is to be explored by means of the questionnaire. For example, you may see from your Research Outline that you need information on the age, education, and marital status of mothers in a neighbourhood. Before concerning yourself with the details of *how* you will ask the question, simply list *what* you need to know. It may be helpful to equip yourself with two sets of index cards of different colours. One set is used to list the items; that is, on separate cards you will write 'Age', 'Education', and 'Marital Status'. Use your second set of cards to phrase the actual questions.

Sometimes, of course, you do not have enough preliminary knowledge to block out the main or sub-points in your Research Outline. You do not know enough yet to distinguish between what is essential to the problem and what seems important but in fact is not. In such cases, a *pilot survey* is useful. Select a variety of people roughly similar to those who you think will be your final respondents. In experimental interviews, try various lines of questioning and types of questions to see what the characteristics of the problem or situation are. A pilot survey, if properly analysed afterwards, can help not only to define your subject but also to give you some preliminary warnings and assistance on problem areas, such as questions which are sensitive or meaningless, or which elicit vague responses. You might even learn that a research technique other than a questionnaire might be the best approach to the subject.

b. Questionnaire Format

The layout of a questionnaire can be as important as the wording of questions. Most research textbooks include examples of format, and it is worth consulting some of those listed at the end of this chapter to develop your ideas about the presentation which is most appropriate for your study. A badly laid-out questionnaire can cause interviewers and respondents to become confused or miss questions. The design of the questionnaire depends on the people you are going to interview and the purpose of your enquiry, but as a general rule, the questionnaire form should be simple, with plenty of space for replies. If the questionnaire is to be self-administered, it is important that the layout be particularly spacious, with a minimum of questions, and clear instructions about completion.

(1) Introduction: in interviewer-administered questionnaires, the first sheet of the interview schedule is used to record 'administrative' information. This is called the 'face sheet'.

Name of organisation here   Schedule number ☐ ☐ ☐

Interviewer:

Call record:

Date: ....   Length of interview: ....

Call on which interview was obtained   1   2   3   4   *(Circle as appropriate)*

Reason for no interview: *(Specify)*

INTRODUCTION: *(statement of reason for interview)*

Many surveys offer a guarantee of confidentiality to the respondent and it is therefore important that there is no indication of his or her name on the questionnaire. Obviously, however, you and your assistants must know who has been interviewed. Keep a master list (under lock and key) of the people to be interviewed and assign code numbers to each person on the list. If there are 300 people to be interviewed, the first person on the list, John Martin, is given number 001. This code is written on the master list beside his name and also on the right hand corner of the face sheet, where you will have provided three boxes for what is called the 'schedule number'.

The INTRODUCTION is the opening statement to be made to respondents as an invitation to cooperate. The full text may not be completely typed out on the questionnaire but the word INTRODUCTION indicates to the interviewer that he or she should refer to what are called 'Notes for Interviewers'. These are found on an additional piece of paper which gives the interviewer precise instructions about the manner in which different sections of the questionnaire are to be introduced, since it is important that all respondents receive exactly the same explanations and instructions.

Most new researchers tend to give lengthy opening statements. With experience, you will discover that two short concise sentences explaining the purpose of the survey, together with some skill in interpersonal relations, are usually enough to engage the respondent's cooperation.

Sometimes the face sheet contains space to record, after the interview, a brief sketch of the circumstances, the respondent's attitude, and anything that may have influenced the interview. Alternatively, this information may be recorded in a space at the end of the questionnaire.

(2) Order: this requires sensitivity to areas of investigation about which your respondents may have special feelings. The usual practice is to place the questions in this order:

    (a) broader, impersonal, easy-to-answer questions which enlist the respondent's cooperation and interest;

    (b) less interesting questions

    (c) sensitive or personal questions, and open-ended questions.

Bridging phrases can be used to avoid sharp transitions from one topic to the next: 'You said earlier that you had three accidents at work. I'd like to ask you some questions now about your company's medical coverage' or 'We've talked a bit about your job and now I'd like to ask you about your leisure activities'. The order of questions should facilitate a natural flow of conversation. In self-administered questionnaires, the bridges can be written into the questions.

(3) Answer choices: the respondent may be given the opportunity to reply to open-ended questions which do not provide an answer category or alternatively the questions may be pre-coded/closed/forced-choice. It is, of course, possible to decide to have a combination of both open-ended questions and pre-coded questions. In the case of the latter a choice of answers is provided on the form; the person answering must make a 'forced choice':

Please indicate your opinion about having a community centre by marking whichever of the statements below is closest to your view. *(TICK ONE)*

No opinion	[ ]
Not desirable	[ ]
Fairly desirable	[ ]
Very desirable	[ ]

    — or —

Please indicate your opinion about having a community centre. *(CIRCLE ONE)*

No opinion	1
Not desirable	2
Fairly desirable	3
Very desirable	4

In the first of the two preceding examples you will notice that the response categories are presented in the form of 'boxes'. If the questionnaire is not typed on a typewriter with bracket symbols, you can use parentheses. In the second example, instead of boxes, the *code number* for each answer is typed on the questionnaire. This has the advantage of specifying to the computer operator the number to be entered later on in the computer processing stage (see pages 82-86).

As indicated earlier, another method of dealing with answer choices is to design a questionnaire which includes both pre-coded/closed/forced-choice questions *and* 'open-ended' questions. Open-ended questions permit a free response: they raise an issue but do not provide answer categories. For example:

> You have been living in Willow Green for five years; will you tell me —
> What do you like *most* about it?

When open-ended questions are asked, enough space must be left for the respondent to answer the questions in his or her own words. This usually means allowing more space than you would ordinarily think necessary, particularly for self-administered questionnaires. Open-ended questions will greatly increase the work of analysis because the replies must be categorised and coded after the questionnaire has been administered. Therefore, it is often useful to aim at designing a semi-structured form in which the respondent replies to a series of forced-choice questions and only a small number of open-ended ones.

(4) Filter questions: sometimes your study group is 'mixed', i.e. composed of people whose characteristics differ so much that some of the questions in the questionnaire will not apply to them. Obviously, 'How many times have you been pregnant?' will not apply to the males of your group, but in the case of 'Do you own your own home? If 'yes', do you have house insurance?', the second of the two questions may apply to only some respondents. If you have a large number of questions which will apply only to one specific group, you might consider using two or more questionnaires, thus making each one more relevant to its own group. This simplifies several processes, notably interviewing, coding and data processing.

If you use only one questionnaire, there are several simple, easily-followed systems which will prevent people from answering or being annoyed by those questions which do not apply to them. One is to use 'filter questions', which direct respondents to a new, special question, depending upon their reply to the first. Filter questions do this by attaching further instructions to the answer choices presented:

8. Do you own a pet? *(TICK ONE)*

　　　　　　　Yes .... [ ] *GO TO Q. 9*
　　　　　　　No .... [ ] *GO TO Q. 10*

Another solution is to use a 'box' for the second question:

8. Do you own a pet? *(CIRCLE ONE)*

Yes 1

.... 2

If Yes: How much to you spend each week on pet food?

nothing 1

less than 50p 2

50p – £1 .... 3 (etc.)

There are other filtering methods, but these are probably among the easiest for the respondent to follow. In planning filter questions, the best method is to write down the question, consider each of the possible answers, and then decide whether you want to know more arising from any of those answers. In the planning example below, the questions are under-lined, and the answer choices are in upper-case.

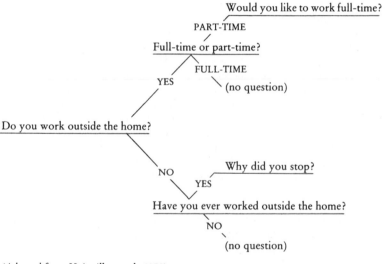

(Adapted from Hoinville, et al., 1978)

c. Question Content

The questions should fit the respondent's frame of reference: they must seem logical and meaningful. They must also correspond to his or her knowledge; that is, people should not be asked questions which they cannot answer, or questions to which they must give socially or legally un-acceptable answers – they may become threatened, conclude that the ques-tionnaire is irrelevant, or make up answers.

Certain types of question content are more sensitive to format than others: Bradburn and Sudman, in a study of responses to 'threatening' questions about gambling, drinking, sexual behaviour, and so forth, found that replies about merely performing the behaviour, in a 'yes' or 'no' form, were not affected by changes in question format. On the other hand, detailed replies involving frequency and intensity of these activities were sensitive to differences in question structure, length, and so on (1979: 18-19).

(1) Problem questions: there are a number of traps to avoid when you write your questions. Some of them are based on common sense, but others might strike you only when you get baffling or useless replies on your questionnaire. For example —

- The Double Question: 'Do you walk to school or carry your lunch?' The wording of some questions makes them difficult or impossible to answer accurately. Sometimes they contain two or more unrelated or even contradictory parts, the answers to which may be different: 'Are you happy in your marriage and job?' Some are simply confusing: 'Would you agree that it is not unlikely that our next mayor won't be a woman?' A question that to you seems extra-carefully worded may be a mind-bender to your respondents.

- The Wrong-Choice Question: 'Is your hair yellow, purple, green or blue?' Pre-testing your questions on a practice group will help to ensure that you give your respondents appropriate questions and all the relevant choices of answers. Horse sense often is not enough here, for what may appear bizarre or unthinkable behaviour to you (and therefore ignored in your questionnaire) may be a way of life to some of your respondents.

- The Kitchen Sink Question: 'Please list all the places you have worked in the past five years, the type of work done and salary received, and why you left.' To save confusion in replying, recording and coding the answers, ask each part of the question separately.

- The 'Fuzzy Word' Question: 'Should middle-aged people live it up?' There are two problems here. 'Middle-aged' does not mean the same age group to everyone, and 'living it up' can mean anything from wearing red to keeping a harem. Fuzzy words can creep into almost any question: 'Do you attend dances frequently?' (or 'rarely' or 'occasionally' or 'often') will give meaningless answers.

- The Cover-the-World Question: 'What do you think of the President?' could refer to the man personally, his job performance, or his status as president of the nation. 'What's this neighbourhood like?' is useful in some interviews (see emic interviews, pp.00-00) but if you know what aspect of the neighbourhood interests you, ask specifically about that.

- Jargon Questions: 'Do you feel that your husband has a self-actualising autonomous personality structure?' is an affront to the respondent as well as to the English language. Also, be careful about words which have one meaning to the professionals in your field and another, or none, to the public. 'Culture', 'personality', 'role', or 'institution' cannot be treated as if all respondents shared a common understanding of the professional meaning you intended.

More generally, the language and style of the questionnaire must be comfortable to the respondent. 'Writing down' is insulting, and using dialect or 'in' words to reach a group of which you are obviously not a member is usually inappropriate.

- 'Dream' Questions: hypothetical questions do not necessarily produce comparable answers from different respondents. 'What kind of education would you like for your child?' might produce a 'sky's the limit' answer from a person who is stating his absolute ideal; from another person, you might receive a modest statement of the best he or she thinks the child is likely to get. Make sure you know whether your question examines wishes or expectations.

- Leading Questions: 'Why are you happy here in Newtown?' or 'Why do you think the community looks up to doctors?' gives the respondent little opening to say he is miserable in Newtown and thinks that most of the people in his community feel that doctors are charlatans.

- 'Hearsay' Questions: 'Do you think your neighbours are happy about the new school?' Do not ask one person the opinions or attitudes of another, unless you wish to compare the first person's impressions with facts which you will establish from t' second person. You cannot cut down on your population numbers by asking a small number of people what they think the attitudes of other people might be.

- 'Fall-out' Questions: these are sets of questions in which something important gets lost on the way. Here is a real-life example: a woman who normally dyes her hair red went to a hairdresser who required that his clients fill out a questionnaire before getting their hair done. Bad dyes of *any* colour will turn hair red. The questionnaire asked:

  1. Do you colour your hair?　　　Yes ....　　No ....
  2. If yes, does it ever turn red?　Yes ....　　No ....
  3. If yes, what product do you use? ....

The conclusion which the hairdresser drew was that anyone who answered 'yes' to Question 2 was using bad hair dye – a conclusion which was invalidated by all the women who purposely dyed their hair red.

Finally, it is obvious that if uninfluenced answers are required, you do not put questions in the form of 'You don't think ...., do you? (Moser and Kalton 1971: 308). But the researcher's biases and preferences can be projected in more subtle ways. In our example of neighbourhood mothers with children under five years of age, the focus of inquiry might be their views about adult educational opportunities for themselves, and their aspirations for their children. The wording of these questions can easily imply that adult education or certain kinds of educational aspirations are something the *researcher* values, and therefore the mother may feel she is expected to make particular choices.

(2) Question checks: within the questionnaire, it is possible to check the consistency of a respondent's answers by rephrasing a question and presenting it a second time, later in the questionnaire. For example:

Government control of family planning is desirable *(CIRCLE ONE)*

Agree 1
Disagree 2
Don't know 3

and later

Family planning should not be in the control of governments *(CIRCLE ONE)*

Agree 1
Disagree 2
Don't know 3

This is not a fail-proof guarantee of accuracy: someone obsessively dedicated to giving you the wrong idea will probably insure that the 'check' question is answered in the same way as the original. Question checks are also useful for testing the reliability of your questions because if people consistently contradict themselves on the same question phrased in two different ways, one or both of the questions is probably unreliable, and should be re-written.

d. Pre-testing

While the pilot survey is a general exploration to determine the focus and approach of the study, the *pre-test* is a final 'dry run' of the entire survey – the questionnaire, the interviewers, the instructions, and the sampling method, if a sample is used (a smaller sample is chosen for the pre-test) to identify unexpected flaws. As is true with the pilot survey responses, the pre-test results should be analysed. In this case, the questionnaire responses should be counted and analysed for weaknesses; the interviewers should be encouraged to write their own and interviewees' comments about particular questions; and reasons for refusals should be investigated.

3. Selecting and training the interviewers

If you use interviewer-assistants, you will be heavily dependent upon their intelligence, accuracy, honesty, reliability and personality. A researcher who is careless or inattentive, or who has a personal bias in relation to the subject or the interviewees can undo much of the effort you have put into constructing the questionnaire and selecting the interviewees. On the other hand, Bradburn and Sudman, in a study of interviewer problems in survey research, found that interviewers' preconceived ideas about problems they might have with the interview or the respondents had little effect on the responses obtained. They also found that previous interviewing experience had some unexpected consequences: more experienced interviewers made more reading errors and variations from the questionnaire, and probed more often. This probably reflected a less-formal approach, and was not significant. (1979: 49, 61-62).

You can check interviewer-related problems, at least to some extent, by monitoring the completed questionnaires as they come in and by comparing the results obtained by various interviews for patterned differences. At the same time, you can also see that all answers are fully completed and legible, and that there is consistency among interviewers in recording and coding. Directors of major surveys sometimes use extensive screening and training procedures for their interviewers. You, too, might save yourself future aggravation by testing potential interviewers for ability in some of the basic tasks of questionnaire administration; specifically, recording accurately and legibly, following instructions, and being able to stick to the sampling procedure. Training, through observing skilled interviewers and doing practice interviews, will help to develop skills such as avoiding diversions from the questionnaire, and presenting an interested and friendly but impartial attitude.

Equip the interviewers with a sheet of instructions explaining —

a. how to go about contacting the prospective respondents.

b. how to introduce oneself and the questionnaire

c. how to record the answers. Open-ended responses should be recorded word-for-word, in the first person ('I like the pre-school programme. . .' rather than 'Mrs Brown likes the pre-school programme. . .')

d. how to explain questions, if necessary, and what probes to use. Probes may be specific comments, or they may consist of ways of behaving. The University of Michigan's *Interviewer's Manual* (1976: 15-16) suggests that when a respondent does not reply fully or clearly, the interviewer might

- repeat the question

- allow an expectant pause

- repeat the respondent's reply

- interject neutral comments, such as 'Why do you feel that way?' 'Anything else?'

- ask for clarification: 'I'm not quite sure what you mean by that – could you tell me a little more?'

e. how to record interviewer's comments – usually in brackets: [respondent seemed confused, even after probes]

It is essential that the interviewers report back to you about any problems or failures to get interviews. In this way, you can correct difficulties as they arise. Once you get interviewers filling in just any response to avoid your wrath, or through boredom or ignorance, the research is undermined.

4. Coding the data

When people think of analysis of survey data, they tend to think of computers. It is well to remember that the decision to use a computer is largely related to the number of people interviewed and the complexity of the information sought. If, for example, you administer a questionnaire to one hundred people, and ask them five or six forced-choice questions each, you can probably analyse the results by manually sorting the questionnaires and counting the answers to each question.

However, you may have interviewed a larger number of people, or may be interested in exploring the relationships between variables (how many of the mothers aged twenty years and under thirty – variable 'AGE' – stated that the thing they liked best about the area – variable 'AREA' – was the school system?' In that case, you will probably decide to use a computer to help you. In either case, it is important to stress that you must consider the method of analysis of your data *at the design stage* of your questionnaire.

a. Quantifying Data

In designing pre-coded/closed/forced-choice questions, you have already given the 'codes' in the form of numbered alternatives: (when using boxes, you can put the codes in small figures inside the boxes)

> Are you? *(CIRCLE ONE)*
> single 1
> married 2
> separated 3
> divorced 4   (22)
> widowed 5

Suppose that for this question the respondent chooses answer '4'. The figure at the far right in parentheses is the column number of the code sheet or line of input on the computer on which the answer, 4, will be entered. Code sheets and lines of input have eighty columns. The first several columns, depending upon the size of the sample or group, are used to record the identification number of the questionnaire. In a sample of 100, three columns would be necessary; the first questionnaire would be number 001, which is recorded in the first three columns of the first line. The response code for the first question is then recorded in line 4, and so on. If more than eighty columns are needed to record all of 001's responses, a second line is used. Questionnaire 002 is entered on the next line, and 002's response codes follow.

If you have more than nine possible answers to a question, you must use two columns for each answer – thus '4' in column 22 now becomes '0' in column 22 and '4' in column 23; '19' becomes '1' in column 22 and '9' in column 23.

Allowing more than one answer choice per question requires special coding:

To which of the following organisations do you belong?

(*TICK AS MANY AS APPLY*)

.... Businesswomen's Association (01)
.... Soroptimists (02)
.... St John's Church Auxiliary (03)
.... Greenville Gardening Society (04)
.... Carmichael Bridge Club (05)
.... Medway Bowling Club (06)
.... Other* *(please specify:)*

(*Additional codes may be assigned to those organisations appearing in 'Other' at the coding stage.)

If you decide to allow the respondent more than one choice of answer to a question, you must first assign a range of codes which will permit inclusion of a list of the usual organisations, together with 'other' which may be coded at the coding stage; second, assign a number of sets of double columns which will enable you to code all the answers given by the respondents. Suppose you decide to assign five sets of double columns for coding the answers to the question on membership of organisations: the respondent who belongs to the Greenville Gardening Society only, will then have the code (04) in the first two columns, (10 and 11) of the ten columns 10 to 19 inclusive assigned for coding the answers. In the example just given where the respondent belonged to only one organisation, it is advisable to enter '00' in the remaining four sets of double columns to confirm the fact that only one organisation was ticked for this respondent. It is preferable to code non-responses so that they are not confused with questions mistakenly skipped while coding.

A questionnaire which is completely pre-coded and has the appropriate column(s) recorded beside each answer has two advantages.

1. It can be entered directly into the computer without an intermediate stage. If the questionnaire codes and column numbers are sufficiently clear, the computer operator can often work directly from the questionnaire. Otherwise, you must first transfer the codes for all replies to each questionnaire onto a computer code sheet, which is divided into twenty rows, each containing eighty columns. Each row represents one line of input. The operator then works from this.

2. I have described the preparation of data for computer analysis in terms of code sheets because in that way it is easier to visualise the process. Increasingly, however, it is usual to enter the data directly onto the Researcher's directory on an interactive system which is linked to the computer memory.

3. If the codes are complicated, or post-coded, you need a record of the appropriate codes and their meanings. A codebook lists, for each question, the column number(s) in which the response codes will be placed, the question number, and the correct codes for each possible response. The codebook is used as a guide in post-coding, and can be useful later as a reference when you are reading the computer print-outs and analysing the

results.

For a study of 352 people, the first items in the codebook might be:

Question	Column	Variable and Code
–	1–3	respondent number (001-352)
–	4	computer code sheet number (1) (if more than one card must be used)

1	5	age
		    1 = 25-34
		    2 = 35-44
		    3 = 45-54

2	6	marital status
		    1 = single
		    2 = married
		    3 = separated
		    4 = divorced
		    5 = widowed

This procedure is repeated for each question. Generally, it is useful to aim for as much detail as possible in coding. In the age variable above, for example, you could assign double columns (columns 6 *and* 7) and use the actual age of the respondent, say 27, as the code.

I mentioned earlier that the analysis of replies to open-ended questions may pose difficulties for the inexperienced. No amount of warning will inhibit the aspiring researcher from using the open-ended question, but the headache of analysis is guaranteed to make one more cautious in succeeding studies. The best procedure for constructing codes for open-ended questions is to list all the responses that have emerged on a sample of the completed questionnaires and see if you can think of a range of categories into which they can be classified. For example, if you have an open-ended question on what mothers like most about their area, an initial check of a random selection will give you an indication that some replies are concerned with the physical location of the neighbourhood; others mention specific facilities such as parks and playgrounds, and still others mention the feeling of neighbourliness. One general rule of thumb is recommended: if the data are coded to maintain a good deal of detail, code categories can always be combined later during an analysis that does not require much detail. If, however, you have coded all your responses into a few gross categories, there is no way during the analysis to recreate the original detail.

If your questionnaire layout is spacious enough, you may be able to write the appropriate codes right on the completed questionnaire, and the operator may still be able to work from the questionnaire itself. More importantly, however, open-ended questions *can* prevent you from assigning columns to any of your questions, including pre-coded/closed/forced-choice ones, until the post-codes are fully worked out, since you may not know how many columns you will need for the open-ended ones. You can avoid this by assigning a number of columns to the open-ended question before administering the questionnaire, and hope that you have enough:

What changes would you like to see in your club?   (38-42)

Five columns have been allowed here for the answers, which will now have to be categorised into five groups or less. Assigning too many columns presents little problem; the extra ones can be left blank. Assigning too few, however, can mean either having to collapse answer categories, losing some of the distinctions you wanted to maintain; or else doing a lot of work changing the columns already assigned.

A practical method of getting to understand this conversion of data from the questionnaire to the computer is available to most aspiring researchers who are willing to work under supervision on the coding stage of a project, where the mechanics of the process will be illustrated.

It is useful to think of three stages in the preparation of your results. First, you have asked the question

1. What is your favourite recreation?

and you have pre-coded the answers, asking the respondent to choose one of seven alternatives. In the second stage, preparing your codebook, you have listed the following information:

Question	Column	Variable and Code
23	30	favourite recreation
		1 = football
		2 = reading
		3 = watching television
		4 = gardening
		5 = boating
		6 = golf
		(etc.)

Note that by using double columns for recreations, your choices are expanded to 99 possibilities, rather than nine.

Stage three, the tabulation of your results, may, as indicated earlier, be simply the manual counting of the number of responses in each category. For example, you have the answers of 352 respondents to the question on recreation. Having sorted and counted the answers, the tabulation might look something like this:

Table 1
RESPONDENTS FAVOURITE RECREATION

Category	Number	Percentage
football	88	25.0
golf	88	25.0
boating	88	25.0
other	88	25.0
N = 352		100.0

Computer print-out tables are similar in structure. Some sheets will contain simple straight counts, as above. Others may show cross-tabulations of the results of two questions. For example, how many of the people in the various age groups (Question 1) voted in the last election (Question 33)? (For a sample print-out, see p. 169).

From these easy beginnings you will soon find your sophistication increasing, and will have little trouble interpreting your print-outs. You do not need to know how computers work, and for most analysis, you do not need to know how to write a computer programme; most computer centres have prepared or 'canned' programmes, such as the Statistical Package for the Social Sciences (SPSS), which will provide the tabulations and statistical tests which you need.

When you are writing your final report or paper, include a copy of your questionnaire, along with the number and kinds of responses to each question. This is usually placed in the Appendix (see page 187).

B. Postal Questionnaires

In using a questionnaire, the researcher has two aims; namely to develop questions which will yield the necessary information, and to persuade people to answer them. Both can be more difficult to achieve with self-administered questionnaires because there is no intermediary to assist and encourage the respondent. The most common type of self-administered questionnaire is the postal questionnaire. The administration and retrieval of a postal questionnaire usually involves several additional stages:

Stage 1. A cover letter, explaining the purpose of the questionnaire and asking for the respondent's cooperation, is sent out together with the questionnaire and a return stamped envelope.

Stage 2. When the first return of replies has declined (beginning about a week after the initial posting) the first reminder letter is sent to those who have not yet returned the questionnaire.

Stage 3. After allowing time (about a week to ten days) for a response to Stage 2, a second reminder letter, together with a second copy of the questionnaire and another stamped return envelope, is sent to non-respondents, on the assumption that the original questionnaire has been lost in the post, misplaced or discarded. Some researchers use an additional stage, in which non-respondents are telephoned, or a third reminder letter sent. You have to judge whether this third reminder is more an inducement than an aggravation to the remaining non-respondents.

Stage 4. Finally, those who responded may be sent a letter of thanks.

In a study involving a large number of respondents, this sequence of stages can entail a sizeable investment in paper, printing and postage. If you send questionnaires to 100 people and get a fifty per cent reponse rate (fifty people); and a fifty per cent reponse rate in stages two and three (twenty-five people and twelve people) for a total response of eighty-seven, you will have to send out 774 pieces of stationery: 387 envelopes and postage, 125 questionnaires, 100 cover letters, 75 reminder letters, and 87 thank-you letters. Such costs, however, are still cheaper than the expense involved in having interviewers personally administer the questionnaire to respondents — hiring, training and paying the researchers, travel expenses, and perhaps maintaining an administrative and clerical staff and office. Ideally, postal questionnaires produce quicker results, since respondents can reply to them simultaneously. They can reach people who live in widely scattered places, or who work at odd hours. They can be completed conveniently and in privacy.

These considerations must be weighed against some obvious disadvantages. People may have less incentive to respond when they do not have face-to-face encouragement; some may not understand the questionnaire; the questions may mean different things to different people; and it may be difficult to figure out who replied and why. Did the respondent pass the questionnaire on to someone else to complete; are your respondents those who have extreme opinions, while people in the 'middle' of the opinion spectrum may not have bothered to reply? Of those who did not reply, were they living at a new address, disinterested, forgetful, incapable, or deceased?

Despite these problems, many researchers have found the postal questionnaire to be a very successful research tool. Here are some pointers for preparing and administering a postal questionnaire.

Once you have satisfied yourself that the questions are appropriately designed to get the information you need, your main concern is to get people to reply. The rules for interviewer-administered questionnaires must be applied even more strictly to self-administered questionnaires. The questionnaire should have a simple, clear format with easily-followed instructions. Shorter questionnaires are better, but not at the expense of cramming too many questions on a sheet and giving it a cluttered and confused appearance. The questionnaire should be accompanied by a brief cover letter, explaining —

- the purpose of the research
- its sponsorship
- how the respondent was selected
- an appeal for cooperation
- an assurance of confidentiality, if appropriate
- directions for completing the questionnaire

The letter may remind the respondent that there are no 'right' or 'wrong' answers. Some cover letters invite the respondent to tick a box at the end of the questionnaire if he or she would like to receive a copy of the results when they are ready.

Given the complexity of postal systems today, it can be difficult to predict on what day of the week a questionnaire will arrive, and in any case, various studies have offered conflicting advice on the most successful (in terms of returns) days or months for posting. Common sense indicates that you have less chance of response during the busy periods of whatever group you are studying, or at holiday times.

If you intend to use reminder letters, you must have a record of who has already replied. For some topics, people are happier not to be asked to put their names on the questionnaire. You can get around this problem by making a master list with the name of each person to whom a questionnaire has been sent, and a code number for each. The code number is placed on the questionnaire, and upon return, is checked off the master list. This list should be held in confidence if you have told people that their names will not be associated with their replies. If you do not intend to use reminder letters, you do not have to keep a list, and can assure people of anonymity. If you computerise the data, each questionnaire must have an identification number, but these can be assigned after they are completed and returned.

How many replies can you expect? Response rates for postal surveys have varied considerably from almost nil to unusually high rates of over ninety per cent. (Bailey 1978: 153) believes that a fifty to sixty per cent response rate is about the best to be expected if no reminder letters are used, but that seventy-five per cent and higher can be had with proper follow-ups.

The following books are very useful for increasing your understanding of questionnaire construction and administration:

Atkinson, Jean, *A Handbook for Interviewers: A Manual for Government Social Survey Interviewing Staff.* London: H.M.S.O., 1967.
Babbie, Earl. *The Practice of Social Research.* Belmont, California: Wadsworth Publishing Co., 1979.
Backstrom, Charles Herbert, *Survey Research.* New York: John Wiley & Sons, 1981.
Bailey, Kenneth D,. *Methods of Social Research.* New York: Free Press; London: Collier Macmillan, 1978.
Bradburn, Norman M., and Sudman, Seymour, *Improving Interview Method*

and Questionnaire Design: Response Effects to Threatening Questions in Survey Research. San Francisco, London: Jossey-Bass Publishers, 1979.

Dillman, Don A., *Mail and Telephone Surveys*. New York: John Wiley & Sons, 1978.

Eckhardt, Kenneth W., and Ermann, M. David, *Social Research Methods: Perspective, Theory and Analysis*. New York: Random House, 1977.

Hoinville, Gerald, and Jowell, Roger, in association with Colin Airey, *et al.*, *Survey Research Practice*. London: Heinemann Educational Books, 1978.

Labaw, Patricia J., *Advanced Questionnaire Design*. Cambridge, Mass.: ABT Books, 1980.

Maclean, Mavis, *Methodological Issues in Social Surveys*, Atlantic Highlands, New Jersey: Humanities Press, 1979.

Moser, C. A. and Kalton, Graham, *Survey Methods in Social Investigation*. 2nd edition, London: Heinemann Educational Books, 1971.

Phillips, Bernard S., *Social Research: Strategy and Tactics*. 3rd edition, New York: Macmillan Publishing Co., 1976.

Nie, Norman H.; Hull, C. Hadlai; Jenkins, Jean G.; Steinbrenner, Karin; and Bent, Dale H., *Statistical Package for the Social Sciences*. 2nd edition, New York: McGraw-Hill Book Co., 1975.

Selltiz, Claire; Wrightsman, Lawrence J.; and Cook, Stuart W., *et al.*, *Research Methods in Social Relations*. 3rd edition, New York: Holt, Rinehart and Winston, 1976.

Schuman, Howard, *Questions and Answers in Attitude Surveys*. New York: Academic Press, 1981.

Sudman, Seymour, *Applied Sampling*. New York: Academic Press, 1976.

——, *Asking Questions*. San Francisco: Jossey-Bass Publishers, 1982.

University of Michigan, *Interviewer's Manual*. Ann Arbor, Mich.: Survey Research Centre, Institute for Social Research, 1976.

Warick, Donald P., *The Sample Survey: Theory and Practice*. New York: McGraw-Hill Book Co., 1975.

Williamson, John B.; Karp, David, A.; and Dalphin, John R., *The Research Craft*. Boston: Little, Brown & Co., 1977.

Wiseman, Jacqueline P., and Aron, Marcia S., *Field Projects for Sociology Students*. Cambridge, Mass.: Schenkman Pub. Co., 1970.

VIII. Sampling

A 'UNIVERSE' or a 'population' is a group in which all the individuals or items are singled out for study. These could be the employees of a factory, the members of a club or the students in a school, and everyone is included.

However, it often happens that the group is so large that to study everyone would be impractical because it is too expensive and too time-consuming. For example, if you wished to know which candidate each person in the USA was going to vote for in the next election, the election would probably be long past by the time you finished the study, and it would cost a fortune to do it. In such a case, you would not study the universe – all the voters in the USA – instead, you would take a sample. A sample is a portion of the universe and, ideally, it reflects with reasonable accuracy the opinions, attitudes or behaviour of the entire group. You would not expect the result from a sample to be precisely the same as the result obtained from studying the universe, but unless the sample is similar, the results are useless. The important thing in sampling, therefore, is to know how close your approximation derived from a sample is likely to be to the result which you would have obtained if you had approached the entire population. This chapter is about how to plan so that your result from a sample will have a calculable margin of accuracy. It will also show (1) how to estimate that margin and (2) the confidence you may place in your estimate.

1. Types of sampling

There are two major types of sampling: probability sampling and non-probability sampling.

a. Probability Sampling

In probability sampling, every member of the relevant universe has a chance of being selected, and the probability of this selection is known. If there are ten marbles in a bowl and each marble is available for selection, the probability that a particular marble will be selected is one out of ten, or 1/10. If two of the marbles are green and the rest blue, the probability of getting a green marble is two out of ten, or 1/5. As long as the probability of selection of a particular sample unit can be calculated (the probability for each item may be unequal, as in the case of the blue and green marbles) one can usually take a probability sample. An important characteristic of probability samples is that one can statistically estimate the difference between the results one would have got by making a total count of the universe (usually not practicable to do), using the same collection methods.

Some commonly used forms of probability sampling are simple random sampling, stratified random sampling, cluster sampling, and systematic sampling.

In random sampling, each member of the universe must have an equal chance of being selected for the sample. For a *simple random sample,* list all the members of the relevant universe. These members can be people, cities, events, companies, or whatever units you are studying. Decide how many members you need for your sample (see page 96). Consult a table of random numbers. (You can find such a table at the back of most statistics texts, or you can get entire books of random numbers.) The numbers may appear in five digit units, for example, 91307. Use as much of the digit, reading from the left, as you need. If you have fewer than 100 people in your population or universe, use only the first two digits of each number, in this case, 91. If your universe contains between 100 and 999 people, use three digits, and so on. Go down the table of random numbers (or up or left to right, or vice versa, but always the same way) and take from your numbered list of the universe any member whose number appears on the table. If some of the numbers on the table are higher than any number on your list, or if you get the same number twice, move on to the next number in the table. Keep going until you have the required numbers of members for your sample. These, then, are the members you will study.

Remember that in many cases you cannot get or make a list of all the members of the study universe. It is impossible, for example, to get a list of all unmarried mothers. If you are looking for a list which might be used to represent the people of your town, you cannot rely on such obvious sources as the telephone directory since not everyone has a telephone, some people are unlisted, and males are over-represented in the directory, since a couple or family is often listed only in the husband's name. You should also examine ready-made lists carefully to be sure of what they represent.

This is simple random sampling, and a far cry from what most people mean when they say 'I took a random sample'. 'Random' as used in statistics does not mean 'haphazard', nor does it mean that a sample chosen according to random procedures will be typical of the universe. All it means is that every individual or item in the universe had the *same chance of being selected* for the sample. A random sample of those attending a dance would have to be taken in such a way that every person there including those on the dance floor, those in the ladies' room, those courting outside on the terrace, and wall-flowers hiding behind pillars had an equal chance of being selected. This would hardly happen if you simply sauntered onto the dance floor and picked the first fifteen people you met.

A second type of probability sampling, *stratified random sampling,* is useful if your universe is a very heterogeneous group: for example, if you were studying job concerns of all the bus company employees, and the drivers, conductors, maintenance people and administrative staff each had very different needs and interests. Perhaps they differ very much in size, as well. In a simple random sample, you might get few or none of the very small number of administrative staff. So in this method, you first divide the employees into strata (four in this case) and take a random sample from each stratum. For some studies, the numbers in the strata are drawn to reflect their proportions in the study population or universe. Thus, if our employees fell into the following numbers:

drivers	80
conductors	60
maintenance staff	40
administrative staff	20
	200

we see that the drivers represent 40 per cent of the total number, so in the sample, they will also form 40 per cent. If our sample is going to be sixty people, we will need twenty-four drivers (40 per cent of sixty), eighteen conductors, twelve maintenance people, and six adminstrative staff. These are selected by random sampling within each group.

A third type of probability sampling is *cluster sampling,* and which usually involves *two* or more samplings. It is useful when it is too difficult or too expensive to get a list of all the members in the universe. If, for example, you wanted to study voters' opinions on a new tax law in a big city, instead of assigning a number to each voter in the city and starting from there, you might do the following:

1.   Divide the city into appropriate areas or regions and draw a sample of areas; and

2.   Take each sample area selected, and draw a sample of voters of each.

This method is cheaper and easier than taking a random sample of the entire city (for which you would have to assign a number to every single voter) but you have to have a good knowledge of the area in order to make a sensible and relevant division of the city into areas. There is also a chance that some small but important group may be omitted from your study; if, for example, the city had only one minority ethnic group, and its members, small in number, lived in one neighbourhood, that neighbourhood could be important, depending on the subject of your study, but might not be selected in your sample.

You can add one or more intermediate stages between 1 and 2 above; for example, after breaking the city up into areas and selecting some randomly, you can then break the sample areas into neighbourhoods and take a sample of those.

A final form of probability sampling is *systematic sampling.* One first decides the size of sample needed. Let us say that you have a universe of twenty and need a sample of four. Using a list of names or numbered items, one picks the first item arbitrarily (say the second name on the list) and then every fifth name after that until four are drawn. If we needed a sample of five, we would select every fourth name and so on.

This method is cheap and simple in ideal circumstances but is not satisfactory if the list of names or items has a pattern or bias. For example, if a group of schoolchildren were seated in rows of ten seats each, and those with the poorest vision, worst or most blatantly helpful behaviour were always placed in the front of the class, one could end up with a sample consisting entirely of the visually handicapped, monsters, or teacher's pets simply by choosing the first child and every tenth child thereafter. When the listing is obviously patterned, it is better either to randomise it before sampling systematically, or to take a proper random sample.

In probability sampling, it is possible to calculate statistically that the distribution of characteristics in the sample group is the same, within certain margins of accuracy, as the distribution of characteristics within the universe. That means that we can talk about being 95 per cent confident of the accurate margins of our sample. (See the examples in Table VIII, 1.) Therefore, we can calculate that the margin of error would be 6 per cent, for example, and we can be 95 per cent confident that our sample will be one of the 95 per cent (of all possible samples which could be taken from the universe) which will give the same results as if we had studied the universe, and *not* one of the 5 per cent that are 'wild'.

b. Non-Probability Sampling

In non-probability sampling, the probability that a person or item will be chosen is not known, and one cannot measure the sampling error. It is difficult to generalise one's findings beyond the study group of the universe. In some studies, however, this is not as important as other considerations. Your priority may be to get a quick, cheap, rough result, or perhaps to test the wording of a questionnaire.

The simplest kind of non-probability sampling is *convenience sampling*, in which one simply asks anyone who happens to be around and available; the people in your office or class, or everyone who happens to pass by a particular streetcorner. It is quick and cheap, but there is no statistical way of knowing how reflective the results are of the relevant population or universe.

Convenience sampling is what many people are thinking of when they refer to 'sampling'. The possibilities for its accidental or deliberate misuse are obvious.

A second type of non-probability sampling is *quota sampling*, which is often used in taking public opinion polls. Here, one first determines the important characteristics of the particular research population. If 20 per cent of the study population are Moslems, 20 per cent of your sample should be Moslems.

In a variation of quota sampling called *dimensional sampling*, one takes into account several characteristics – sex, age, occupation, residence, religion, or whatever characteristics might be appropriate – and then ensures that there is at least one person in the study to reflect any relevant combination of these characteristics.

Whether the quotas are based upon a single characteristic or on more, the selection of members of the sample is not done randomly. Instead, the researcher just finds enough people in each of the important categories.

2. Size of sample

Not only do many people misuse the words 'random' and 'sample', but once they are aware of the need for a sample, the only question which interests them is 'How many people do I need?' and are astonished that there is no single answer, such as 15 per cent of the universe, or 262 people. Probability sample size depends on a number of things, most of which can be easily understood by the average person, but the basis of which is too detailed to present here. I will therefore simply mention the following points, and advise you where to go from there.

First, the larger the sample, the more likely it is that its proportions or characteristics are similar to those of the universe, or parent population. If, for example, you had 1000 people in your population, and took a 'sample' containing 999 people, you are fairly safe in assuming that your results would be very much like those you would have got had you studied all 1000. On the other hand, taking such a large sample might be expensive and time-consuming, and, it is also known that, above a certain sample size, you really are not gaining proportionately in accuracy. But what is that certain sample size?

Sample size is determined mainly by the type of sample, degree of precision required, and degree of variability of the population. You might say that you want complete precision. In that case, throw out the idea of a sample and study everyone. But do you really need such precision? In a study for the construction industry, you may only need to know what price people are prepared to pay for a new house to the nearest £1000, not to the nearest penny. Getting it to the penny would be costly and probably foolish.

Degree of variability of the study population affects precision. If your population is very homogeneous in its characteristics – all nuns, for example – and you want to know their preferences in entertainment, you could probably get reliable results with a smaller sample than the one you would have to take if your group consisted of Middle-Eastern potentates, Mormon teenagers, geriatrics, long-term prisoners and Olympic athletes.

Table VIII. 1 shows the characteristics of various sample sizes drawn from the British electorate during poll-taking. Notice that as the sample size increases, the precision of the results increases. With a sample of 1000, about one in twenty polls taken is likely to be more than 6.2% wrong. However, with a sample of 12,000, the likelihood is that results from a sample will be more accurate – one in twenty will be more than 1.8% wrong.[1]

---

[1] This chart is based upon two-stage sampling: first a sample of constituencies is taken, then a sample of voters within the selected constituencies. As a result, the margins of error are nearly twice as high as those which would be obtained by using the formula given on p. 9 5

TABLE VIII, 1
'The Chances of Getting a Wild One'

Sample Size	Confidence Level and Margin of Accuracy	'Wild Ones' or Sampling Error
and the sample is 1000	then you can be 99% sure it is is accurate to within 8.1%	which means 1 poll in 100 will be more than 8.1% wrong
	then you can be 95% sure it is is accurate to within 6.2%	which means 1 poll in 20 will be more than 6.2% wrong
	then there is an evens chance it is accurate to within 2.1%	which means 1 poll in 2 will be more than 2.1% wrong
and the sample is 1500	then you can be 99% sure it is is accurate to within 6.6%	which means 1 poll in 100 will be more than 6.6% wrong
	then you can be 95% sure it is is accurate to within 5.0%	which means 1 poll in 20 will be more than 5.0% wrong
	then there is an evens chance it is accurate to within 1.7%	which means 1 poll in 2 will be more than 1.7% wrong
and the sample is 2500	then you can be 99% sure it is is accurate to within 5.1%	which means 1 poll in 100 will be more than 5.1% wrong
	then you can be 95% sure it is is accurate to within 3.9%	which means 1 poll in 20 will be more than 3.9% wrong
	then there is an evens chance it is accurate to within 1.3%	which means 1 poll in 2 will be more than 1.3% wrong
and the sample is 12,000	then you can be 99% sure it is is accurate to within 2.3%	which means 1 poll in 100 will be more than 2.3% wrong
	then you can be 95% sure it is is accurate to within 1.8%	which means 1 poll in 20 will be more than 1.8% wrong
	then there is an evens chance it is accurate to within 0.6%	which means 1 poll in 2 will be more than 0.6% wrong

Even if a poll is perfectly conducted —

NOTE: Reprinted by permission of the publisher from *The Sunday Times* (London), 7 June 1970.

Please note the phrase 'even if a poll is perfectly conducted': if bias has occurred in the selection of the sample, a large sample size will not eliminate it.

In determining your sample size, you must decide the maximum margin of error which you can accept. Let us say that you decide that an acceptable margin of error is 4 per cent, that is, if the results from the sample were 50 per cent 'yes', you are 95 per cent sure that the 'yes' percentage in the universe, had you studied the universe, would be between 46 per cent and 54 per cent or 4 per cent either way of 50 per cent.

First, solve the following formula:

$$n = \frac{4p\,(100-p)}{E^2}$$

n = sample size
p = % of population expected to have the characteristic in question
100−p = % of population expected not to have the characteristic
E = margin of error

So if 50% of the population is expected to have a certain characteristic, the formula is solved as follows:

$$n = \frac{4 \times 50\,(100 - 50)}{4^2}$$

n = 625

If you do not know the number in your universe, this is the formula to use. However, if it is possible to relate the size of your sample to the size of a finite universe, there is a refinement which can be inserted into the formula, after solving the first equation.

$$E = 2\sqrt{\frac{p\,(100-p)}{n} \times \left(1 - \frac{n}{N}\right)}$$

The relationship between the size of the sample and the size of the universe will have only a negligible impact on the size of the margin of error unless the sample approximates one-tenth or more of the universe. Using the results of our first calculation, suppose that we have a finite universe of 5000. The correction for that universe will reduce the margin of error, according to the following calcuation:

$$E = 2\sqrt{\frac{50 \times 50}{625} \times \left(1 - \frac{625}{5000}\right)}$$

E = 3.7%

Thus, the correction for a finite universe reduces the margin of error in this example from 4 per cent to 3.7 per cent.

There is a more precise formula for calculating sample size, but this one gives sufficient accuracy for most purposes. Most statisticians feel that one needs a sample of at least thirty in order to perform most statistical analyses such as some of those described in Chapter XI, and some put the desirable minimum higher, at 100. For comparing groups, of course, one needs this minimum in each group.

This discussion is simply intended to show that sampling is useful in some studies, and that it is not a hit and miss procedure. If you are going to sample, you need to know more about types and applications of sampling, and selection of sample size. A very simple, interesting discussion can be found in —

Slonim, Morris James, *Sampling* (originally titled *Sampling in a Nutshell*). New York: Simon & Schuster, 1960.

From there, you might proceed to —

Moser, C. A. and G. Kalton, *Survey Methods in Social Investigation.* New York: Basic Books; London: Heinemann Educational Books, 1971.

or to the chapters on sampling in most of the books listed at the end of Chapter VII. You may also need special advice. Consult a sociologist, psychologist, statistician or other specialist trained in the use of statistics in your field. Explain your study, the group which you propose to study, and what you need to know your results. Do this after you have worked out your Research Statement and Research Outline but before you begin the research.

IX. Written Sources

BE CAREFUL in your selection of written sources. The simple act of getting a book into print does not make the author an expert. Check his or her credentials — what is the author's standing in his field? What do the reviewers say of his work? Can his statements be substantiated by whatever criteria are appropriate. If they are based on research, what *is* the research? Does he explain the basis of his findings? Bring an informed, critical attitude to your reading. Unless the book has the Dewey Decimal Classification number 226.—, it is not the Gospel. This chapter presents a selected list of reference works to guide you in your selection. Abstracts and indexes which are available both in print and in computer-readable form are indicated by an asterisk.

No bibliography is ever 'up-to-date'; in the time it took to get his book to press, many new and useful works have been published. The following chapter is intended as a guide. As you become familiar with the reference sources in a particular field, you will learn how to locate additional works as they appear.

A. Guides to Libraries

1. International
International Library Directory. 3rd edition. London: A.P. Wales Organisation Publication Division, 1968.

2. Canada
Anderson, Beryl Lapham, *Special Libraries and Information Centres in Canada: A Directory.* Rev. ed. Ottawa: Canadian Library Association, 1970.

3. Great Britain
Association of Special Libraries and Information Bureaux, *Aslib Directory.* Edited by Brian J. Wilson, 3rd ed. 2 vols. 1968-1970.
Libraries in the United Kingdom and the Republic of Ireland. London: Library Association, 1979.

4. United States
American Library Directory. R. R. Bowker Co. 1923–. (Guide to more than 30,000 libraries in the U.S. and 3000 in Canada; published every two years)

B. Guides to Reference Books
There are a number of excellent guides to the use of reference books. Two, in particular, are quite comprehensive:
Sheehy, Eugene P., Comp., *Guide to Reference Books.* 9th ed. Chicago: American Library Association, 1976. *Supplement,* 1980. (International: USA emphasis.)
Walford, A. J., ed., *Guide to Reference Materials.* 3rd ed., 3 vols. (London) Library Association, 1975-1977. (International, British and Continental emphasis)

Other useful guides are:

Bell, Marion V. and Swidan, Eleanor A., *Reference Books: A Brief Guide*. 8th ed. Baltimore: Enoch Pratt Free Library, 1978. (USA, some foreign references)

Cheney, Francis Neel, *Fundamental Reference Sources*. Chicago: American Library Association, 1971. (USA, some foreign references)

Galin, Saul and Spielberg, Peter, *Reference Books: How to Select and Use Them*. New York: Vintage Book Co., 1969. (USA)

McCormick, Mona, *The New York Times Guide to Reference Materials*. New York: Popular Library, 1971. (USA)

Ryder, Dorothy, ed., *Canadian Reference Sources: A Selective Guide*. Ottawa: Canadian Library Association, 1973. *Supplement*. 1975.

C. Traditional Standard Sources

In addition to the more familiar sources such as encyclopedias, dictionaries and atlases, there are the following useful sources:

1. Periodical literature

The following are guides to periodical literature, which includes regularly published newspapers, magazines, and scholarly journals.

a. Newspapers: most libraries keep back copies of local newspapers, at least, but few newspapers have publicly-available indexes. There is no guide to newspapers comparable to the *Readers' Guide To Periodical Literature*. (below) Some guides to library collections of newspapers are:

British Library, Newspaper Library, Colindale, *Catalogue of the Newspaper Library*. Colindale, London: published for the British Library Board by British Museum Publs., 1975. (Catalogue to about half a million volumes of daily and weekly newspapers and periodicals, from 1700 onwards; also contains Commonwealth and foreign newspapers)

Parch, Grace D., ed., *Directory of Newspaper Libraries in the U.S. and Canada*. New York: Special Libraries Association, 1976.

Webber, Rosemary, *World List of National Newspapers: a Union List of National Newspapers in Libraries in the British Isles*. London: Butterworth & Co., [1976].

Because of storage problems, many libraries are now microfilming newspapers. Two guides to newspapers in microform are —

U.S. Library of Congress, Catalog Publication Division, *Newspapers in Microform: Foreign Countries, 1948-1972*. Washington, D.C.: Library of Congress.

Newspapers in Microform: United States, 1948-1972. Washington, D.C.: Library of Congress, 1973.

A multiple index is —

Newspaper Index: The Chicago Tribune, The Los Angeles Times; The New Orleans Times–Picayune, The Washington Post. Wooster, Ohio: Newspaper Indexing Center, Bell and Howell, 1972-1974. (After 1974, the index for each paper is issued separately.)

Probably the two best-known newspaper indexes are —
New York Times Index, New York: New York Times. 1913–. (Earlier indexes
from 1851 to 1913 are on microfilm.)
Times [London]: *Official Index.* London: *Times,* 1906–.

For a guide to USA newspaper indexes, see Milner, Anita Cheek, *Newspaper
Indexes: a Location and Subject Guide for Researchers.* Metuchen, N.J.:
Scarecrow Press, 1977. (USA)

b. Magazines and Scholarly Journals
Ayer & Son's Directory of Newspapers and Periodicals. Philadelphia: Ayer
Press, 1880 – (USA and Canadian; annually).
British Humanities Index. London: Library Association, 1962– (British; con-
tinuation, in part, of *Subject Index to Periodicals,* 1919-1962. quarterly).
The New Periodicals Index. Boulder, Colo.: Mediaworks, 1977 (indexes 'alter-
native' periodicals on ecology, health, feminism, etc.).
Poole's Index to Periodical Literature. 1801-1881. 7 vols. Gloucester, Mass:
Peter Smith Publisher, 1963 (covers 19th century, mainly popular USA and
British magazines; items listed by subject only).
Readers' Guide to Periodical Literature. New York: H. W. Wilson Co., 1900
(covers 20th century, mainly popular USA and British magazines; items
listed by author, subject; if fictional work, by title; published twice a
month).
The Standard Periodical Directory. 5th ed. 1977 (arranged by subject; title
index; annually).
*Ulrich's International Periodicals Directory. A Classified Guide to a Selected
List of Current Periodicals, Foreign and Domestic.* New York: R. R. Bowker
Co., 1932– (arranged by subject; title index; published every two years).
Irregular Serials & Annuals; an International Directory. (companion to
Ulrich's; arranged by subject; title index; published in alternate years to Ul-
rich).
Bowker Serials Bibliography Supplement. (brings both of the above up-to-date;
issued intermittently).

One USA and British index, the title of which has changed several times is —
Readers' Guide to Periodical Literature Supplement. 1909-1919. New York: H.
W. Wilson Co., 1916-1920.
International Index. 1920-1965. New York: H. W. Wilson Co., 1924-1965.
Social Sciences and Humanities Index. New York: H. W. Wilson Co., 1965-
1974.
Social Sciences Index. 1965-1974. New York: H. W. Wilson Co., 1966-1974.
Humanities Index. 1974. New York: H. W. Wilson Co., 1974–.

To find out which USA or Canadian libraries have the periodicals you need,
consult —
Canadian Periodical Index. Ottawa: Canadian Library Association, 1964–
(period 1948-1963 covered by *Canadian Index to Periodicals and Documen-
tary Films;* period 1928-1947 covered by *Canadian Periodical Index*).
Danky, James Philip. *Undergrounds: a Union List of Alternative Periodicals in
Libraries of the United States and Canada.* Madison, Wis.: State Historical
Society of Wisconsin, 1974.
New Serial Titles: A Union List of Serials Commencing Publication After Dec.

31, 1949. Washington, D.C.: Library of Congress, 1953–.

Ottawa. National Library. *Periodicals in the Social Sciences and Humanities Currently Received by Canadian Libraries*. Ottawa: 1968 (interim publication for full Canadian union list).

Union List of Serials in Libraries of the United States and Canada. 3rd ed. 5 vols. New York: H. W. Wilson and Co., 1965 (to 1949; journals in all languages).

For periodicals in British libraries —

Stewart, James D., *et al.*, eds. *British-Union Catalogue of Periodicals: A Record of the Periodicals of the World, From the Seventeenth Century to the Present Day, in British Libraries*. London: Butterworth Scientific Publications, 1955-1958. Supplement to 1960.

British Union-Catalogue of Periodicals, Incorporating World List of Scientific Periodicals. Edited by Kenneth I. Porter. 1964– (continuation of *British Union-Catalogue*).

c. Book Reviews

Book Review Digest. H. W. Wilson Co., 1905– (United States and British general fiction and non-fiction hardbound works; items listed alphabetically by author; also has title and subject index; monthly except February and July, cumulative every five years).

Book Review Index. Detroit: Gale Research Co., 1965 (USA emphasis, some Canadian and British titles; scholarly and general; fiction and non-fiction, humanities, social sciences; items listed alphabetically by author; bimonthly in recent years).

2. Books in print

a. International:

United States Catalogue. 4th ed. New York: H. W. Wilson Co., 1928.

Cumulative Book Index; a World List of Books in the English Language. New York: H. W. Wilson Co., 1933. (*United States Catalogue* lists books in print on January 1, 1928; new titles are added in the *Cumulative Book Index,* published eleven times yearly, cumulative annually. Recent books not yet listed can be found in the weekly periodical *Publishers' Weekly*).

b. Canada:

Canadian Books in Print: Author and Title Index. Toronto, University of Toronto Press, 1976– (continuation of *Canadian Books in Print,* 1968–; annually).

Canadian Books in Print: Subject Index. Toronto: University of Toronto Press, 1976– (continuation of *Subject Guide to Canadian Books in Print,* 1973-1974; annually).

c. Great Britain:

British Books in Print: The Reference Catalogue of Current Literature. London: J. Whitaker & Sons; New York: R. R. Bowker Co., 1967– (annually).

British Museum. Dept. of Printed Books. *General Catalogue*. 263 vols. London, 1959-1966. Ten year supplement, 1956-1965; five year supplement, 1966-1970 (guide to most comprehensive collection of British publications).

British National Bibliography. London: Council of the British National

Bibliography, British Museum, 1950– (description of every new work appearing in Britain weekly).

d. Ireland:
Dublin. *National Library of Ireland. List of Publications Deposited.* Dublin: Statistical Office, 1930-1937 (annually).
Irish Publishing Record. Dublin: School of Librarianship, University College, Dublin, 1968– (covers both the Republic of Ireland and Northern Ireland; annually).

e. United States:
Books in Print: An Author–Title Series Index to the Publishers' Trade List Annual. New York: R. R. Bowker Co., 1948 (annually; includes only titles published or exclusively distributed in the United States).
Subject Guide to Books in Print: An Index to the Publishers' Trade List Annual. New York: R. R. Bowker Co., 1957 (annually).
Publishers' Trade List Annual. New York: R. R. Bowker Co., 1873– (United States emphasis; some Canadian titles).

3. Pamphlets and Paperbacks
Canada. Public Archives. *Catalogue of Pamphlets in the Public Archives of Canada.* 2 vols. Ottawa; Acland, 1931-1932.
Vertical File Index: a Subject and Title Index to Selected Pamphlet Material. New York: H. W. Wilson Co., 1935– (USA; monthly except August).
Paperbacks in Print. London. J. Whitaker & Sons, 1960– (books printed and sold in Great Britain; annually).
Paperbound Books in Print. New York: R. R. Bowker Co., 1955 (twice yearly).

4. Dissertations
a. International
Dissertation Abstracts International. Ann Arbor, Mich: University Microfilms, 1938– (covers abstracts of dissertations submitted by North American and European Universities; published in three parts: *A. The Humanities and Social Sciences,* monthly; *B. The Sciences and Engineering,* monthly; and *C. European Abstracts,* indexed by keywords in titles; quarterly).

b. Canada
Ottawa. National Library of Canada. *Canadian Theses.* Ottawa: 1962– (annually).

c. Great Britain and Ireland
Aslib. Index to Theses Accepted for Higher Degrees in the Universities of Great Britain and Ireland. London, Aslib, 1953– (annually).

d. United States
Comprehensive Dissertation Index. 1861-1972. 37 vols. Ann Arbor, Mich: University Microfilms, 1973 (comprehensive for USA; includes some others; author and subject index to approximately 400,000 dissertations; indexes also available for 1973-1975).

5. Guides to abstracts

International Federation for Documentation. *Abstracting Services.* 2nd ed. 2 vols. The Hague, The Federation, 1969 (covers science, technology, medicine, agriculture, social sciences, humanities).

Kruzus, Anthony Thomas. Encyclopedia of Information Systems and Services. 3rd ed. Detroit: Gale Research Co., 1978 (an extensive list of abstract services across a range of subjects).

6. General bibliographies

a. International

Besterman, Theodore. *World Bibliography of Bibliographies.* 4th ed. 5 vols. Lausanne: Societas Bibliographica, 1965-1966. (Supplement by Alice F. Toomey, 1964-1974.)

Bibliographic Index: A Cumulative Bibliography of Bibliographies. New York: H. W. Wilson Co., 1937– (covers popular and scholarly books, periodicals, pamphlets and bulletins in a number of languages; published every three months from 1937 to 1964; every six months since 1965; cumulative annually and every four years).

b. Canada

Lochhead, Douglas, comp. *Bibliography of Canadian Bibliographies.* 2nd ed. Toronto: University of Toronto, 1972.

c. Ireland

Eager, Alan R. *A Guide to Irish Bibliographical Material.* 2nd ed., rev; Westport, Conn: Greenwood Press, 1980.

(For British and USA bibliographies, see '2. Books in Print'.)

In addition to these, there are specialised bibliographies on almost any subject one can think of – from economic development to physical fitness. A few are listed in Section B: Reference Books on Specific Subjects. Some bibliographies are simple listings of author, title, and publishing information. Others are annotated, providing a brief description of contents, and others are critical, providing a review of the material. In the last fifteen years, computerised bibliographic lists have become available, and are rapidly replacing any printed bibliographies which need to be up-to-date. For a discussion of computerised bibliographies, see 000.

7. Biography

a. International

Biographical Dictionaries Master Index. 3 vols. Detroit, Gale Research Co., [1975] (index to more than fifty biographical dictionaries).

Biography Index. New York: H. W. Wilson Co., 1946– (contains listings of a great variety of biographical sources on world figures published since 1946; organised alphabetically, and indexed by profession and occupation; quarterly, cumulative in annual and three-year volumes).

International Who's Who. London: Europa Publications, 1935– (basic summaries of living public figures; revised edition published annually).

Ireland, Norma Olin. *Index to Women of the World From Ancient to Modern Times: Biographies and Portraits.* Westwood, Mass: F. W. Faxon Co., 1970.

Thorn, J. O., *et al.,* ed. *Chambers Biographical Dictionary.* London: W. & R. Chambers; New York: St Martin's Press, 1897– (revised edition published periodically).

Webster's Biographical Dictionary. Springfield, Mass: G. & C. Merriam Co., 1953– (basic information on current and historical figures; revised edition published periodically).

b. Canada

Dictionary of Canadian Biography. Toronto: University of Toronto Press, 1966-1976.

Canadian Who's Who. Toronto: Trans-Canada Press, 1910– (published every two years).

c. Great Britain

Dictionary of National Biography. 22 vols. plus supplements. London: Oxford University Press, 1921– (covers deceased figures through 1960; historical and current; latest [7th] supplement 1971).

Who's Who. London: A. & C. Black, 1849– (covers living figures; brief information, supplied by the subjects themselves; revised edition published annually).

Who Was Who. 6 Vols. London: A. & C. Black, 1897– (covers deceased figures through 1970 taken from *Who's Who;* latest volume 1972).

d. Ireland

Crone, John Smyth. *A Concise Dictionary of Irish Biography.* Dublin: Talbot Press, 1937 (does not cover living figures).

Thom's Irish Who's Who. Dublin: Thom's Directories, 1923 (ends with 1923).

Who's Who, What's What and Where in Ireland. London: Chapman Publishers, 1973 (covers both the Republic of Ireland and Northern Ireland).

e. United States

Dockstader, Frederick J. *Great North American Indians. Profiles in Life and Leadership.* New York: Van Nostrand Reinhold Co., [1977].

Who's Who in America. Chicago: A. N. Marquis Co., 1899– (covers living figures; brief information supplied by subjects themselves; published every two years).

Who Was Who in America. 6 vols. Chicago: A. N. Marquis Co., 1942-1976 (covers deceased figures from 1897 to 1976, taken from *Who's Who In America*).

Johnson, Allen, *et al.,* eds. *Dictionary of American Biography.* 20 vols. New York: Charles Scribner's Sons, 1928-1958. Index, supplements through 1977 (covers deceased figures through 1955; most objective and reliable source for United States).

8. Almanacs and yearbooks

Almanacs and yearbooks are collections of facts, often presented in table form. They contain summaries and statistics on population and political, economic, scientific, biographical and historical information, plus a great deal of miscellaneous material. There are very specialised almanacs and yearbooks, but some general ones are —

a. International

Europa Yearbook. 2 vols. London: Europa Publications, 1946– (volume one covers international organisations and Europe; volume two covers Africa, Asia, Australia, the Middle East, North and South America; annually).

International Yearbook and Statesman's Who's Who. London: Burke's Peerage, 1953– (covers international organisations and statistical and political information on all countries of the world; biographical information on world leaders; annually).

The Stateman's Yearbook. London, New York: Macmillan & Co., 1864– (covers all countries of the world; annually).

Statistical Office, Statistical Yearbook. New York: United Nations, 1948– (covers all countries of the world; annually).

United Nations Statistical Office. *Demographic Yearbook.* New York: United Nations, 1949– (covers vital statistics of most countries of the world; 1963 volume contains index to all previous volumes; annually).

b. Canada

Canada. Statistics Canada. *Canada Yearbook.* Ottawa, 1906– (annually).

Canadian Almanac and Directory. Toronto: Copp Clark Co., 1847– (annually).

c. Great Britain

Great Britain Statistical Office. Annual Abstract of Statistics. London: Statistical Office, 1854– (annually).

Whitaker, Joseph. *An Almanack.* London: J. Whitaker & Sons, 1969– (covers Britain, with some information on other countries; annually).

d. Ireland

Ireland Central Statistics Office. Statistical Abstract of Ireland. Dublin: Statistics Office, 1931– (annually).

Northern Ireland, Ministry of Finance. Registrar General's Division. *Ulster Year Book.* Belfast, 1926 (irregularly).

e. United States

Information Please Almanac. New York: Simon and Schuster, 1947– (covers the United States, with historical and current affairs information on all countries of the world; less comprehensive than *World Almanac;* annually).

U.S. Bureau of the Census. Statistical Abstract of the United States. Washington, D.C.; Government Printing Office, 1897– (annually).

World Almanac and Book of Facts. New York: Newspaper Enterprise Association, 1868– (covers the United States with some information on all countries of the world, annually).

9. Censuses

In addition to the general sources listed below for Canada, Great Britain, Ireland and the United States of America, to take but four countries for which censuses are available, census officials frequently issue specialised and summarised reports and analysis on various facets of the census. To find these for the four countries mentioned, consult —

a. Canada

Canada. Statistics Canada. *Census of Canada.* Ottawa, The Queen's Printer (taken in years ending in 6 and 1).

Canada. Statistics Canada. Vital Statistics and Disease Registries Section. *Vital Statistics.* Ottawa: Statistics Canada (annually).

b. Great Britain
Great Britain. Central Statistics Office. *Annual Abstract of Statistics*. No. 1 1840/
1853–, London. (Each number contains statistics for fifteen preceding years.)
Great Britain. Office of Population Censuses and Surveys. *Census*. London:
HMSO (taken in years ending in 1; quinquennial edition added in 1966).
Guide to Census Reports, Great Britain 1801-1966. London: HMSO, 1977
(excellent introduction explaining the history and characteristics of the cen-
sus, and a chapter on the comparability of the various censuses).
The Registrar General's Statistical Review of England and Wales. London:
HMSO.

c. Ireland
Ireland. Central Statistics Office. *Census of Population of Ireland*. Dublin:
Stationery Office. (Taken in years ending in 6 and 1, except for 1921 and
1976. Special abbreviated census for 1979.)
Statistical Abstract of Ireland. 1931–. Dublin: Stationery Office (annually,
irregularly).
Report on Vital Statistics. 1953–. Dublin: Stationery Office (periodically).

d. United States
American Statistics Index. 1973–. Washington: Congressional Information
Service, 1973 (guide to U.S. government statistical publications; annually).
U.S. Bureau of the Census. *Census of Population*. Washington, D.C.: Govern-
ment Printing Office, 1980 (taken every ten years in years ending in 0).
Directory of Federal Statistics for Local Areas: A Guide to Sources. 1976.
[Washington, D.C.: Government Printing Office, 1978.]
Vital Statistics of the United States. Washington, D.C., Government Print-
ing Office, 1939– (covers United States vital statistics – birth, death,
marriage and divorce; annually).

10. Guides to associations and manufacturers
a. International
Directory of European Associations. Beckenham, Eng., CBD Research;
Detroit, Gale Research Co., 1971–.
World Guide to Scientific Associations and Learned Societies. 2nd ed. Edited by
Michael Zils. New York: R. R. Bowker Co., 1978.
World Guide to Trade Associations. 2 vols. New York: R. R. Bowker Co.,
1973.

b. Canada
The Corpus Almanac of Canada. Toronto: Corpus Publishers Services (annu-
ally).
Directory of Associations in Canada. 2nd ed. Toronto: University of Toronto
Press, [1975] (non-government and non-profit associations only).

c. Great Britain
Directory of British Associations. Beckenham, England: CBD Research, 1965–
(Great Britain and Republic of Ireland; revised frequently).
*Trade Associations and Professional Bodies of the United Kingdom: A Directory
and Classified Index*. London: CBD Research, 1962– (revised periodically).
Current British Directories. Beckenham, England: CBD Research, 1953–
(irregularly).

d. Ireland

Administration Yearbook and Diary. Dublin: Institute of Public Administration, 1967– (annually).

Thom's Commerical Directory. Dublin: Thom's Directories, 1960-1967.

Thom's Directory of Ireland: Professional Directory. Dublin: Thom's Directories, 1960-1967.

e. United States

Enyclopedia of Associations. Detroit: Gale Research Co., 1956– (published approximately every two years).

National Trade and Professional Associations of the U.S. and Canada and Labor Unions. Washington, D.C.: Columbia Books, 1966– (annually).

Thomas Register of American Manufacturers. New York: Thomas Publishing Co., 190? (annually).

Klein, Bernard, ed. *Guide to American Directories.* 9th ed. New York: B. Klein, [1975] (new editions published irregularly).

D. Government Resources and Publications

You should also be aware of the fact that national and local government departments, agencies, and public and private organisations frequently have information services which will provide information on subjects related to their activities. Much of this information is published in pamphlet or booklet form, but sometimes you can enlist the assistance of the body's research or information staff to get information which is tailored more closely to your research needs. It does not hurt to try asking a likely sounding body for help; your chances of success are best if —

1. You know what you are doing — that is, you have a Research Statement and Research Outline, and are able to convey a clear picture of what your study is about;
2. You are polite, suitably respectful, and prepared to share some of your own findings, if asked;
3. You follow up your requests with notes of thanks, and in cases of extensive help, a copy of your research results.

In consulting public and private bodies for research information, remember that some may have a vested interest in presenting only one side of a case or issue, and even the 'research' upon which their information is based may be the product of a biased orientation. An intelligently critical approach is your best safeguard in assessing the worth of the information which you receive.

Here are some sources to help you in your search. For each country, *guides* to the use of publications are given first.

1. International guides

Brown, Everett Somerville, *Manual of Government Publications: United States and Foreign.* New York: Johnson, 1964.

Childs, James Bennett, *Government Document Bibliography in the United States and Elsewhere.* 3rd ed. Washington, D.C.: Government Printing Office, 1942.

International Committee for Social Sciences Documentation, *A Study of Current Bibliographies of National Official Publications.* Paris: UNESCO, 1958.

Palic, Vladimar M., *Government Publications: A Guide to Bibliographic Tools.* 4th ed. Washington, D.C.: Library of Congress, 1975.

2. Canada

a. Guides

Higgins, Marion Villiers, *Canadian Government Publications: A Manual for Librarians*. Chicago: American Library Association, 1935.

b. Publications

Canada. Department of Public Printing and Stationery, *Canadian Government Publications: Catalogue. 1953-1969*. 17 vols. (annually); continuation of *Catalogue of Official Publications of the Parliament and Government of Canada, 1928-1948*.
Monthly Catalogue, Jan. 1953–Dec. 1969. Ottawa: Queen's Printer, 1953-1970.

Canada. Information Canada. *Canadian Government Publications. Catalogue, 1970–*. Ottawa, 1971–.
Monthly Catalogue, January 1970–.

Canada. *Revised Statutes of Canada*. Ottawa: Queen's Printer, 1970 (arranged by law; supplemented by annual *Statutes of Canada*, arranged by subject).

3. Great Britain

a. Guides

Bond, Maurice F., *Guide of the Records of Parliament*. London: H.M.S.O., 1971.

Ford, Percy and Ford, Grace, *A Guide to Parliamentary Papers*. Shannon: Irish University Press, 1972.

Pemberton, John E., *British Official Publications*. 2nd ed., rev. Oxford: Pergamon Press, 1973.

Stavely, Ronald and Piggott, Mary, *Government Information and the Research Worker*. 2nd. ed., rev. London: Library Association, 1965.

b. Publications

Golding, Louis, *Dictionary of Local Government in England and Wales*. London: English University Press, 1962.

Great Britain. Laws, Statutes, etc., *Halsbury's Statutes of England*. 42 vols. 3rd ed. Managing editor, A. D. Yonge. London: Butterworth & Co., 1968-1972.
Consolidated Tables and Index for Volumes 1-45. London: Butterworth & Co., 1977.

Great Britain. Parliament. *Parliamentary Debates*. London: 1804–.
House of Commons. *General Alphabetical Index to the Bills, Reports, Estimates, Accounts and Papers Printed by Order of the House of Commons and to the Papers Presented by Command, 1801-1948/49*. 4 vols. London: Statistical Office, 1853-1960.
Parliament. House of Lords. *General Index to Sessional Papers Printed by Order of the House of Lords or presented by Special Command*. 3 vols. London: Eyre, 1860-1886.

Great Britain Stationery Office, *Catalogue of Government Publications. 1922–*. London: Statistical Office, 1923 (annually).
Government Publications Monthly List. London: Statistical Office (monthly).

Municipal Yearbook and Public Utilities Directory. London: Municipal Journal, 1897–.

4. Ireland

a. Guides

Maltby, Arthur, *The Government of Northern Ireland. 1922-1972: A Catalogue and Breviate of Parliamentary Papers.* Dublin: Irish University Press; New York: Barnes and Noble [1974].

Smyth, John Christopher McGowan, *The Houses of the Oireachtas.* 3rd ed., rev. Dublin: Institute of Public Administration, 1973.

b. Publications

Ireland. Dáil. *Parliamentary Debates. Official Report.* Dublin: Stationery Office. Sept. 9, 1922–.

Ireland. Seanad. *Parliamentary Debates. Official Report.* Dublin: Stationery Office. Dec. 11, 1922–.

Irish Free State. Laws, Statutes, etc. (Indexes) *Index to the Statutes, 1922 to 1963, With Chronological Tables and 1964-1965 Supplement.* Prepared in the Statute Law Reform and Consolidation Office. Dublin: Stationery Office [1966]. Ireland (Éire). Laws, Statutes, etc. (Indexes) *Index to the Statutory Instruments, 1964 to 1970.* Prepared in the Statute Law Reform and Consolidation Office. Dublin: Stationery Office [1972].

5. United States

In the USA a source of information on where to look for help is the National Referral Center at the Library of Congress, which, from a file of 13,000 organisations, can find experts in virtually any subject area who are prepared to provide free information. The organisations include federal and state agencies, libraries, information centres, research bureaus, hobby associations, citizens' organisations, professional societies, and any organisation, in fact, which can provide specialised information and which will do so free. The National Referral Centre compiles directories of information resources, under the general title —

A Directory of Information Resources in the United States. Washington, D.C.: Government Printing Office, with the following subtitles:
Federal Government, With a Supplement of Government-Sponsored Information Analysis Centers. Rev. ed., 1974.
Social Sciences. Rev. ed., 1973.
Biological Sciences. 1972.
Physical Sciences, Engineering. 1971.

a. Guides

Andriot, John L., *Guide to U.S. Government Publications.* 4 vols. McLean, Va: Documentary Index, 1976-1978.

Cumulative Subject Index to the Monthly Catalog of United States Government Publications, 1900-1971. Compiled by William W. Buchanan and Edna M. Kanely. Washington: Carrollton Press, 1973– (to be in 15 volumes).

Downey, James A., *U.S. Federal Official Publications: The International Dimension.* Oxford: Pergamon Press, 1977 (directed particularly at foreign users, with information on how to get the publications).

Leidy, William Philip, *A Popular Guide to Government Publications.* 4th ed. New York: Columbia University Press, 1976 (several thousand selected titles from materials issued by various agencies of the U.S. government, mainly between 1967 and 1975).

Index to U.S. Government Periodicals. 1972–. Chicago: Infordata International, 1974 (quarterly; cumulative annually).

Jackson, Ellen, *Subject Guide to Major U.S. Government Publications.* Chicago: American Library Association, 1968.

O'Hara, Frederic J., *Reader in Government Documents.* [Washington, D.C.]: National Cash Register Co., 1973.

Schmeckebier, Lawrence F. and Eastin, Roy B., *Government Publications and Their Use.* 2nd ed., rev. Washington, D.C.: Brookings Institution, 1969.

Wilcox, Jerome Kear. *Manual on the Use of State Publications.* Chicago: American Library Association, 1940.

b. Publications

(1) National:

*CIS *U.S. Serial Set Index.* Washington, D.C.: Congressional Information Service, Inc. [1975-1978] (a twelve-part collection of U.S. government publications compiled under the direction of Congress, covering 1789-1969).

Congressional Information Service. *Index to Publications of the United States Congress.* Washington, D.C.: Congressional Information Service, 1970– (monthly).

United States Congress. *Congressional Record.* Washington, D.C.: Government Printing Office, 1873– (daily newspaper; contains all business presented before both chambers, plus articles, letters, comments).

Official Congressional Directory. Washington, D.C.: Government Printing Office, 1809– (Congressional organisation, committees, biographical data on Congressional members and officials; published every two years).

United States Government Manual. Washington, D.C.: Government Printing Office, 1935– (lists and describes all government branches, departments, corporations, boards, committees, commissions, and quasi-official agencies, and the names of officials attached to each; annually).

United States Laws, Statutes, etc. (Indexes) *Index to the Federal Statutes General and Permanent Law.* 2 vols. Washington, D.C.: Government Printing Office, 1911-1933 (indexes federal legislation 1789-1931).

United States Statutes at Large, Containing the Laws and Concurrent Resolutions Enacted from the Organisation of the Government in 1789. Boston: Little, Brown & Co., 1845-1873; Washington, D.C.: Government Printing Office, 1875–. (It contains laws passed by Congress during each year. Many of these supercede or are superceded by earlier or later legislation).

United States Code. 1976 ed. Washington, D.C.: Government Printing Office, 1977 (all laws in force on January 3, 1977; issued approximately every six years).

U.S. Superintendent of Documents. *Catalog of the Public Documents of Congress and of Other Departments of the Government of the U.S. for the Period March 4, 1893–Dec. 31, 1940.* 25 vols. Washington, D.C.: Government Printing Office, 1896-1945.

*U.S. Superintendent of Documents. *Monthly Catalog of United States Government Publications.* Washington, D.C.: Government Printing Office, 1895– (continuation of preceding catalog; author, title and subject indexes cumulated annually; two decennial indexes for 1941-1950 and 1951-1960).

(2) State and Local

Bollens, John Constatinus; Bayes, John R.; and Utter, Kathryn L., *American County Government: With An Annotated Bibliography*. Beverly Hills, Calif: Sage Books, 1969.

The Book of the States. Chicago: Council of State Governments. 1935– (guide to the States' governments; published every two years).

Council of State Governments. *State Bluebooks and Reference Publications (A Selected Bibliography)*. Rev. ed. Lexington, Kentucky: The Council [1974].

The County Year Book. Washington, D.C.: National Association of Counties, International City Management Association [1975–] (county counterpart of *Municipal Year Book;* annually).

Index to Current Urban Documents. Westport, Conn: Greenwood Press, 1972– (covers official publications of larger cities and counties; quarterly).

Municipal Year Book. Chicago: International City Managers Association, 1934– (government and statistical information on U.S. cities; directory of officials; annually).

National Directory of State Agencies. Washington, D.C.: Information Resources Press, 1974–.

U.S. Library of Congress. Exchange and Gift Division. *Monthly Checklist of State Publications*. Washington, D.C.: Government Printing Office, 1910– (monthly).

E. Publicly-available Online Information Services

Data bases are 'organized collections of . . . individual bits of data' (Sessions, 1974-41). These individual bits can be almost anything, for instance, a book title, one person's I.Q. score, the population of France. The telephone directory or your family's recipe file are data bases of a sort, but the term commonly refers to computer-readable material. Computer-readable data bases, of which there were more than 500 publicly-available in 1980 (Williams 1980: 240) are going to become more widely available to researchers in the next few years through online data base information systems — systems in which the computer, or central processing unit, sends (and usually can also receive) data through electronic links to a receiving terminal, which can be a great distance away from the terminal itself.

Online data base information services fall into two categories:

1) *bibliographic files,* which are reference lists and/or abstracts of books, documents, periodicals (and sometimes information sources such as organisations and persons) on a particular subject or aspect of a subject; and

2) *data banks,* which contain numeric and/or 'factographic' information on a subject — frequently, economic and demographic material, physical properties of compounds, data banks on full legal texts, and terminology data banks (Tomberg 1979: 343) The terminal at the airline ticket desk draws on a data bank.

Data bases began after World War II, with the development, particularly by the USA government, of science and technology and health care service files. Commercial developers added other files, in business, public administration, and the humanities. In 1972, however, nearly half of all bibliographic files still fell into the category of the sciences.

Government online services developed in the mid and late sixties; others began in the early seventies. In the later seventies, several new trends occurred: an increased emphasis upon data banks, especially U.S. business data banks, as opposed to bibliographic files; and the increasing dominance of Europe in the production of bibliographic files (Tomberg 1979: 343-346).

What can you do with online information services?

Online *bibliographic files* can give you quite specific information. You might ask, for example, what has been published recently on the psychological testing of twins who have been separated and reared in different environments; neurobiologists' opinion on the meaning of brain size in dolphins; the use of MAO inhibitors and trycyclics in the treatment of agoraphobia; what assessment has the professional art world made of the cartoons of writer James Thurber; or something much simpler, such as 'Give me some simple books that will explain computers to me'.

Three major bibliographic online systems used in the USA are those of Lockheed Information Systems (DIALOG), System Development Corporation (ORBIT) and Bibliographic Retrieval Services. Canada uses these plus Canada Institute for Science and Technology, and QL Systems. The major systems in use in the United Kingdom are DIALOG, ORBIT, and those of the British Library (BLAISE) and the European Space Agency (DIALTECH). Each of these offer multiple data bases; DIALOG, for example, has over 110, including ERIC (Educational Resources Information Center); Child Abuse and Neglect; and the Social Sciences Citation Index; ORBIT has over 65, including Sport and Recreation Index, and Current Index to Journals in Education; BRI has approximately 30, including Exceptional Child Education Resources; Alcohol Use/Abuse Information File; and Comprehensive Dissertation Index (Moore 1980: 3,5,7).

Online data base networks such as Euronet DIANE, with access to European computers, are available in Ireland, but the number of terminals in Ireland is limited, and, as of 1980, the necessary supporting telecommunications system, particularly outside Dublin, is poor. Currently there is no online Irish data base; users of DIANE, for example, are drawing upon data bases developed elsewhere (National Board for Science and Technology 1980: 25-26). However, three online data bases – legal, industrial and agricultural – are currently in pilot stages, for use in 1983-84 (Murphy, 1982). For a discussion on other expected and potential developments in Ireland, see Sweeney, G. P., 'On Line Networks in Ireland: Present and Future' in *A Leabharlann* (Winter) 1978: 116-133.

Online *data banks* can contain almost any kind of information. One can, for example, get very specific census breakdowns, business statistics, market statistics, and the actual numerical data used in the preparation of a large number of social science projects.

Two widely used data banks in Europe are ARIANE, a French civil engineering data bank, and the United Kingdom's dataSTREAM International. The latter, in fact, is used nearly three times as often as all the bibliographic files together (Tomberg 1979: 346). Some American data banks include the USA census, the Human Relations Area Files and Grant Information System, which provides grant information about U.S. Government, commercial and private organisations.

You can get access to online information services through academic libraries, mainly university and polytechnic libraries. In the United States of America, approximately 80 per cent of academic libraries use online services; in the United Kingdom, approximately 70 per cent. These are mainly bibliographic file services. The most frequent users of these services are faculty and graduate researchers; however, a large number of libraries (about 40 per cent in the UK, for example) make the service available to outsiders. Most libraries charge outsiders for the service, and there is a wide variation in the cost and method of assessing the charges (by the hour, by the search, by the individual reference). On the other hand, if you are fortunate enough to be an *academic* user in the UK, you probably will not be charged at all; the practice in American libraries, however, is to charge academic users (Akeroyd and Foster 1979: 202).

Sometimes, you are allowed direct access to the services: the Library of Congress, for example, permits access to listings of 1.2 million books, periodicals and documents through terminals connected to its computerised information system, SCORPIO. Each information retrieval system is operated slightly differently.

As an example, this is the way SCORPIO works. To begin, you type in a simple letter code at the terminal, and press a key marked 'ENTER'. The video screen of the terminal greets you, and invites you to continue. Perhaps you are interested in consumer education and want to know what the library has on the subject. You type 'consumer education', then type 'B' for 'browse' and 'ENTER'. On the screen will appear a long, alphabetised list of books on consumer education. Each item is numbered, and when you see one that interests you, press 'D', for 'display', and the full reference, giving author, publisher, place of publication, date, Library of Congress call number, and Dewey Decimal System number appears. SCORPIO will also, if you wish, provide you with a list, printed on paper, of all you have seen. You then signal 'ends' to the computer, and that finishes your exchange. You then look for the book in the library.

However, information retrieval systems can perform far more complicated acts than that, and normally, if you use a library-sited online information service, you will probably have to state your research interest to a trained 'search' specialist, who will then conduct the search for you. The searcher will try to plot a strategy which is most likely to produce as many references as you wish on topics related to what you want to know. The information can then be displayed on the computer terminal screen itself, or can be printed at the computer center and sent to you.

Abstracts and indexes which are available both in print and in computer-readable form are indicated by an asterisk (*) in the reference lists presented here in Chapter IX. For a comprehensive description of available data bases, consult —

Williams, Martha; Lannom, Laurence; O'Donnell, Rosemary; and Barth, Stephen, *Computer-Readable Data Bases: A Directory and Data Sourcebook.* Urbana, Ill: American Society for Information Science, 1979.

Other guides include —

Annual Review of Information Science and Technology. Washington, D.C.: American Society for Information Science, 1966– (annually).

Data Bases in Europe: A Directory to Machine-Readable Data Bases and Data Banks in Europe. Edited by Alex Tomberg. 3rd ed. London: Published for EUSIDIC by ASLIB, 1977.

Hall, James Logan, *On-line Bibliographic Data Bases: 1979 Director*. London: ASLIB, 1979.

On-line Informational Retrieval Sourcebook. London: ASLIB, 1977.

Kruzas, Anthony T., *Encyclopedia of Information Systems and Services*. 3rd ed. Detroit: Gale Research Co., 1978.

National Technical Information Service. *A Directory of Computerised Data Files Software and Related Technical Reports*. [Washington, D.C.]; National Technical Information Service, 1978 (directory of materials available to the public from U.S. federal agencies).

On-line Review: The International Journal of On-line Information Systems. Oxford and New York: Learned Information, 1977– (quarterly).

Sessions, Vivian S., ed., *Directory of Data Bases in the Social and Behavioural Sciences*. New York: Science Association/International, 1974.

F. Archival Sources

In addition to standard published reference materials, there is an enormous body of archival sources and records which may be useful to your research project. Anyone who has ever done a genealogy or family tree knows the variety of records one may have to draw upon; birth, marriage and death records, church records, wills, deeds, census returns, immigration forms, ships' passenger lists, naturalisation, school, military service, voter registration and employment records, newspapers, photographs, and even tombstones, and these are often only a beginning.

'Archival sources' will be used here to refer to public records and any other kinds of materials which may have been kept for government, legal, commercial or associational purposes. If your study involves getting information on local history, or tracing specific people or families, you will recognise the need for documentary sources. There are other kinds of studies which you need them for. For example —

There is a belief in the west of Ireland that while the family farm used to go to the eldest son, more recently it went to any child in the family, and failing that, any relative who would take it. Today, through sale, it often passes out of the family altogether. I was interested to know, for a specific area in south-west Donegal, if this was a historically accurate description of the pattern, and to what extent farms were being sold out of families today.

The first step was to get Ordnance Survey maps of the area. Two local farmers were able to list the current owners of each farm and in most cases, trace the ownership back three generations and give the relationships in each case. To trace the owners from earlier generations, I consulted the maps and records of the General Valuation Office, Dublin, which lists occupiers, owners, acreage and valuation of each property. Since these records do not indicate relationships, however, I had to consult other sources to discover the connection between occupier or owner, and his or her successor. This search covered many of the records listed in the first paragraph of this chapter. This genealogical detective work finally produced informaton for all but a very small number, and a series of patterns of inheritance emerged.

In a second study, I was interested in the factual bases of stereotypes; in this instance local people believed that the residents of a neighbouring village had a high rate of hospitalisation for mental illness, and that the cause of this was the high rate of intermarriage among close relatives, such as first cousins. My interest was not in whether intermarriage causes mental illness; I wanted to discover if, in fact, there was any factual foundation to this belief: *did* the village have a higher rate of hospitalised mental illness; and were those hospitalised the offspring of people related within certain degrees of kindred?

To discover this, I had to make a list of everyone in the village. I then checked the local mental hospital records to get the name of each person admitted from the village; I also investigated locally to find out whether anyone was or had been hospitalised elsewhere. To determine relationships between parents, I checked the parish registry. Since the entire population was Roman Catholic, and the Roman Catholic Church requires a dispensation for marriage of people related within the third degree of collateral kindred, the parish registry recorded each marriage and noted any in which a dispensation for intermarriage was required. This was only the beginning, of course; I then had to find out how this village compared with neighbouring villages, both in incidence of hospitalisation and rate of intermarriage.

In using archival sources, it is essential that you understand their limitations. Most documentary information is collected for purposes entirely unrelated to those to which researchers put them. Some old school records, for example, record a child's name each time he re-entered school after an absence longer than a specified period. In farming communities, where, historically, children had to be absent for weeks during critical agricultural activities, the same child might be entered on the rolls two or three times in one year. Sometimes, the only identifying character listed for the child is the name of the father, and in a small rural community, many people may have the same last name, and sometimes the same first name, as well. You cannot always be sure, therefore, whether you are dealing with one child, or two or three.

Each type of document has its own peculiar characteristics, and documentary sources differ considerably from one country to another by kind of record, location, and conditions of use. While many of the guides listed below refer to 'genealogy', their use extends beyond that, since they explain the location, purposes and limitations of many social and legal records.

1. International

Fang, Josephine Riss and Songe, Alice H., *International Guide to Library, Archival and Information Science Associations*. New York: R. R. Bowker Co., 1976.

Filby, William P., *American and British Genealogy and Heraldry: A Selected List of Books*. Chicago: American Library Association, 1970.

Greenwood, Val D., *The Researcher's Guide to American Genealogy*. Baltimore: Genealogical Publishing Co., 1973 (covers USA and Canada).

Wellauer, Maralynn A., *A Guide to Foreign Genealogical Research: A Selected Bibliography of Printed Material with Addresses*. Rev. ed. Milwaukee: Wellauer [1976] (intended for USA users, but covers most countries of the world).

Pine, Leslie Gilbert, *American Origins*. Garden City, New York: Doubleday & Co., 1960 (guide to European genealogical sources).

Stevenson, Noel C., *Search and Research, the Researcher's Handbook: A Guide to Official Records and Library Sources for Investigators, Historians, Genealogists, Lawyers and Librarians.* Rev. ed. Salt Lake City: Deseret Book Co., 1964 (mainly United States; also includes Canada, England, Scotland, Northern Ireland and Republic of Ireland).

Thomas, Daniel H. and Case, Lynn M., *Guide to the Diplomatic Archives of Western Europe.* Philadelphia: University of Pennsylvania Press, 1959.

2. Canada

Association of Canadian Archivists, *Director of Canadian Records and Manuscript Repositories.* Ottawa: Bonanza Press, 1977.

Canada. Public Archives, *General Inventory: Manuscripts.* Ottawa, 1974-1977 (in progress).

Union List of Manuscripts in Canadian Repositories. Rev. ed. Ottawa: Queen's Printer, 1975.

3. Great Britain

British Museum. Department of Manuscripts, *The Catalogues of the Manuscript Collections.* London: Trustees of the British Museum, 1962.

Galbraith, Vivian Hunter, *Introduction to the Use of Public Records.* London: Oxford University Press, 1952.

Gardner, David E. and Smith, Frank. 3 vols. *Genealogical Research in England and Wales.* Salt Lake City: Bookcraft Publishers, 1964-1966.

Great Britain. Public Records Office, *Catalogue of Microfilm.* [London: Public Record Office, 1977].

Public Record Office, *Guide to the Contents of the Public Records Office.* 3 vols. London: Statistical Office, 1963-1968.

Hamilton-Edwards, Gerald Kenneth Savery, *Tracing Your British Ancestors: A Guide to Genealogical Sources.* New York: Walker & Co., 1967.

Iredale, David, *Enjoying Archives: What They Are; Where to Find Them; How to Use Them.* Newton Abbot: David and Charles, 1973 (guide to British documents and archives).

Stephens, W. B., *Sources for English Local History.* [Manchester]: Manchester University Press [1975].

4. Ireland

Heraldic Artists Ltd, *Handbook on Irish Genealogy: How to Trace Your Ancestors and Relatives in Ireland.* Dublin: Heraldic Artists, 1976.

Ireland, Public Records Office, *A Guide to the Records Deposited in the Public Records Office of Ireland.* Dublin Statistical Office, 1919.

MacLysaght, Edward, *Irish Families: Their Names, Arms and Origins.* Dublin: Hodges Figgis, 1957.

Nolan, William, *Sources for Local Studies.* [Dublin: The Author], 1977.

———, *Tracing the Past: Sources for Local Studies in the Republic of Ireland.* Dublin: Ardagh Press, 1982.

Northern Ireland. Public Record Office, *Sources for the Study of Local History in Northern Ireland.* Belfast [1969].

O'Neill, Thomas P., *Sources of Local Irish History.* Dublin: Library Association, 1958.

5. United States

American Genealogical-Biographical Index to American Genealogical, Biographical and Local History Materials. Vols 1-102 (in progress). Middletown, Conn: Godfrey Memorial Library, 1974-1978.

American Genealogical Research Institute Staff, *How to Trace Your Family Tree.* Garden City, N.Y.: Doubleday & Co., 1973.

Brooks, Phillip Coolidge, *Research in Archives: The Use of Unpublished Primary Sources.* Chicago: University of Chicago Press, 1969 (United States sources, especially those in the National Archives and Library of Congress).

Crouch, Milton and Raum, Hans, *Directory of State and Local History Periodicals.* Chicago: American Library Association, 1977.

Directory of Historical Societies and Agencies in the United States and Canada. Madison, Wis: American Association for State and Local History, 1956– (published every two years).

Evans, Frank Bernard, *Modern Archives and Manuscripts: A Select Bibliography.* [Washington, D.C.]: Society of American Archivists, 1975.

Guide to the *National Archives of the United States.* Washington, D.C.: U.S. National Archives and Record Service, 1974.

Hamer, Philip M., *A Guide to Archives and Manuscripts in the United States.* New Haven: Yale University Press, 1961.

National Union Catalog of Manuscript Collections. Washington, D.C.: Library of Congress, 1962 (cumulative index in each volume; published approximately once a year).

Stemmons, John D., *The United States Census Compendium: A Directory of Census Records, Tax Lists, Poll Lists, Petitions, Directories, etc., Which Can be Used as a Census.* Logan, Utah: Everton Publishers. [1973].

U.S. Bureau of the Census, *Directory of Federal Statistics for Local Areas: A Guide to Sources, 1976.* Washington, D.C.: [Government Printing Office] 1978.

U.S. Library of Congress, *United States Local Histories in the Library of Congress: A Bibliography.* Edited by Marion J. Kaminkow. Baltimore: Magna Carta Book Co., 1975.

Yantis, Netti Schreiner, *Genealogical Books in Print.* [Springfield, Va: By the author, 1975.]

G. Personal Documents

Another type of source falls into a category which has been called 'personal documents'. These are records, accounts, diaries, budgets, letters, local histories, plays, poetry, proverbs, songs, etc., which are often unpublished, 'unofficial', and unique. These documents may have been produced for reasons entirely unrelated to your study. For example, the anthropologist Ruth Benedict, in her study *The Chrysanthemum and the Sword* (1946), drew upon already existing films, novels and other written sources to provide an analysis of Japanese culture during World War II when access to the culture itself was impossible. But you need not rely upon your luck to stumble across useful materials. You can also ask people to produce them for you. Townsend (1957) in his study of elderly people in London, asked people to keep diaries of their activities during the day; in other studies, people have been asked to keep budgets, records of whom they visited, work patterns, and exchanges of goods and services with neighbours. You can also ask people to write more impressionistic accounts; life histories, descriptions of particular events, attitudes towards people or phenomena and so forth.

Here are two examples. The first consists of excerpts from letters written home by Irish immigrants to the United States of America in the latter half of the nineteenth century:

(1884) . . . i had a very stormey passage, i advise every girl not to come out [from Ireland] in the month of March to this country i was thinking of home on patrick day the hatches were closed for five days and we thought we were going to drop. . . i often think of home and of my dear parents and of my brother and sister and i taught long the first month i came here if my parents would see me now they would not know me i got awful fleshy since i came to this country. . .

(1884) . . . this country is not as good as it was they are not aloud to sell no more liquor in the state of Iowa they are aloud to make it but cannot sell it. this country is not as different as i thought it was. they are good & nice people in this town. . . i think this is a healthy state the stoutest and fleshest peapol i ever saw in this town. . .

(1892) . . . I am still at Mapleton & getting along first rate but it is hard to tell how long I will be we have a new road master here since the first of October he fired every Irishman the first two months he was here only me [and] a fellow from Tipperary and he had to quit the first of January he was all the time giving him hell himself & I had got along all right so far but he hates the ground an Irishman walks on he is a Norwegian as you are well aware an Irishman is not badly stuck on him either. . .

(1897) . . . I could get a job in the road masters office in the beginning of September at $25 a month but would not take it. He generally pays $35 but said because I was a foreigner and inexperienced he thought I should work cheap. But I politely thanked him and said 'No Sir'.

(1897) Keep —— to school ask him to write me again. Sometime I will write to him and tell him all about snakes, squirrels, wolves, Indians, negros, Germans, Swedes & Norwegians, & Yankees, the Community I live in is composed of all these classes. They all hate the Irishman, but there is no love lost and Irishman does not care for these.

An examination of the entire collection of the letters from which the examples are taken shows a set of common themes, even though they are written many years apart by people who never knew each other: an interest in the crops and agricultural activities of their home villages; the hard working conditions in the United States, as well as the 'good' pay; suspicion of other ethnic groups in their new communities; and an interest in both Irish and American national political and economic affairs. One man, for example, sent a very detailed account of the presidential campaigns of McKinley and Bryan, and an explanation of a major election issue: the gold standard versus the '16 to 1 silver and gold standard' to his family who had to get a literate person to read it to them.

A second example falls into the 'commissioned' category. I had asked teen-aged girls in Donegal to write accounts of what happened at local dances. Here is one —

A Typical Dance in Our Local Hall

We usually go to the hall about midnight; going there before this time is useless as the boys do not get up to dance until then.

With the exception of a few who get up to dance the majority stand about and have their chat, smoking cigarettes. Then very bravely they snub the cigarette, and march across. The brave ones are the ones who come across straight away, others are not quite as fortunate.

Towards midnight, I can usually see the drama taking shape. A young boy 17-18, who may wish to dance a girl, will stand right opposite her. If he is one of the fairly shy ones he will not come straight across, and ask her up to dance, he will see if anyone noticed him: if not, he will try again, he will come then, more or less, sideways: the quickest, and easiest way he can manage it. He will then shoot out his hand and say 'Dance'? One usually replies, okay.

He will then try his hand at conversation. A typical conversation between a boy of 17-18, and his partner goes as follows: 'Are you enjoying the dance?' ('It's not so bad.') 'The band is good.' (It's great.') 'Do you come here often?' (And he has probably seen the particular girl a hundred times.) ('I come here every Sunday night. Why?') 'Oh, no reason at all, it's just that I didn't see you.' (This is said in case he might let the game away on himself. Boys don't usually like girls to know they have noticed them, that is the impression they give anyway.)

Silence usually follows, so I know the big question is coming up. He looks up at the band so as to avoid coming face to face with his partner and asks, 'Would you like a mineral?' [soft drink] ('No.') 'Then you *must* be going with someone?' The purpose of the mineral – accept a mineral from me, you, in other words are you going to allow me to see you home tonight; reject the mineral, and you are rejecting me.

Another way of getting around to the question of saying, 'It is hot in here, are you *sure* you wouldn't like a mineral, or anything?' The 'anything' usually means crisps, sweets etc.

I noticed if a boy intends asking a girl out, he will dance fairly close to her, he may do this at all times, but if she refuses his mineral, he will casually say, 'Shake or Jive'? The reply is usually ('I can't Jive') to which he replies, 'Well, I am *sure* you can shake, everyone can shake.' By this time, one usually knows he is fed up, and waiting for the dance to be over.

If one accepts the mineral, he expects she will let him walk her home, or to her car, if she has come by car.

Making a date for another night he usually says, 'Will I see you again?' Unless a boy is going steady, or doing a line with a girl he will not pay her in to the dance. This is the way among the younger boys anyway.

Such material is useful if your Research Outline specifies this kind of information and asking people to keep accounts and such like, may prove the best method of getting it. Alternatively you may come across useful material by chance. The utility of specific kinds of records, such as budgets, is obvious; life histories, diaries, letters, and 'attitudinal' materials can give you clues as to what a person thinks is important enough to write about, his conerns, and preoccupations; collections of such material from a particular culture can give us this information for the culture itself as well as some insight into what the people of that culture think is appropriate to write about, and how they organise and present material.

The more impressionistic and attitudinal kinds of material, such as diaries, should usually only be used to give you research ideas which can then be pursued through other methods. A local proverb which says 'Put a hat on a stick and you'll get a wife in Ballyglass' might suggest that you look further at the relationships between the two places. You should not try to 'psychoanalyse' the material, looking, for example, for sexual repression, aggression, or mental or emotional disturbance. Even experts are wary of using personal documents alone, without other more carefully controlled supporting materials, for such analysis.

For more information on the use of this kind of material, consult:

Gottschalk, L., Kluckholn, C., and Angell, R., *The Use of Personal Documents in History, Anthropology and Sociology.* New York: Social Science Research Council, 1945, Bulletin 53.

Social Science Research Council, *The Social Sciences and Historical Study.* New York: The Council, 1954.

Winks, Robin, ed. *The Historian as Detective: Essays on Evidence.* New York: Harper and Row Publishers, 1969.

PART THREE

Preparing the Results

X. Recording and Organising the Information

A. Basic Written Notes

MOST PEOPLE, when they imagine a research project, see it as having two parts: collecting the material and writing up the results. These are the phases most familiar to the average person, and one may tend, therefore, to overemphasise their place in the research, and to put too little importance on the other 'invisible' parts of the research process. In fact we have dealt with one of these already: the Research Design process. A second major one is the way you record and organise your information. Together, these two general areas take up at least as much time as it takes to collect the information, and unfortunately, they are not nearly as interesting. Most people want to spend as much time as possible interviewing people, reading new material, or observing something interesting. That, after all, is what they consider 'research' to be. Few want to spend time psychoanalysing themselves ('What do I mean by *juvenile delinquency?*' 'What do I mean by *broken homes?* What do I really want to study?') and even fewer want to go through the boring job of recording and organising the information they collect. We think of our research time as precious and limited; therefore, most of it should be spent on the 'meat' of the project, collecting the information. No need to write it down in any great deail; it wastes research time, and anyhow, you will remember it. Take a few rough notes and catch up later. Right?

Wrong. There are some hard truths in life —
1. You will *not* remember it.
2. You will *never* catch up.

So when you begin to plan your research, allow time for recording and organising. Depending on the method you use, it can take three to five hours of recording and organising time for every hour's worth of information you collect. Questionnaire forms, once prepared, usually take less, but certain specialised kinds of information, such as recording of body movements and gestures, take more. This may seem like a lot of time, particularly for a part of the research you may not have known existed, but proper recording, in addition to its more obvious benefits, will save you weeks or even months of time when you go to write up the work. In some cases, it has been known to make the difference between completing a research project and not.

There are a number of methods of recording information. The one you have probably seen most often is the questionnaire, which is not only a guide for getting information, but also a form for recording it. You can also develop a similar form to record interviews when you are going to ask the same questions of a number of people.

But what if your interviews involve putting different questions to each person? Suppose you are making a study of your community's history and you want details on the kinds of work which were done sixty years ago. You will look at any records and literature that you can find, but you will also ask elderly mill-workers, housewives, shopkeepers or whoever for descriptions of what their work involved, what skills were needed, the daily and yearly round, how they learned their jobs, and so forth. Some of the questions will be the same for all, but many will differ, and will be determined by what the person tells you. Or perhaps you are observing behaviour, such as how disputes are settled in a playground, or ways in which workers break the monotony of the working day, or how people actually use the services of a community association.

Here is one method, which can be used for recording —
- observations of people, processes and events
- interviews
- material extracted from books and other written sources

We will use an observation situation for the first example. Suppose that there has been a lot of divisiveness between officials of the local hospital nurses' union and the members. You are studying these divisions as they relate to specific issues which you have found to be important in the union:

Bases of Disagreement (I) Between *Nursing Union Officials* (II) and *Members* (III) in *Greenville Hospital* (IV).

I. *Bases of Disagreement*
    A. Working conditions
        1. night work
        2. performance of 'non-nursing' tasks
    B. Admission standards
        1. admission of foreign-trained nurses
        2. admission of nurses' aides

You have decided that one of the techniques which will give you information on point B. 2, 'admission of nurses' aides' is observation of union meetings at which this issue is frequently discussed. Assume that you have sat through your first meeting, and have taken notes in as much detail as possible during the meeting. You now have a set of rough notes. The aim is to convert them into as detailed a record as possible, in a form which will allow you to retrieve and use the information when you need it.

Step 1: Objective: to have as accurate an account as possible of what occurred in your observation, where, under what circumstances, and in what sequence.

Materials: hardbound notebook, with sheets sewn in to keep notes secure and in chronoiogical order.

Use only the pages on the right-hand side of the book. Do not write on the backs of the sheets, or on the backs of any other sheets which you might use. The importance of this will be seen later.

Take all your rough notes in this notebook, including notes of interviews, observations of events, rough diagrams, and notes from books or documents. Avoid using other paper of different sizes, loose sheets, old envelopes and the backs of programmes, except when using a notebook would be inappropriate or impossible. Number each notebook with a Roman numeral (I, II etc.), and each page in the notebook with an Arabic number (1, 2 etc.).

Step 2: Objective: to add details and information on circumstances, physical features, background, and factors which may have influenced the type and quality of the information.

Materials: the hardbound notebook.

After the meeting, re-read your rough notes and add anything which you did   not have time to write during the meeting. Do this as soon as possible after the meeting. At the end of the notes add any of the following, if relevant:

a. circumstances and background: how you came to attend the meeting (who suggested it or invited you, or whose permission you got, etc. This is important: if the person who sent you or gave you permission is disliked or suspected by the people at the meeting, or by an interviewee, you may not be aware of it at the time, but it may help to explain later, why, when you are more familiar with the situation, a particular meeting or session went the way it did.)

b. physical description of the setting, furnishings, lighting, temperature, etc.; descriptions of the participants, their placement, movements from these positions, etc. A floor plan or diagram may be useful.

c. any background information on the participants or the event which you may know. This may include occupations, length of employment, and anything else which might be helpful but which you did not learn during the course of the meeting. For example:

> Mrs Brown is about thirty-five and transferred a year ago from Greenville Hospital to Ward Three here, where she is a ward sister. She is a widow with three children under six years old and is secretary of the hospital branch of the nurses' union.

> or

> A meeting of this organisation is held every month. At the last two meetings, only five people attended and a notice was circulated on July 19, 1980 ordering all members to attend or lose their membership. According to minutes of meetings held in the past year, only issues of policy are discussed. As can be seen above, the last motion of today's meeting was a departure from that policy.

d. Record anything which you think may have affected the quality of your notes, such as the fact that you suspect that people may have been inhibited in your presence, or that you may have been a participant yourself, and possibly restricted in what you could observe; or the fact that you could not take any notes during the meeting itself and are writing entirely from memory now.

Step 3: Objective: to extract the material from your hardbound notebook in such a way that you can retrieve the information later and write up your report.

Materials: typewriter (if possible); 8" x 5" paper; carbon paper; file folders.

The 8" x 5" sheets are simply standard typing paper sheets cut in half. However, you can also use specially treated paper, such as NCR paper, which allows you to make copies without using carbon paper. Whatever paper you use, choose a size roughly similar to 8" x 5", and keep to the same size.

Now type or re-write the notes from your hardbound notebook onto the half-sheets of paper. Make an original, or top copy, and three or four copies of each sheet. Begin the first sheet and every sheet with these headings in the upper right-hand corner:

When you complete the circumstances and background, which may take several pages, begin on the notes proper from the hardbound book. Use as many half-sheets as you need, making three to four carbons of each sheet. Begin *each* new sheet the same way as the example given, that is, with the four headings shown.

As you finish transferring each page from the notebook to the half-sheets, cross out the page in the notebook. If for any reason you do not take all the material from the notebook (it may seem irrelevant at the time, perhaps) put an 'X' or other clear mark beside the material and check back through the notebook from time to time to see if this 'X'-marked material is still not useful.

Number each half-sheet when you type it. You can number 1-5000 through all your notes, or simply begin again at 1 for each day's notes. You may also wish to give the number, on each typed page, of the notebook from which you are typing, in case you ever need to go back to the original rough notes. Having numbered each notebook with a Roman numeral, and each page of the notebook with an Arabic numeral, list them in one corner of the half sheet — III: 36.

When you have the entire observation written up on half-sheets, go back over each sheet and fill in the headings. Numbers 2, 3 and 4 will be easy. Here they are for our sample half-sheet on page 125:

2. Nurses' Association meeting
3. Greenville Hospital auditorium
4. May 16, 1980

1. Topics
2. (Event observed or
   interviewee's name)
3. (Place of event
   or interview)
4. (Date)

Circumstances and Background:

(Begin here with the material you wrote at the end of your hardbound notebook account — that is the material under points a-d on page 000. It will read something like this:)

I went to the meeting of the Nurses' Association at 8 p.m. with Sister Martin. It was held in the hospital auditorium. There were approximately seventy-five people present, all nurses. There were eight speakers on the platform: Mrs. Williams (1), Miss Marshall (2), (list) They were seated on the platform according to the diagram below:

```
        x   x
        7   8

x   x   x   x   x   x
3   2   1   4   5   6
```

(scale: 1 inch =)

Observation:

At 8:05 Mrs Williams went from her seat to the rostrum and said, "The meeting will come to order. We are here this evening to discuss the proposal made last week by Miss Little that the Nurses' Association admit nurses' aides to membership. Would anyone like to comment?" For approximately sixty seconds, no one spoke. A woman in the front row waved her right arm at full length but Mrs Williams didn't call on her. III:36

Point 1, if you remember, is 'Topics'. You will get the topics this way: scan each sheet and decide what subjects are covered. For your nurses' meeting, a page may contain the topics 'staff wages', 'work hours', 'grievance procedures'. For point 1 in our example, the topics would probably be —

1. Topics: circumstances; nurse's aide admission proposal.

Proceed to the next page and do the same thing: fill in all the points, and get the topics by reading that page. Your topics may remain the same for several pages, or may change for each page. Nevertheless, put all four points on *each* page, even if you are repeating the same points.

You may have one topic on the page, or three or four. You will probably have seen your topics somewhere before: if you are really using your Research Outline to collect your information, your notes will obviously reflect the points in your Outline, and your topics will be similar, if not the same as your Research Outline points. If they are *not,* you should stop and try to figure out why.

After some practice, your rough note-taking, writing organisation and memory will improve, and you can stop writing out points a, b, c and d of Step 2 in your hardbound notebook — but, of course, you still have to record them on your half sheets. In other words, when you get home from your interview or observation with your few rough notes, you no longer have to record these points twice — once in the notebook and once on the half-sheets. Go directly to the half-sheets, writing the circumstances then filling in points a–d as you work your way through your rough notes.

Step 4: Objective: to file the half-sheets so that you have —
(a) one complete account of the observation or interview; and
(b) a file folder for each topic that appears in your notes.
Materials: typed half-sheets, stapler or paper clips, file folders.

When you have finished writing up your entire observation on the half-sheets, let us imagine that you have filled up ten half-sheets. If you made three carbons or copies of each, you now have forty sheets of paper; the ten originals, or top copies, and thirty carbons.

Take the ten originals or top copies and staple them together, from page one to the last page. This means you now have one complete copy of the observation or interview, if you ever need to read the whole thing in proper order from the beginning to end.

Now you have in front of you ten piles of carbon-copy half-sheets with three sheets in each pile. Take the first pile. Read the first topic listed at the top of the page:

1. staff wages; work hours; grievance procedures.

In our example, it is 'staff wages'. Make a file folder called 'Staff Wages' and put the *first sheet in the first pile* into it. Now take the second sheet in the *same* pile. The second topic is 'work hours'. File it in a folder titled 'Work Hours'. Take the third sheet and file it under the third topic 'Grievance Procedures'. So far, all you have done is file copies of the same pages.

Now move on to the second pile, and do the same, filing one copy under each of the topic headings listed on that page. If the page has as its topics —

1. nurse doctor conflicts; grievance procedures; pensions plans

file one copy under each of the three headings. You do not have to make a new file folder for 'Grievance Procedures' because it appeared as a topic before and you already have a folder. Your folder headings correspond to your topics, which in turn correspond to the points in your Research Outline.

What if you have only two topics on a page? You have three copies. File the first copy under the first topic, the second under the second, and throw the third one away. What if you have four topics and only three copies? If you see this happening often, start making four copies. If it happens occasionally, file the first three copies under the first three headings, and for the fourth topic, put a note in the file folder for that topic, saying 'See May 16, 1980, page 6'. When you need to look at that page, go back to your stapled pile of top copies, which you should keep all in one place, and read page 6 of May 16.

You can continue sentences and topics from one page to the next. It is easier if you do not continue just one line when the topic is going to change, but otherwise, simply type your notes without worrying about your filing system. If a topic continues on a new sheet, that new sheet will contain the topic in its heading and therefore the two sheets will be filed together. You can staple them if you want to ensure that they stay together.

You can probably now see why you are using half-sheets of paper; it limits to a few the number of topics you can get on a page. If you used standard-sized paper, you might get eight or nine topics to a page, and be forced to make as many copies in order to file a sheet on each.

The recording method described above is used for interviews as well as observations, for diagrams and maps, and for material from books and documents. For books, use the heading this way:

1. Topic(s).
2. Author's full name, book title, publisher and place of publication, date of publication.
3. Location of the work (this is useful for documents, especially if you are using sources scattered among a number of libraries, agencies or offices, and wish to find them again).
4. Date (of your note-taking).

Write your notes from books or records, or draw your maps and diagrams, directly on the half-sheets. You can also photocopy material, for instance, paragraphs from books, and paste them on the half-sheets. This way, any of your information that is not recorded on questionnaires or other standardised forms will appear on these half-sheets. When you are finished with your research, you will have one pile of top copies of all your notes stapled together from earliest to most recent. You will also have a set of file folders containing your carbon copies. They will correspond to the topics in your Research Outline. You can keep the files in the same order as the points in your Outline, and number them, if you wish, to match the points in your Outline.

From time to time you can go over your Outline points and check each corresponding file to see that you are getting the information that you need. You may, of course, have to add or cut points in your Outline, and your file folders will reflect this.

When you finish your research and want to write it up, look at your Research Outline to see if you can use it as the outline for your paper. Often, you can. Sometimes you have to re-order the points: in our Outline for

Changes (1945/1980) in *Selected Characteristics* of *Convicted Juvenile Delinquents Aged 13-18 Years* in *St Michael's Correctional Institution.*

if you had happened to place the point 'Location' in the middle or near the end of the Outline, you now might want to re-order the points and make it first, because you will probably want to describe the location of the institution near the beginning of your paper.

When you get the outline points in an order suitable for your paper, line up your file folders in the same order. Take your first points, read the corresponding folder, analyse or summarise the material in it, and write it up. Sometimes you may have to group points together, but the procedure is the same. But do remember — there are two outlines involved here. One is a guide to the information you need to collect, and one is a plan for writing your paper. When you are planning your research at the beginning, never work out your Research Outline as if it were going to be the outline for your paper. If it can be used that way at the end of your research, fine. If not, make a separate outline for writing your paper.

There are other note-taking procedures, but most are variations of the one described above. All require an investment of time and patience but are well worth it in the end. Whatever method you choose, the essential thing is that you use it regularly and keep up-to-date.

Tape recording is useful if it is essential that you get exact words, tones or music, or if writing would disturb the flow of conversation, or if you have to be free to do something else during the interview or event. You can also, of course, tape record yourself giving a running account of the event.

In these cases, tape recording is simply a substitute for the hardbound notebook. The second stage, putting the material on half-sheets, is still necessary. Here are some points to bear in mind if you tape record:

1.   Many people resent or are frightened by tape recording, and, of course, secret tape recording represents a serious ethical breach. Never use a tape recorder without announcing its presence and seeking permission to use it. Keep your tapes in confidence, just as you would your written notes. Try both written recording and tape recording to see how each influences the presentation and availability of material.

2.   Tape recording in itself does not produce certain types of information which may be important to your study: 'kinaesthetics' such as body movements and gestures; facial expressions, and physical characteristics of people and settings. (Written notes, on the other hand, do not produce facsimiles of sound, but the caution is necessary since sometimes technical aids give one a false security of having recorded 'everything')

Therefore, at the end of the tape recording, you must either tape or write the information called for in points a–d of Step 2; circumstances, physical descriptions, background and influencing factors, plus the points mentioned in the preceding paragraph.

3.   Tapes must be transcribed and 'edited' immediately after they are made. Your research time may be very limited; perhaps you have had to travel some distance and want to spend all your precious time collecting and wait until you get home to transcribe the tapes. This is usually a serious mistake, because by that time you will have forgotten all the details called for in point 2. You may think that you will not; how could anyone forget such clear impressions? The clear impressions tend to run together, however, and vague recollections will not be good enough in your notes.

4.   It is possible to include all the information called for in points 2 and 3 by reciting it into the tape recorder at the end of the interview; however, letting untranscribed tapes pile up can lead to other problems. If you do not have the information on half-sheets, classified by topics, it can be difficult to tell how you are progressing — whether you have enough on a particular topic, whether you are unintentionally skipping research points. The sheer volume of work can also present a formidable obstacle when you finally do begin to transcribe.

None of the above should deter anyone whose research requires accurate recording of sound. It is intended as a cautionary note for those who think tape recording offers the easy way out.

B. Other written recording techniques

1. Kinesic notation

Sometimes it is important to record exact details of human physical movement, expressions and gestures. Surprise, scepticism, anger, friendliness, pain can all be communicated through body movement, independently of what is said. A factory manager who appears to be saying and doing all the 'right' things may still experience serious antagonism from his workers; is he, perhaps, conveying hostility or contempt through non-verbal communication?

This study of communication through body motion is called *kinesics,* and experts in this field have developed a shorthand notational system which permits quick recording of body movement. A person with a headache, for example, might be recorded as having R/H̄ (right hand to frontal region above brow); H f b b (brows knit); and L/L (lips compressed) (Birdwhistell, 1970). Learning the system well enough to record fast, ongoing movement requires considerable practice but it is worthwhile if your project requires extensive, accurate recording of body motion. For the complete notational system, see —

Birdwhistell, Ray, L., *Kinesics and Context: Essays on Body Motion Communication.* Philadelphia: University of Pennsylvania Press, 1970.

2. Grids

There are specialised forms for recording other types of information. One is useful for recording types of fast action, or repetitive material on interaction among people. A grid like the following is used:

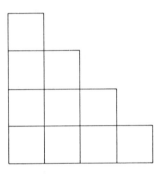

Figure X. 1

On this grid, you can record types of interaction between any two people. For example, suppose you are observing how children interact in a playground. You watch for five minutes, and this is what you see: Mary hits John, jumps rope with Sarah, kicks Tom, and dances with Jane. John dances with Sarah, kicks Tom, and has no interaction with Jane. Sarah kicks Tom and has no interaction with Jane. Tom hits Jane. You can record all of this very fast on a blank grid prepared before the observation. Develop a code for the various activities (this requires that you make a few practice observations first):

> H = hits
> J = jumps rope
> K = kicks
> D = dances
> O = no interaction

You can record other information about each person in boxes drawn in beneath the grid:

Mary

H

John

J	D

Sarah

K	K	K

Tom

D	O	O	H

Jane

(Place beneath grid)

	Mary	John	Sarah	Tom	Jane
1.	5	4	4	5	3
2.	X	0	0	0	X
3.	6	0	1	3	1

Figure X. 2

In these lower boxes, the first row is assigned to Mary and appears directly under her name; the second row to John, and the third to Sarah. We can use them to record ages (Row 1); whether or not they come from broken homes (X, Row 2); number of other children in the family (Row 3); etc. In the example about the neighbour women below, we can record length of time lived on the street, approximate family income, number of children, level of education, and so on. (Remember that you record these items only if your Research Outline calls for them. You are not merely thinking up kinds of things to record because you have blank spaces on your grid.)

Our grid shows only one-way interaction; we know that Mary kicked Tom, but we do not know if Tom retaliated. You can convert the grid to show two-way action: Mrs Ryan babysits for Mrs Smith, who in turn sets Mrs Ryan's hair. Mrs Moore gives her children's outgrown clothes to Mrs Ryan. Mrs Ryan gives Mrs Moore a lift to church on Sunday. Mrs Allen's son helps Mrs Ryan in her garden, and in return, Mrs Ryan does sewing for Mrs Allen, and so on. We develop a code, and record it on the two-way grid:

B = babysits   H = hairdressing
C = gives clothing   G = gardening
L = gives lifts   S = sewing

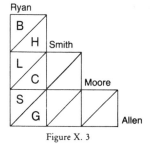

Figure X. 3

You can also use grids to record change. If you were working in a Spanish-American neighbourhood and were interested in knowing who spoke Spanish to whom in which situations, you could use one grid to show who spoke what to whom in the local bar; another in the streets, another at work, etc.

The main value in the grids as shown above is that they simplify and speed up recording. But in many cases, they can be used to spot a pattern; everyone kicks Tom; one child plays only with children younger than herself; Mrs Ryan always gives services; Mrs Moore always gives goods. Or Mrs Smith is always the receiver and never the giver; or women with higher family income (recorded in boxes below the grid) do not participate as much. One person may always speak English at work, or speak English to people of higher status; another person may always speak Spanish to a particular person even though everyone else on the grid always speaks English to that person. The bar may be the place where all older men speak Spanish, and so on.

3. Genealogical charts

A final recording device is one use for making genealogical charts or 'family trees'. You might make a genealogical chart in the course of doing someone's life history, to keep the characters straight in your mind; or you might use the chart as an end in itself, to show, for example, as I did on one American Indian reservation, that all nine hundred of the residents were interrelated. You can also use the charts to record a variety of information other than what appears through the figures on the chart; information such as age, length of marriage, religion, language spoken, emigration destination, political preference, level of education, and almost any characteristic that you care to note.

Do not feel that you have to understand terms like 'second cousin' or 'third cousin once removed' to do a genealogical chart. The only words you need to know are mother, father, sister, brother, daughter, son.

There are several ways of making genealogical charts; none is ideal because kinship systems are unwieldy. Here is the most commonly used method, beginning with the basic symbols *(Figure X. 4)*.

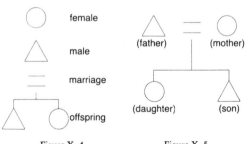

Figure X. 4   Figure X. 5

An example may be seen in *Figure X. 5*.   Brothers and sisters are shown 'hanging' off the line (in order of birth, where practicable). Here are the other symbols you may need:

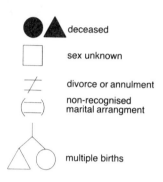

deceased

sex unknown

divorce or annulment

non-recognised marital arrangment

multiple births

Figure X. 6

With these symbols, you can show any set of family relationships, no matter how complicated.

1.   Use a big piece of paper. If you are more interested in going back through history, beyond great-grandparents, and are not too concerned with modern-day second cousins and beyond, a large square piece of paper is probably the best. On the other hand, if you are going back only three or four generations, or want to include distant cousins, or if there is a large set of brothers and sisters anywhere on the chart, a wide rectangular piece of paper, such as a length of shelf or wall paper, is essential. Leave a lot of space between each person so you can insert spouses, and below them, any children.

2.   Do not worry if people who are in the same generation, such as two sets of cousins, do not appear on the same horizontal plane on the chart; you can end up with one set in the middle of the chart and one at the bottom right-hand corner even though they are not younger. Except in very small families, to get people of roughly the same generation at the same level on the chart, you may have to use an enormous piece of paper, and there is no great advantage to it. You can achieve what you have lost visually simply by putting the date of birth under each person's name.

3.   Since the chart makes the relationships evident, there is no need to write the relationship under the symbol, since the same person may be Son in one connection and Father and Brother and Husband in others. However, if the chart is organised from the point of view of one person (see Ego on the next chart) then you can, if you wish, write the relationships under the symbols to save having to trace them out each time. The words can be abbreviated; use the first two letters of the relationships, plus 'Gr' and

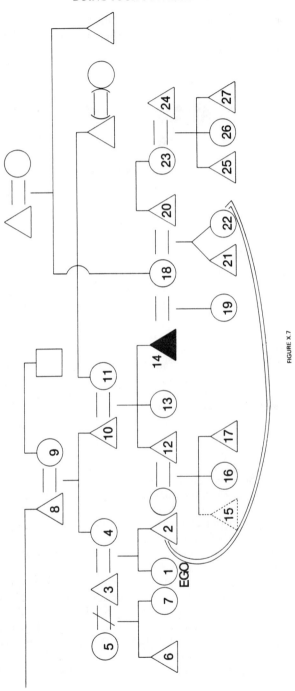

FIGURE X 7

'GrGr' for grandparent/great-grandparent and grandchild/great-grand-child relationships. For example, Fa, Mo, So, Da, Br, Si, Hu, Wi, GrFa, GrMo, GrGrFa, GrGrSo, and MoSiDa, BrDaHu. Each person gets only one relationship written under his/her name — whatever relationship he or she bears to the Ego, the central person.

There is also no need to use more than one colour, or special markings, except in one case: if you ever have to cross a line with a second one (with very good planning, you should not) draw it in a different colour, or distinguish it in some other way. In the example below, I use a humped line to show this (no. 18 on the chart).

4.   People often ask, 'Shall I put in-laws on the chart?' Of course. Your aunt's husband is an in-law, and in order to show their children (your cousins) you are going to have to put him on the chart. Whether you go further, and put your uncle-in-law's brothers and sisters on the chart, or your spouse's brothers and sisters and their families, depends on what you are trying to show. If you do, there is no need to distinguish them artificially; their relationship, like all others, will be obvious from the chart.

Figure X. 7 illustrates the use of the symbols, in a chart of about average complexity.

I am numbering some of these symbols in order to simplify my explanation, but ordinarily, you do not have to number them. I will explain the chart from the point of view of Number 1, whom I will call 'Ego'. Ego has a brother (2) and two living parents (3 and 4). Ego's father (3) was married before, and then divorced from 5. He and 5 had two children, 6 and 7. (These are a half-brother and half-sister to Ego and her brother, if you are interested.)

Ego's grandparents on her mother's side (8 and 9) are still living (we cannot see her father's parents on this section of the chart). Her aunt (10) and uncle by marriage (11) have three children: 12, 13 and 14. No. 12 (Ego's first cousin) has three children: 15, who is adopted, 16 and 17. Ego's first cousin 13 is not married, and her first cousin 14 is dead. No. 14 married 18, and had one daughter, 19. When 14 died, his wife 18 married 20, and they have twins, 21 and 22.

What would happen to the chart if 22 were tiresome enough to marry Ego's brother, 2? Just draw a *very* long marriage sign all the way across the chart between them, the best way you can, and 'hang' any children off the sign.

Notice that some of the people on this chart have no biological connection to Ego; in fact, they do not even have a marriage connection to any of Ego's biological relatives. For example, when Ego's cousin 14 died, his wife 18 married 20. We show 20's sister (23) and her husband (24) and their children 25–27. You will also notice, in case you wondered, that it is quite all right for 22 and 2 to marry; they are not related by blood.

Try a practice exercise on your own family. You can begin with any generation you like. Let us say that you will begin with your own generation, with yourself. Here is the drill:

1. Draw a horizontal line and 'hang' your brothers and sisters from it. Leave a lot of space between them. Then start with your eldest sibling (brother or sister). Let us say it is a brother. Whom did he marry? Draw her. How many children do they have? Draw them, once again leaving a lot of space in between them, if they have spouses. Then go on to your next brother or sister. Do the same again, and repeat the exercise for every brother and sister. Draw the children of each one.

2. Draw a vertical line connecting you and your brothers and sisters to the marriage sign between your parents. Draw your parents. Now take each of your father's brothers and sisters in turn. Whom did each marry? How many children did each have? Whom did each of the children marry? How many children did they have?

Do the same for your mother's brothers and sisters.

3. Draw a vertical line connecting your father and his brothers and sisters to the marriage sign between their parents. Take your father's father. Who were his brothers and sisters? Whom did each marry? How many children did each have? Grandchildren?

Do the same for your father's mother.

Do the same for your mother's father.

Do the same for your mother's mother.

Go back as many generations as you like, repeating these steps for each generation.

The first time you do this, you will probably have to transfer the figures to a larger piece of paper and allow more space between each person but you will soon see the basic simplicity of the system.

Finally, under each symbol you can list any information you like: name, date of birth, and if appropriate, marriage and death; religion, level of education, etc. If this clutters up your chart too much, you can give each person a number and then list the numbers and information on an accompanying sheet.

If you would like to know more about making genealogical charts, consult—

Schusky, Ernest L., *Manual for Kinship Analysis*. 2nd ed. New York: Holt, Rinehart and Winston, 1972.

C. Sound Recording, Photography, Film and Video

by Lelia Doolan

Sound recorders and cameras, including stills, film and video, provide additional tools to help in gathering, organising and presenting research materials. Frequently a situation that would otherwise take pages to describe can be recorded in a single picture; interviews and conversations can be taken 'live' without the interference (or possible inaccuracy/incompleteness) of written notes, and sequences of ongoing action can be caught as they happen. In terms of presentation, verbatim aural or visual materials can both illustrate a piece of research, giving it immediacy and authenticity, or in itself provide a documentary text to be accompanied, where required, by a verbal commentary.

Everyone has at some time taken a snapshot, or been the subject of one. Family albums are often as valuable as prehistoric hoards, containing information on family relationships, dress and hairstyles, food, furniture, architecture, casts of characters for different social activities and occasions. Old newspapers, books of photographs, histories of art, social and indust-rial documents and commentaries, pictures and maps of urban develop-ment; old discs (or up-to-date ones) of music and drama offer audio-visual research data readymade. Before rushing out, then, to buy or borrow a recorder or camera, check to see whether what you need is not already available. Elsewhere in this book (chapter IX) there is information on sources of research materials that are available in national and local institu-tions. Often these institutions hold archives of sound recordings, slides, film, videotapes. Some of them may also have audio-visual equipment for limited use by competent applicants.

What follows is not intended as a detailed do-it-yourself. Rather, it indi-cates some general principles and procedures. *You* must decide for yourself precisely which tool you need to use, and why it is essential. A short list of relevant books is included at the end.

1. Sound recording

a. Equipment

In this, as in every other instance, choosing the right machine for the job is important. There is nothing more frustrating than loading yourself up with heavy gear and then discovering that all you needed was a pocket cassette machine or an Instamatic camera.

There are two types of sound recording machine: the quarter inch open-reel type and the cassette machine (which uses a narrower gauge, one-eighth-inch). The quarter inch recorder has advantages in terms of its variety of recording speeds – 1⅞, 3¾, 7½, 15 inches per second, with 3¾ or even 1⅞ being adequate for speech (and the faster speeds suitable for music) thus offering better quality of sound reproduction and easier editing facilities. The cassette recorder has only one recording speed but is gener-ally more portable and unobtrusive. So, unless you need really good quality sound that will stand on its own, apart from your written research, you may find a cassette machine adequate, and more comfortable to use. The recording of music is rarely adequately done by a cassette recorder, the tape being too narrow to contain the full range of timbre, pitch and tonality. If, however, you merely need to record the words of a song for later inscrip-tion, or wish to note your own comments on the figures and movements of a dance, or the actions and positions of speakers, with the background sound of the relevant dance or meeting, you should be safe enough with a cassette recorder.

Almost more important than the choice of recorder is the choice of microphone. Most cassette recorders have built-in microphones. This kind of arrangement provides reasonable intelligibility when a small number of people are involved and they sit close to the machine. Interviews in crowded circumstances, for instance during a noisy meeting, in a busy workplace, or on the street, are better handled by using an external microphone, preferably uni-directional. The omni-directional microphone, as its name suggests, picks up sound in a wide arc and you are liable to get too much background interference. Most people will be familiar with the sight of television news reporters speaking directly into a microphone which they hold close, and to news interviews where the reporter first asks a question into the microphone and then 'offers' it to the person being interviewed. This technique assists in separating the voice of each from the surrounding buzz. So, an external, if possible uni-directional, microphone, which can be plugged into the side of the recorder is good basic equipment for an interview situation.

Finally, you will need tape. Cassettes come in various lengths, usually 15 minutes, 30 minutes and 45 minutes per side (often identified as C30, C60, C90). Quarter inch tape comes in 5", 7" and 10" spools. Unless you contemplate a very long interview or need to record, uninterruptedly, a lengthy sequence of action or speech, it is often easier to use a shorter length of tape. This minimises spooling back and forth afterwards, and in the case of cassettes the tape is less likely to stretch.

Cassette recorders (and some smaller open-reel machines) have a dual power system, using either batteries or working off mains electrical current. It is useful to carry a spare pack of batteries where no direct current is available but, on the whole, mains electricity is a steadier and longer-lasting power source, so use it when you can.

b. Situation

Check out the location in advance of any recording. Things to look for are: power sources, types of plug socket, position of persons involved. In most cases you may simply be recording an interview with one other person. Position the microphone and the machine so that the person you are talking to will be comfortable, and place yourself so that you will be near enough to have your questions recorded, but not to intimidate the other person. A small microphone stand, so that you can place the microphone securely on a flat surface, will allow you to conduct interviews in a relaxed way.

Where a large number of people are involved, you are better to remain mobile (i.e. using batteries or an extension cord as your power source) and, with your external microphone, to hold such separate conversations as you require. In the case of a large meeting or event, where you wish both to carry some sense of the activity as it happens and also to record your impressions/comments on it, you could either use two machines, each with its separate microphone or, as I have indicated above, combine a general recording of the event using an omni-directional microphone, into which you speak (holding it close to your mouth) when the need arises. Placing microphones to record music, especially for group performance, is a tricky business. If you can use only one microphone, place it where it will catch the general balance of the sound, being careful to allow for the extra penetration that drumming or other percussion instruments create. If the event is a once-off occasion, you would be well to set up two machines in case of breakdown.

A general rule-of-thumb for this, as in all other research situations, is to reconnoitre the ground in advance, decide on a strategy and stick to it. Portions that are missing may be picked up later, either at a repeat recording session, or by re-interviewing.

The likeliest failures, apart from inadequate preparation or incomplete questioning, are mechanical failure or flat batteries. Some simple mechanical failures — such as the tape sticking — can often be released by pressing fast forward or rewind button; most machines have a battery power indicator with a needle, showing the danger zone in red. Many machines also have a three-figure counter which gives a rough estimate of the length of tape already inscribed. It is useful to make a note of the number reached after each section or interview. Similarly, if you have a gauge which shows sound level, check that the voice of your interviewee is, in fact, registering. The movement of the needle will indicate this, and you can adjust the volume control to keep the needle midway. When each recording session is complete, mark the tape with the date, name of the activity or interviewer, location; then mark the tape box with the same details *and* a number relating it to your Research Design.

c. Presentation

You now have tapes or cassettes with raw material for selection, sifting and inclusion in your written paper, or for arrangement as an accompanying appendix or section. In the first instance, the material needs to be transcribed in written form. This can be speeded up by getting a foot control unit for playback, so that your hands may be free to write or type. It is also useful to listen to all the material right through, noting relevant parts, and the counter numbers of these, so that inessential bits are discarded. You can then go back and transcribe only what you really need. If possible, where a lot of recorded material is involved, this should be done as soon after the recording session as possible. Not only is your memory fresher, permitting you to add in what you think important by way of description of location, dress, facial expression or movement, but you avoid the daunting task of transcribing miles of tape at the very end.

In the second instance, where you want to present a completed tape separate from your written paper, the material has to be edited together into a new order. There are two procedures for doing this: cutting and splicing, and 'dubbing'. Cutting and splicing involves the physical cutting of the tape and its subsequent joining together at a new point, using splicing tape to make the join. A small splicing block, a felt pen to make the necessary marks where you wish the fresh join to occur, a razor and splicing tape are the necessary tools. A few practice splices will help your nimbleness. Do your best to hold the tape by its edges so as not to get it covered in fingerprints. These small oily deposits can clog the heads of the machine, causing unwanted noise. Check each splice as you go to make sure it is satisfactory. This procedure means that you must use ¼-inch tape as the cassette tape is really too narrow to permit manual editing.

'Dubbing' is the device of recording from your original copy onto a fresh tape on another machine. In this way you can dub from a cassette onto a ¼-inch tape and then make manual edits on that tape, in the way described above. Or, using either cassette tape *or* ¼-inch tape as your original, you can dub those passages you require in their new order directly onto the new tape, building up a complete sound essay as you go.

2. Photography

a. Equipment

Cameras range from the simple, fixed-lens-type box camera into which you fit film on a cassette, to the most sophisticated single lens reflex (SLR) camera with all kinds of built-in exposure meters, electronic wind-on devices and so on into which you fit a spool of film by winding it in manually. A third type of camera, the Polaroid, has a fixed lens and takes film in packs, usualy eight to each pack. It has the advantage of producing pictures 'on the spot'.

Film stock for twelve, twenty or thirty-six exposures comes at different ASA/DIN speeds: the lower the number, the slower the film. A high ASA/DIN rating — say, 400 or 1000 — allows you to work well in poor lighting conditions; a low rating (64-125) is fine for sunny weather or a bright but dull day, and will give plenty of depth to your pictures. These ratings work for both black and white and colour. It may suit you better to use slides, particularly if you mean to present your material to an audience. Slide film stock comes in similar ratings. ASA/DIN ratings really only apply to cameras with a range of film speeds and aperture openings (that is the 'eye' which opens and closes as you click the shutter). These are marked on the lens. Be sure to set up the meter on your camera to the ASA/DIN rating of the film you are using or you will get some funny results.

The standard lens is adequate to a range of normal uses: portraits, group shots, buildings, even landscapes. It 'sees' pretty much as your own eye does. A wide-angle or 'fish-eye' lens allows you to include more subject matter. A long or telephoto lens brings distant objects into close-up. Each lens has numbered rings or collars for setting aperture opening, shutter speed and distance. The greater the aperture opening (say, $f2·5/3·5$) and the lower the shutter speed ($\frac{1}{15}$/$\frac{1}{30}$th sec.), the more light will fall on your film for work in poor lighting conditions. A higher f stop (16 or 22), with a faster shutter speed allows less light through the lens for very bright conditions. You will find the right combinations through trial and error. Focusing can be done on single lens reflex cameras by looking through the viewfinder and moving the distance ring until your subject is sharp and clear. As you cannot 'see' the subject in this way through a fixed lens camera viewfinder, you can measure the distance with your own eye and set the numbered collar accordingly. It is possible to get extra lenses for extreme close-up work, or macro-photography as it is sometimes called.

b. Situation

Do not be discouraged if all you can afford is a Polaroid camera or a fixed lens type. Many fine pictures have been taken with such equipment. Your chief concern should be to work out in advance what kind of material you need and the use to which you mean to put it. Obviously, your Research Outline will guide you here. If, for example, you mean to show a range of pictures of the buildings and grounds of St Michael's Correctional Institution, augmenting those you have found in the *Greenville News* picture archive, you must decide whether to keep these in the same style by using black and white film, or to contrast/update your material by using colour. A fixed lens or Polaroid camera may well prove adequate. If, however, you hope for publication in colour, it may be necessary to use slide film. These technical details should be settled early on.

Cameras need light to work in. Most problems with photography involve to much, or too little, light. A camera lens is nothing like as sensitive as the human eye and objects which are visible to you may be quite obscure when transposed to film. Outdoor conditions, and objects which stay fairly still, all help your situation. If you are photographing people and you want to show their faces, get as near as you can. Group photographs, with everyone the size of a pin in the far distance, make poor picture material. If people want to pose, let them; just get close enough to make the shot expressive. Unposed pictures can be dramatic and revealing but it is well to check in advance that nobody minds your doing this.

Obviously, a procedure, such as a laboratory test or industrial pattern, is best shown in a series of mid and close shots, with perhaps a wide shot of the location and participants, in which to place the various stages. Beware of placing people in front of reflective backgrounds, for instance windows or the sun, or you may end up with a dark silhouette against a dazzling background. Similarly, fine landscapes which delight the human eye and show the pleasant tourist amenities enjoyed by the people of Aznavour and their visitors, may gain in depth and interest on film if you use a foreground object to frame the view. For indoor photography, you will need to be especially careful to have enough light. A flash attachment can help but will sometimes 'wash out' faces, or make them look blinded. Experimentation will help you to get better results.

c. Presentation

Film can be processed either by yourself or by a laboratory. Black and white film can be developed quite easily, using a small developing tank. The manufacturer's manual gives instructions on kinds and amounts of chemical. A bathroom can be converted for part-time use as a darkroom, and paper, an enlarger, some measuring jugs and plastic baths, chemicals and a timer will enable you to make contact prints and, from them, prints of various sizes for inclusion in your text, or for presentation in a separate folio. Colour printing is more expensive and you are here in the hands of a commercial firm. With slides, you can get the film processed and then cut the separate slides and mount them yourself. Boxes of slide mounts can be bought from camera dealers or film companies.

3. Film

a. Equipment

The cine camera, like the stills camera, is simply a black box with a hole or 'eye' which records on film the scene in front of it. This time, the film is driven past the opening or 'eye' by a motor which runs on batteries or mains. This motor moves the film onward at a steady rate, allowing it to 'see' complete sequences.

Cameras come in different sizes and sorts of complexity. Most films made for cinema showing are shot with big sound cameras which take film that is 35mm in width. Documentary and news film shown on television is normally made on 16mm film, using either sound or silent (frequently called 'mute') cameras. 'Home' movie-makers have traditionally used single 8 or super 8mm cameras, the latter having a sound facility as well. Recently, growing numbers of professional film-makers are using super 8mm, and some television companies favour its use for news coverage. Super 8 cameras are lighter and smaller and cheaper. Also, recent improvements in body and lens design have provided them with an impressive range of capability. Their chief disadvantage is perhaps a certain 'flatness' of picture quality, and in the fact that super 8 films cannot be shown to very large audiences withou a powerful projector and a big screen. They can, of course, be copied onto 16mm or even 35mm film without major loss of picture quality.

As with film for the stills camera, cine film stock comes in various ASA/DIN ratings. In the United States ASA is sometimes marked as E.I. (exposure index). Again this means that film with a high rating (160) is good for work in dim lighting; a rating of 25 or 40 works well in the outdoors or for well-lit interiors. There are two kinds of film: negative and reversal. Reversal film processing produces a print in a single process; negative film is developed first as a negative image and from this prints are made. Reversal film was introduced so that 'amateur' film-makers could avoid the extra cost of having a print made. Black and white negative film is available in 16mm but is rare in the 8mm formats. Reversal film in black and white is available in all formats and some 8mm types may be processed as negative. Colour negative is rarely used in 8mm and is becoming less popular with 16mm film-makers. Colour reversal film is widely used on both formats, and further prints can be made from your original camera print. The term 'chrome' tacked on after the manufacturer's brand name signifies that the colour film is reversal. The word 'color' indicates that the film is negative. The motion picture industry invariably uses negative film. The ratio of costs between 16mm and the 8mm formats varies according to the individual film-maker's practice. 16mm is a lot more expensive than 8mm, costing from five to ten times more to put one minute of 16mm sound film on the screen than the same length on 8mm film. The quality of super 8 film is rapidly catching up on 16mm and, with improved sound cameras and projectors, and advantages in terms of costs, it is an attractive research tool.

Film stock comes in 50-foot cassettes/cartridges for 8mm formats; fifty feet of film runs for about three minutes. Some sound cameras can take up to 200 feet. 16mm comes in reels of 100, 400, and 1200 feet.

A word about silent and sound cameras/film stock: sound film usually has a magnetic stripe running along one side of the film; on this synchronised sound can be recorded. Sound cameras are often slightly bigger than the mute kind. A sound camera can always take mute film though the reverse is not true. Decide how you are going to use the film before you shoot it. It is frequently necessary to shoot only mute film, recording a 'wild' (unsynchronised) sound-track as you go, on a separate tape recorder. Picture and sound can be matched up satisfactorily afterwards. The only time you must synchronise picture and sound exactly is when someone is talking directly to the camera, or when you are recording interviews. These require precise synchronisation, called 'lip sync'.

Microphones are obviously quite important here, too. Everything in the preceding section on sound recording applies, with a few additions and reminders about uni- and omni-directional microphones. (There are bi- and poly-directional types; lapel and neck microphones for interview situations; rifle and bazooka microphones for recording distant sound or speech accurately.) In each case, the microphone cord (from the camera or recorder to the subject) must be long enough to allow comfortable movement. If hand-holding the microphone is not essential, microphone stands or a microphone on a pole or 'boom' are useful. Some super 8 cameras have built-in microphones. While they are often of good quality, there is a danger that they may pick up and record camera noise, so it is wise to test for this before you embark. A wind sock or shield to protect the microphone from wind-buffeting can be made from foam rubber or other soft, porous material. It is wise to cover the microphone in this way in all outdoor work.

b. Lenses

The zoom lens is now the most commonly used in all cine cameras in the 16mm and 8mm formats, replacing the complement of normal, wide angle and long lenses. You can, therefore, use the zoom lens as a 'fixed' lens at various points on the zoom (close shot, mid shot, wide angle shot) for the total length of a shot. Or, you can 'zoom in' close to your subject, or 'zoom out' to a wide shot *during* the course of taking a sequence of action. As with a stills camera, the lens has collars for setting the opening or f stop and for focusing, as well as the zoom collar with its zoom stick.

c. Situation

Your research topic dictates the kind of film footage you will need. Film can provide data upon which to base a piece of research, say, decison-making in encounter groups. In a case like this, a filmed record of people's actions, gestures or speech can form the ground for investigation and comparison against your own observation. Psychologists, biologists, other natural scientists, time-and-motion researchers, students of human and animal behaviour, have found film a useful tool for the study of processes and procedures. Explorers and anthropologists have used film to record aspects of the lives of people they visited. Film of ritual celebrations, child-rearing practices, hunting and food gathering activities have been used to supply a 'you-were-there' authentication to written material. It is not an exaggeration to say that anything that can be lit can be filmed.

There are, however, hazards. Obviously, you cannot base your research on the filmed procedures of an encounter group if the camera has only shot parts of it. Similarly, there is scarcely any need to film every element of a football match if the only topic under investigation is the behaviour of the goalkeeper, or the crowd on the terraces/bleachers. The second hazard with a camera is that it intrudes and alters the 'natural' state of affairs, especialy in small groups or indoors. People begin to 'act' for the camera. Alternatively, they may become shy or inhibited. This can often be dealt with by spending some time in familiarising everybody concerned with the camera. It may be possible to leave it in a fixed position until people get used to it and then, perhaps, operate it by using a remote 'on/off' switch. The third hazard is an operational one. Machines need maintenance and care in use; they often break down and, depending on the complexity of your work, they may require two or more people to operate them. These factors can sometimes get in the way of what you actually need to do. One researcher who was studying barter among the Chinese boat people said that she could not possibly have covered with a camera the number of transactions she could physically manage by her own unaided effort. She felt herself hampered by having to look through the camera viewfinder when she needed to keep the whole scene under constant review in order to run quickly to and fro among the various parties to each negotiation. With practice, many of these technical difficulties can be overcome. When you are familiar with its capabilities and quirks and become fluent in using it as a note-taker, the camera can do a lot of the running for you.

A few reminders will help you. Everything in the section on photography about keeping objects and people close when you need to observe detail; not shooting into a light or placing your material against a reflective surface, are worth remembering. In addition, if you wish to move the camera to right or left (panning) or up and down (tilting) or to move physically with the camera towards your subject or away from it (tracking), remember that you must make these movements slowly and smoothly. If you do not, your shots will tend to blur and jerk. A tripod on which you can mount the camera is a help here, and if you can get a base with wheels, you can move easily across flat surfaces. If you are using a sound camera, remember that it is safer to fix the microphone in a static position. If this is impossible and the microphone must be hand-held, try not to move your fingers up and down on the microphone but hold it steady as the movements of your hand can cause interference. In all sound shooting, you should begin each shot by filming a hand-clap or clapperboard. Finally, make a check-list of all the equipment you need for a given situation, and test that everything is in working order before you begin filming.

d. Presentation

A print of the film you have shot can be shown by projecting it onto a screen exactly as you filmed it. Or, you can have single frames or sequences of frames printed up to interleave your text as illustration. A third alternative, and one commonly adopted, is to select shots or sequences of shots and to edit them together in the order you choose, forming a completed film.

Editing is not difficult at all. It is largely a matter of learning a routine and getting plenty of practice. You will need the following pieces of equipment: a viewer/editor with winding reels so that you can spool it through, see each frame and mark your cutting points; a splicer to make the cuts; tape or cement to make the joins; a rack with pegs or pins on which to hang single shots or sequences, numbering each peg to match your written numbered list so that you can quickly locate what you need; a chinagraph pencil to mark where to make the edit, and to identify the 'head' and 'tail' of a shot. If possible, you should wear a pair of white cotton gloves. Film can easily get smudged or dirty and, especially if you are editing your camera print (less expensive than having a 'work' print made), you need to be extra careful. Finally, you need a projector.

The first thing to do is to project your camera print, one reel at a time, onto a screen at approximately the size of the image you mean to show in public. The viewer has a very small screen and if you simply run it through this you may miss details of gradation, focus and timing. You need to get a feel for the rhythm and 'look' of what you have done, *as your audience will see it*. Project each reel several times, making a numbered shot list as you go, identifying takes that are no good and building up a rough idea of where each shot should be in the finished film. Do this with each reel, then, using the viewer, cut the print up, shot by shot, hanging each shot on its numbered peg and marking that peg number beside its corresponding shot on your list. You can then splice these together to form a 'roughcut' and run this roughcut through the projector to see how it looks before making your final edits.

Editing sound film is only a bit more complicated. For this, you will need a sound head on the viewer so that you can hear what has been recorded on the magnetic stripe. It is possible to cut the camera print but you must be very attentive to jumps in sound level at editing points as this can be irritating when you come to project it. There is also the problem that, as the sound runs ahead of the picture by a few frames, you may get sound 'over-lap' on your edits. Experience and native cunning will help you to find ways around this but, in the meantime, there is an inexpensive solution. This involves transferring the sound on your magnetic stripe onto a sprocketed sound tape the same width as your film (this tape is often called 'fullcoat' or 'sep mag' – separate magnetic – tape). With a small piece of equipment, a synchroniser, you line up this tape to match the camera print, run them synchronously (the hand clap or clapperboard at the beginning of each shot will help you to identify the exact frame where they are in 'sync), cut them at the same point, and hang them together on your numbered peg. Then simply join the selected takes in the sequence you require.

That's all there is to it.

4. Video

a. Equipment

Videotape recording (VTR) combines sound and vision on a tape of vari-ous widths (¼, ½, ¾, 1, 2-inch) which can then be played back and viewed on a normal television screen, or on a monitor. Because of this instant playback facility, you can immediately see what you have recorded and, if necessary, re-shoot. The same tape can be used and re-used.

Portable video units, or portapaks, comprise a camera, with built-in microphone, and a videotape recorder. Without going into elaborate elec-tronic detail, what happens is this: the subject 'seen' through the lens is picked up on a tiny circular screen inside the camera. From this screen (called a 'tube'), the image with its accompanying sound is passed through the cord connecting camera to videotape machine. Recording heads on the video machine then 'inscribe' the image and sound onto the tape. By con-necting a cable from the recorder to a monitor or TV set you can see what is being recorded. Mains electricity or batteries provide power to drive both recorder and camera.

There are three main kinds of portable video format: open reel-to-reel, VHS (Video Home System) and U-Matic, the latter two using cassette tapes. The U-Matic and VHS systems record in colour; open reel machines usually record in black and white. Tape duration varies; open reel tapes run for thirty minutes on a portapak; a portable U-Matic tape lasts for twenty minutes; VHS machines can take a tape of up to three hours. VHS and open reel portapaks are, on the whole, cheaper than the U-Matic type.

As video is one of the fastest-moving development industries in the world, new formats are being piloted all the time. The video disc system (using disc rather than tape), two-in-one portapacks (camera and recorder as one unit using various ¼", ½" and ¾" tape cassettes) are among those coming on the market and it is expected that a full video system will soon be as lightweight and portable as a small super-8mm cine camera.

Black and white and colour cameras vary in price and quality. As with cine cameras, there is a lens, a viewfinder, and the box itself with its built-in or detachable microphone. Most lenses have a zoom capacity and they always have a collar for setting aperture opening and another for focusing. The camera microphone is almost always omni-directional but there is, on each recorder, a socket into which an external microphone can be fitted. Again, microphone stands or booms, and a tripod and dolly for the camera are useful adjuncts to the unit.

b. Situation

Video is a valuable 'action-research' tool because of its instant playback facility. This implies that your research involves a certain amount of *doing*, by the person or group undertaking the research, or by those people being studied. You might, say, be studying ways adopted by a certain committee of highlighting problems in house construction or land division, or any one of a number of pressing needs within a particular urban neighbourhood or rural district. Your Research Design will identify a range of options — door-to-door canvassing, public meetings, putting up posters, lobbying politicians, writing articles for local or national press, getting on radio or television, making a video documentary in the locality. Your research could either take the form of an edited video report showing the ways adopted and their outcomes; or, it could be part written paper, part video; or, again, you could have the committee participate with you in making a video pro-gramme about their grievances and base your research paper on selected aspects of their process.

Video has often been used in this way, to gather evidence for making a case about a specific issue. One tenants' organisation in a Belfast suburb used video to stimulate its own members into concerted action about bad housing conditions. They showed a videotape of some of the major defects at a meeting in their community hall, gathered fresh instances from the dis-cussion that followed the showing, selected volunteers from the meeting to make a total inventory of all complaints, and incorporated these in a new videotape. This was then shown to officials from the housing authority, resulting in a limited range of improvements. Similar examples for other cities abound.

Of course, video can also be used for more conventional research needs, including those mentioned in the film section above. One research team, studying certain aspects of family relationships within their domestic setting, kept videotape machines and cameras recording continuously over a lengthy period. From the videotapes, patterns of recurrent behaviour were identified; these provided data for a study of hierarchies in domestic groups.

There are a number of things to watch when using video. The day of the lightweight, all-in-one camera and video recorder is almost upon us but, until then, there is a good deal of lugging about of video gear to be done. Portapaks *are* portable by one camera operator. However, they seem to grow heavier with each minute of carrying, or standing to shoot. It is not difficult to make a halter from strong materials and so hang the recorder comfortably in front of you (if you carry it on your back, rucksack style, you will not be able to get at the 'Record' or 'Play' levers nor will you be able to see if the tape is moving properly). If you have to do a lot of moving about during shots, it is advisable to borrow something that moves on wheels, a wheelchair or supermarket trolley, or whatever, and have someone push you along. Or you can use a car, shooting through an open side window or from the back window (make sure it is clean).

The chief failures encountered in portapak work are caused by loosely connected cables and flat batteries. Batteries hold power for about thirty minutes' use and can be recharged by a battery charger which doubles as a mains transformer. With reel-to-reel recorders, tape spools sometimes jump off the guide tracks (given agitated movement, such as in running with the machine or setting it down suddenly) and tape then snarls up. A final warning about cameras: the tube or tubes inside the camera is very light-sensitive and can be damaged by pointing the lens directly into a bright light or at the sun. This 'burns' part of the tube and causes spidery lines and blotches on your later pictures. It can to some extent be remedied by pointing the camera at a brightly-lit flat white surface for up to half an hour (making the 'burn' cover the tube surface uniformly in effect). The placing and use of microphones is similar to that for film.

It takes practice to learn the best method of operating the unit to suit your needs, although learning the basic principles takes no more than an hour. With experience, you will realise that constant zooming in and out, or swinging from side to side to follow the speakers in a conversation must be done much less frequently than the eye might do it. Constant change in the size of a person in shot ultimately draws more attention to the workings of the camera than it does to the topic in view. So try to reduce your rate of action to slow motion. Placing yourself or the camera at the right point to 'see' the whole scene, or the special bit you need, is one of the most important choices you make in this part of your research. In every case, reconnoitre, plan, get to know the terrain. Even work out, roughly, the shots in advance. Again, if is often useful to familiarise your subjects with the 'presence' of video by spending some time at the beginning in showing them what you are doing, and how they look on TV. Finally, and most importantly, always allow the recorder to run for ten seconds or so before focusing in on the action you wish to 'take'.

c. *Presentation*

This is where you discover how good your Research Design was and whether you have followed it thoroughly and accurately. If you have done so, the business of preparing your material for presentation is a mechanical one.

The first option is to edit. You need a videotape recorder with an edit facility, a fresh reel or cassette of videotape, and a monitor (TV set), together with the machine you have used to make the recording and its monitor. It is also necessary to have a stop-watch or seconds counter for the timing of edits. The procedure involves 'dubbing' (re-recording) from your original tape onto the new tape, assembling those pieces you need in the required order. The monitors allow you to see the material you wish to dub (on the 'preview' or original recorder's monitor) and the way it looks and sounds when dubbed onto the new tape (on the 'edit' monitor). Reel-to-reel editing is a tedious process as you must line up each edit point mechanically, count back ten seconds and then roll both machines simultaneously for ten seconds, hitting the 'Edit' button (on the edit machine) precisely at the chosen point. This ensures that both machines are running in 'sync' and avoids bumpy edits. It will save time to view your tapes beforehand and to note down the counter numbers of the relevant sections.

Most U-Matic videotape recorders now possess an electronic edit device, consisting of a unit which controls both the preview and the edit recorder. This unit, in fact, does the counting for you, rewinds the tape and keeps both machines running in perfect step.

There is another way of editing your material and that is to do it, television style, on the spot. Instead of using just one camera, like a film camera, and afterwards editing together the shots you have taken from various angles and viewpoints, you can use two or three cameras, link them into a switcher and cut from one to the other during the action, recording your selection directly onto the videotape recorder. This requires quite a team of people and a great deal of preparation in advance, but it does save time afterwards. There are other variants that you can try as you gain expertise.

Of course, it may not be necessary to edit at all. If the videotape records a 'happening' in its entirety, then obviously that is the way it must be shown. For showing to an audience, remember that no more than twenty or thirty people can see a normal-sized TV screen (23 inches or so) or hear its output. Larger, film-sized screens are becoming available for showing to bigger groups and for this you can always get an amplifier and speakers to improve sound distribution.

It is possible to photograph (on a monitor) 'freeze' frames from the videotape and insert them as illustration of your textual matter. While these may look a bit fuzzy or 'grainy', they can still carry the requisite information effectively.

One final important point: there is a difference between video line standards in various countries; for instance, the United States has a 525 line standard, whereas a 625 line standard operates in the United Kingdom. Tapes recorded on one standard cannot be replayed on machines using another. Conversion is possible but costly.

The additional research tools mentioned in the preceding sections will be of no avail if you have not identified for yourself precisely the material you need and the best means of acquiring it. If your research involves a comparison between regional accents or speech forms, you are obviously better off with a simple tape recorder than with a film or video camera. If, on the other hand, you are studying children's play-songs, you may need to see the matching of action to word. You will know from your Research Design whether it is the 'look' or the 'sound' of a topic that you wish to study, and where you need to be aware of both. Photographs are a simple, direct way of presenting documentary evidence. Film is useful for detailed, complex processes, and in situations where electrical current is unavailable and portability essential. Videotape has multiple documentary uses, is a good 'live' recorder of events, and a valuable action-research tool.

Ethical considerations involving invasions of privacy or using people as 'booty' must be carefully taken into account. Permission to use pictures of people should be sought in advance, wherever possible. Perhaps a good question is 'Would *I* mind if this were done to me?'

d. Sources

Buying the various items of equipment mentioned here can be prohibitive for the beginning researcher, and hiring can lead to a heavy daily cost, especially if you are unfamiliar with the machinery. It is advisable, therefore, to look around for likely places from which to borrow. Schools, colleges, universities and adult education institutes usually have this type of equipment, and may also provide some training as well. In most cities in the United States and Canada, and in the United Kingdom, community resource centres or co-operative groups of independent film and videomakers exist to provide training and operational and editing facilities. Cable TV studios are also a likely source. In Ireland, there is little development in either community media workshops or in the cable companies as a resource; it is to be hoped that this situation can only get better.

Some useful books on these topics are —

Sound:
Gardener, John, *Master Creative Tape Recording.* New Jersey: Hayden Book Co., [U.K.] Newnes Technical Books, 1977.

Photography:
Carey, David, *How It Works. . . The Camera.* Loughborough, England: Ladybird Books, 1970.

Film:
Lipton, Lenny, *Independent Film-making.* New York: Simon and Schuster, 1972.

Video:
Atienza, Loretta J., *VTR Workshop: Small Format Video.* Paris: UNESCO, 1977.
Dranov, Paula, *Video in the 80s.* White Plains, N.Y.: Knowledge Industry Publications, 1980.

General:
Collier, John Jr., *Visual Anthropology: Photography as a Research Method.* New York: Holt, Rinehart and Winston, 1967.
Dehavenon, Anna Lou, and Harris, M., 'Hierarchical Behaviour in Domestic Groups: A Videotape Analysis' in *Cultural Materialism,* edited by Marvin Harris, pp. 42-45. New York: Vintage Book Co., 1980.
Hockings, Paul, ed., *Principles of Visual Anthropology.* Paris: Mouton and Co., 1975.
Worth, Sol and Adair, John, *Through Navajo Eyes: An Exploration in Film Communication and Anthropology.* Bloomington, Ind.; London: Indiana University Press, 1972.

XI. Analysing the Results

by Richard Scaglion

A. General data

ONE OF the biggest obstacles to analysing and writing up research results is disorganised notes. After months of work on a research project no one wants to spend almost as much time again sifting through bits and scraps of paper and incomplete notes. People who do not follow a Research Outline have an additional problem at this point: they do not know when they are finished and they drag the project on endlessly, thinking that perhaps there is one more book they should read or one more aspect they should study. They become paranoid when they hear about anyone else's research and wonder if they, too, should include something like that. . . on and on it goes, and the study, now the Book of the Century, never sees the light of day.

However, if you have followed the suggestions in Chapters II and X, you are now at the most rewarding point in your project: analysing and writing up your material. Analysing is the processing which your brain, sometimes assisted by technical aids, performs on what you have collected. Some of us are better processors than others, but most of us can improve by better organisation. In analysing your information, whether on your own, or if appropriate, with the help of a computer, you will probably be categorising information, trying to see patterns and relationships, discarding the irrelevant, summarising, and drawing conclusions. These processes can be done verbally or quantitatively or both. Remember, however, that quantification, no matter how sophisticated, does not confer accuracy; if your material is poor, clothing it in figures will not help.

If you have used the filing system described in Chapter X, you can begin preliminary analysis. Since you have filed your notes according to the topic(s) on each page, and the topics correspond largely to the points in your Research Outline, you can choose any point in your Outline, find the file for it, and see what information you have. For some topics, such as the history of the location of a place, probably all you need to do is summarise the information. In other cases, you may need to find categories or patterns. In still other cases, you may have to compare the contents of one file with those of another.

It is possible, of course, to *code* and process your half-sheet notes, genealogical charts, grids and so on, just as you code and process questionnaires. Material in written notes, for example, can be categorised according to presence or absence of a particular phenomenon or behaviour, or according to type. For example, if you had extensive notes on a group of football supporters at a game, you might code the types of participants, the behaviours exhibited during the observation, their frequency and any changes in frequency during the episode. If you had a large number of different observations, this would be a convenient way of analysing the more clear-cut aspects of your data. If you have collected a number of genealogical charts, you might code them according to number of relatives, number the informant remembered on father's side versus the actual number finally achieved from all sources of investigation; number remembered on mother's side; size of each nuclear family, average age of marriage in each generation, levels of education, etc.

Standardised systems of categorisation are available for certain kinds of material: for example, Bales' twelve interaction categories, which are used for studying groups involved in problem-solving or decision-making. The categories include such activities as 'shows antagonism', 'deflates other's status, defends or asserts self' and instances are coded to indicate both the actor and the recipient (Bales 1952: 149). The entire coding, however, is done *at the time* of observation; extended notes of the sort described in Chapter X are not taken.

B. The Contribution of Statistics

No matter how you have organised your data, you should remember that the data analysis, like the write-up, is just like telling a story. You start out with a general description or idea of what is going on. You then go into more detail, giving examples to illustrate your points. At the conclusion, you should provide a summary of your main findings. In a purely qualitative treatment, you would accomplish the above tasks by using words alone. The evidence you give to support your observations would be in the form of illustrative descriptions. By adding quantitative data, you can be more convincing.

Think about the following statements:

'Many of the inmates in St Michael's Correctional Institution are from the lowest of three socio-economic classes.'

'More males than females have migrated from Ballyglass in the past ten years.'

What exactly did the authors of these statements mean by 'many' and 'more'? What is the basis for their statements? Is it intuition, observation or what? Would we share their opinions? Suppose the first sentence read, 'Thirty-five of the one hundred inmates of St Michael's we interviewed were from the lowest of three socio-economic classes.' In this instance one might not consider that number to be 'many' since one would expect about one-third of the inmates to be from the lowest class just by chance. What, though, if the sentence had read, 'Ninety-three of the one hundred inmates we interviewed were from the lowest of three socio-economic classes?' This is much more 'convincing' in the sense that the reader is more likely to believe that socio-economic class is really a factor.

At this point it is important that you should not think of quantitative analysis as a mysterious or magical process in which numbers are 'fed' into a machine which 'digests' the information, analyses it for you, and spews forth numbers which are incomprehensible to the average person. You do the analysis. The computer only does what you tell it to do. Basically, the computer is a counting device which saves you the time and trouble of counting. In the above examples, you could certainly count up the number of juveniles from St Michael's whom you interviewed and sort them into socio-economic classes in whatever way you have defined class. Similarly, you could count up the males and females from Ballyglass in your sample and sort them out according to sex and according to whether they migrated or not. However, when you have as many variables as you probably do, and as much data as you have probably gathered, it becomes quite tedious to sort all this data into so many categories by hand. There are many questions to ask: what factors are associated with migration from Ballyglass? Is it a function of age, sex, occupation, number of siblings, whether other family members have migrated, or some combination of these factors? The computer helps us to look at all these relationships, and more, without wasting a lot of time in hand tabulation. Quantitative analysis helps us to be more precise in our descriptions.

In reading this chapter remember the distinction made in Chapter VIII between a *sample* and a *universe* or complete *population* of people or items. This chapter is written from the perspective of analysing a sample, since most of our data generally involve samples of populations which can be considered as samples of still more general populations. If you are working with a universe, you should be careful, because certain quantitative measures such as the standard deviation (see pp. 157-58) have slightly different formulae depending on whether a sample or a population is being described. Generally speaking, the *statistical tests of association* listed in Table XI.10 on p. 168 are used to draw conclusions from a sample only, whereas many of the other quantitative measures described in this chapter, such as the measures of central tendency and dispersion (see pages 155-62), are useful ways of expressing results whether they have been derived from a sample or from a complete population. If you are working with a complete population, you might want to consult a standard statistics text such as one of those listed at the end of this chapter.

1. Univariate analysis: frequency distributions

Suppose you have refined your concepts (such as 'socio-economic class'); collected your data and coded it for analysis as previously described. What do you do next? The first step is to get an overall idea of what is going on. You should look at each variable in turn to see how it is distributed. In our examination of St Michael's Correctional Institution, we were interested in knowing about the population – for the staff: ages, sexes, occupations, and so forth; for the inmates: ages, sexes, offences committed, lengths of sentences, and so on. Each of these is a variable. We want to find out how many persons or things in our sample fall into each category of each variable. This type of analysis is called a *frequency distribution* because we want to know about the distribution of each variable – the frequency in each category. It is also called *univariate* analysis because we are only interested in looking at one variable at a time.

Some of your data will be in non-numerical categories: marital status, occupation and colour are variables of this type. Other data will be numerical: income, number of children, weight, height, etc. In the non-numerical or grouped data, categories should be *exhaustive* (everything fits into some category) and *mutually exclusive* (nothing fits into more than one category). In some cases, the categories fit into some sort of order (like cold, warm, hot) and in some cases they do not (like, single, widowed, married, divorced, separated). When there is no inherent rank ordering of categories, that is, where each category is on the same 'level', we call the data *nominal*. An example is colour: we cannot say that red is 'higher' or 'above' green; they are simply different things. *Ordinal* data is similar to nominal data except that ranking is present. We know that 'cool' is below 'hot' on a temperature scale. Numerical scales form *interval* data. Here we know more than a rough ordering: we know *how much* higher or lower one number is than another. In the temperature scale, for example, we know that 15 is 5 degress lower than 20. We can perform numerical computations with such scales. We can say, for example, that five degrees plus five degrees is equal to ten degres. It is absured to say, however, that cold plus cool equals hot. Yet researchers sometimes make such statements!

Computer data processors have an acronym to describe what happens when one is not careful with data analysis: 'GIGO', or 'garbage in, garbage out'. Consider the marital status code we devised on p. 000:

single 1
married 2
separated 3
divorced 4
widowed 5

Now suppose that we had interviewed ten women in each category. If we looked at the distribution of this variable it would look something like this:

Table XI. 1
MARITAL STATUS

Category	Code	Number of Women
Single	1	10
Married	2	10
Separated	3	10
Divorced	4	10
Widowed	5	10
	TOTAL	50

We could ask the computer to find the 'average' of the variable 'marital status'. It would compute the *mean* or average, using the code numbers we have given it, and would find a mean of three. Does this mean that the average woman in our study is separated? Of course not; this is an example of 'GIGO'. We fed the computer with meaningless data and we received meaningless results.

Suppose the distribution looked like this:

Table XI. 2
MARITAL STATUS

Category	Code	Number of Women
Single	1	12
Married	2	31
Separated	3	2
Divorced	4	1
Widowed	5	4
	TOTAL	50

Here the average or mean would be about 2.1. 'Married point one?' Again, garbage. However, suppose we want some sort of measure of what the 'average' woman is like. Statisticians call such indices *measures of central tendency*. The measure of central tendency most commonly used for nominal data, called the *mode*, is rather obvious: it is simply the most common category. Here the mode is 2, meaning that most women in our survey are married.

Suppose we had the following frequency distribution for ordinal data:

Table XI. 3
MIGRATION LOCATIONS

Category	Code	No. of Migrants
Elsewhere in same country	1	5
Different county same province	2	14
Different province within Ireland	3	39
Outside Ireland, within Europe	4	7
Outside Europe	5	10
	TOTAL	75

Again, the *mean* or average is meaningless. The *mode* or most common category is 'different province within Ireland'. For ordinal data we have an additional measure of central tendency: the *median* or middle value. For ordinal categories, the median category is the category at the 'half-way' point.

In the above example, there are a total of 75 migrants. Half of this number is 37.5. There are 5 in the first category and 14 in the second, making a total of 19 who migrated somewhere within the province. The next category has 39, making a total of 58 who migrated somewhere within Ireland. The midway point has been passed; thus 'different province within Ireland' is the median category, and is a good measure of central tendency for this sample.

What about interval data? What measure of central tendency should you use? Actually you can use all three we have mentioned, although the mean is usually the most efficient. Consider Table XI. 4:

Table XI. 4
AGES OF MIGRANTS

Age	Number of Migrants
16	1
17	5
18	6
19	7
20	6
21	7
22	9
23	5
24	5
25	3
26	4
27	2
28	0
29	0
30	1
31	1
32	1
33	0
34	1
35	1
36	2
37	1
38	0
39	1
40	1
TOTAL	70

Here, if we list all the separate ages and compute the mean, we get 23.2. The mode, or most common category, is 22, and the median age is 23. All of these measures of central tendency show that the migrants are fairly young, in their early twenties. Which is the best measure? The mean is fairly high because of some older migrants, but all are fairly close. You could report any or all of these measures.

You may have noticed that for the nominal and interval data, the tables were interesting and useful and the measures of central tendency were not so revealing. For the interval data, the table was rather long, and we really did not need to look at it if we had all the measures of central tendency. This is because for interval (metric) measures we can be much more precise in inventing *descriptive statistics* which 'describe' how the variable is distributed.

We have talked about measures of central tendency, which give us some idea of where the midpoint of 'average' of the sample lies. But we also need some idea of how 'spread out' the data are. For example, in Table XI. 4, we can see that data are 'clumped' in the early twenties, then spread out for older persons. In other words, most of the data are fairly close to the mean. The *standard deviation* is a measure of how dispersed from the mean the data are. Roughly two-thirds of all the cases in our sample will fall within one standard deviation (plus or minus) of the mean. For the above data, the standard deviation is 5.6. Thus, about two-thirds of the migrants are between 17.6 and 28.8.

How is the standard deviation computed? Since we are interested in how far each number or variate is from the mean, first we must compute the mean, which is simply the average of the numbers. We then find the difference between each variate and the mean to get an idea of how far apart they are. For example, 21 is close to the mean (a difference of only 2.2) whereas 48 is far from the mean (a difference of 24.8). If you subtracted the mean from each variate, you would get some negative numbers (for example, 21 − 23.2 = −2.2) and some positive numbers (48 − 23.2 = +24.8). We would like to add up all the differences between variates and the mean to get an idea of the total amount of dispersion, but the combination of the negative and positive numbers would cause the total to be around zero. In order to eliminate this problem, statisticians have decided to square the differences to eliminate the negative signs. Then they add them up. But there is still one problem: the bigger the sample, the bigger this sum. If we had twice as many persons in our migration sample, and the sample were to be distributed exactly the same, this sum would be twice as big even though the sample would not be 'spread out' any more than before. To eliminate this problem, we divide the total sum by the sample size (actually, the sample size minus one, for reasons we need not go into). In mathematical notation, the formula discussed above is as follows:

$$S^2 = \frac{\sum\limits_{i=1}^{n} (X_i - \bar{X})^2}{n-1}$$

Where

> S^2 is the square of the standard deviation
>
> $\sum\limits_{i=1}^{n}$ means the sum of all the quantities
>
> x_i means each variate
>
> $\bar{x}$ is the mean
>
> n is the size of the sample (the total number of persons, etc.)

This formula says exactly what we said in words. You read it 'from the inside out'. First, you take each variate, subtract the mean, and square the difference. Then the symbol $\sum\limits_{i=1}^{n}$ tells you to add all these up. Finally, you divide this sum by the sample size minus one. You may have wondered why the above formula gave the *square* of the standard deviation and not the standard deviation itself. This is because the square of the standard deviation is another useful measure of dispersion called the *variance*. Needless to say, there are many descriptive statistics, each having a particular purpose. It is not my intention to describe all of these but rather to give you some appreciation of the more commonly-used statistics and why we use them.

As you can imagine, computing the standard deviation by hand is an unenviable task, and one to be avoided at all costs. The computer can do this for us in a micro-second. Thus it is enough for us to know that the standard deviation is a *measure of dispersion* or an indication of how spread out the data are. Keep in mind that our overall purpose in this section is to look at (or describe) the distribution of each of our variables. The most efficient way to accomplish this is to have the computer do it for you. There are many computer programmes to accomplish all sorts of research tasks. Most of these programmes have been put together in 'packages' so that you do not have to do any computer programming as such. You have only to define your variables and the categories for each variable, then tell the computer what general sort of analysis you want to be done.

Perhaps the most commonly-used of such 'packaged programmes' is SPSS or the *Statistical Package for the Social Sciences*. Suppose you want to use SPSS to do your univariate distribution analysis. There are two programmes which you would find particularly useful: the *Frequencies* programme and the *Condescriptive* programme. The first is particularly useful for nominal and ordinal data, the second for interval data. If we had used the *Frequencies* programme to analyse the marital status data described earlier in this chapter (Table XI. 2), our results would resemble the following:

Table XI. 5
MARITAL STATUS

Category label	Code	Absolute freq.	Relative freq. (%)	Adjusted freq. (%)	Cum freq. (%)
Single	1	12	23.5	24.0	24.0
Married	2	31	60.8	62.0	86.0
Separated	3	2	3.9	4.0	90.0
Divorced	4	1	2.0	2.0	92.0
Widowed	5	4	7.8	8.0	100.0
	0	1	2.0	Missing	100.0
	Total	51	100.0	100.0	

One 'missing case' has been included here to illustrate how this type of data is handled. A missing case would occur where, for example, an interviewee declined to give marital status.

The 'category label' has been defined for the computer, as has the code number. The *absolute frequency* gives the number of persons in each category. The *relative frequency,* expressed here as a percentage, is simply the percentage each category forms of the total sample (where missing data are included in the total). The *adjusted frequency* is a similar percentage, except that here, missing data are excluded from calculations. The *cumulative frequency* adds succeeding categories of adjusted frequencies. In Table XI. 5, for example, 86.0 per cent of the sample for whom there are data are either single or married. Cumulative frequencies are sometimes useful for ordinal data. For example, if we had a *frequencies* table for the ordinal variable of migration locations discussed earlier (Table XI. 3), we could use the cumulative frequencies to show the percentages of migrants at increasing distances from their place of birth. We could say that, for this sample, 77.3 per cent migrated to places within Ireland.

Naturally, you could easily compute these percentages by hand after doing the necessary tabulations. The computer is used merely as a counting device to make your work easier. In your final report you would not want to include tables showing the distribution of every variable, of course, but would select only those which were most important. Similarly, you would not want to list all the percentages which the computer calculated for you; you would use those which were critical in supporting your main findings. One of the problems facing social researchers who use computer analysis is to sort through the massive amount of information available and select the most important to report. No one can do this better than you can.

The *condescriptive* programme of SPSS can be used to analyse your interval variables. No tables are produced, since, as we have seen, these are not really useful for interval variables. Instead, a list of descriptive statistics is produced. A sample is given in Table XI. 6.

Table XI. 6
TIME SPENT AT ST MICHAEL'S

Mean	2.239	Std err	0.098	Median	2.044
Mode	2.000	Std dev	0.922	Variance	0.850
Kurtosis	0.051	Skewness	0.942	Range	3.000
Minimum	1.083	Maximum	4.093		
Valid cases	88	Missing cases	7		

For many readers who are not familiar with statistical analysis, Table XI. 6 may seem imposing. Each statistic has a particular purpose: each tells something about the distribution of the variable 'time spent at St Michael's'. While it is not our purpose to explain how each and every statistic is calculated, we will give a brief description of the purpose of each. First are the measures of central tendency, the mean, mode and median, with which you are now familiar. These give us some idea of the 'average' time inmates have spent at St Michael's, which is around two years. The standard deviation and variance, as measures of dispersion, tell us how 'spread out' the data is. Here we see that about two-thirds of the inmates have spent between 1.3 and 3.2 years at St Michael's (one standard deviation or 0.922 years either side of the mean, which is 2.239 years). The *minimum, maximum* and *range* simply indicate the least and most time spent at St Michael's, and the difference between these respectively. The *standard error* is useful for certain statistical tests which need not concern us here.

Skewness and *kurtosis* are two useful indices which provide information about the 'shape' of the distribution of the variable 'years spent at St Michael's'. For certain statistical tests, we are concerned that the distribution of the variable be reasonably 'normal'. By this we mean that we expect most cases to be fairly close to the mean, with fewer and fewer cases the further we go from the mean. Thus, we would expect most inmates to have spent about two years at St Michael's, with fewer having spent three years, fewer still having spent four years and so on. When we plot the 'normal' situation (what we would expect) on a graph, the shape resembles a bell, as shown in *Figure XI. 1.*

This shape is the well known *normal distribution* shape or bell-shaped curve. Many statistical tests require that the distribution of a variable be approximately this shape for the test to be valid. Indices of skewness and kurtosis tell us about the shape of our variable's distribution.

Skewness is a measure of symmetry, indicating how 'lop-sided' the distribution of our variable is. The normal curve has a skewness index of zero, because it is perfectly symmetrical. Positive skewness indicates that cases are clustered to the left (below) the mean, with extreme values found mostly to the right. Consider the distribution of the variable 'ages of migrants' described earlier in Table XI. 4. This distribution would have a positive index of skewness (the actual index is +1.3) because most extreme values (older migrants) are to the right of the mean. The higher the index of

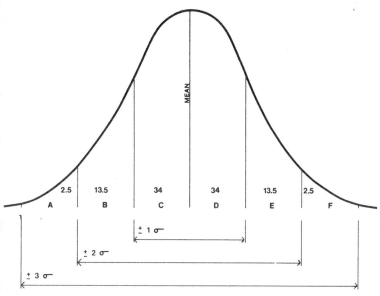

Figure XI. 1
NORMAL DISTRIBUTION CURVE

skewness, the more lop-sided the distribution. Negative skewness indicates that the distribution is skewed in the opposite direction, with cases clustered to the right of the mean and most extreme values to the left.

Kurtosis is a measure of how 'narrow' or 'flat' the distribution is. Again, the normal curve has a kurtosis of zero. A positive index of kurtosis indicates that the distribution is narrower than the normal curve; such a curve would look 'tall' and 'thin' in comparison with the bell-shaped curve. The variable 'ages of migrants' is such a distribution curve; it has a kurtosis of 4.1. *Figure XI. 2* illustrates the distribution of this variable.

Comparison of this curve with the normally shaped curve *(Figure XI. 1)* shows that the former looks 'thin' and also 'tails away' to the right. Thus, a negative index of kurtosis indicates a flat curve; a positive index indicates a narrow curve. The greater the index the narrower the curve.

It should be clear by now that the various statistics describe how interval variables are distributed. They provide the statistician with a sort of 'short-hand' in which a quick scanning can convey quite a lot of information, and eliminate the need to 'plot' most variables. So long as the variables are reasonably normally distributed, with low indices of kurtosis and skewness, relatively small standard deviation, and measures of central tendency which are relatively similar, the researcher can confidently proceed with further analysis. If any of these statistics seems to be much different from what we might expect, the tables provided by the *frequencies* programme

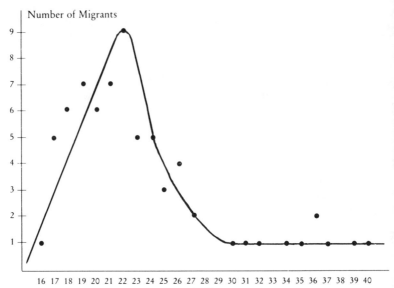

Figure XI. 2
ACTUAL DISTRIBUTION SHAPE FOR "AGES OF MIGRANTS"

can be utilised to provide additional information about the distribution of the variable in question.

2. Bivariate analysis: association and correlation

By now, you should have a fairly clear idea of the broad outline of your data. This was the purpose of the univariate or distribution analysis. You have looked at each variable in turn. You know how many of your sample of persons or things fall into each category of each variable, and you know something about what the 'average' person or thing is like. This will help you in describing what your sample is like. You should now be able to give a clear picture of the population of St Michael's Correctional Institution, for example. You know, for instance, what percentage of staff hold which positions, for what sorts of offences the inmates have been committed and how long they have been in St Michael's.

Now you want to carry this analysis one step further. You want to know about the relationship between two variables. You now know *how many* of the inmates from St Michael's are from the lowest socio-economic class, and you can be more precise about one of the statements which opened this chapter. But is the socio-economic class related to the type of offence? Or to the length of sentence, time spent in St Michael's, age of inmate, and so on? To answer these types of questions we need to do a *bivariate* analysis or an analysis of the relationship between two variables.

In order to undertake such an analysis, once again you need to consider the level (nominal, ordinal or interval) of the data. Suppose that we wanted to examine the relationship between eye colour and hair colour. These are both nominal variables. In order to look at this relationship, we need to construct a table with the categories of one of the variables along one axis and the categories of the other variable along the other axis. Such a table is called a *contingency table*. If we actually did such an analysis, we might construct a contingency table like the following:

Table XI. 7
HAIR COLOUR

		Red	Blonde	Brown/Black	
Eye Colour	Blue/Green	4	23	30	57
	Brown/Other	6	33	45	84
		10	56	75	141

An examination of this table does not seem to show very much relationship between hair colour and eye colour. True, persons with brown or black hair were more likely to have brown eyes than blue/green, but this was also true for other hair colours. In fact, since brown was the most common eye colour in this sample, it is not surprising that persons of whatever hair colour would be more likely to have brown eyes. This distribution is about what we would expect by chance. Contrast the above table with the following:

Table XI. 8
HAIR COLOUR

		Red	Blonde	Brown/Black	
Eye Colour	Blue/Green	10	33	14	57
	Brown/Other	0	23	61	84
		10	56	75	141

The second table seems to show some relationship between the variables in question. Nearly all of the persons with brown or black hair also had brown eyes. All of the redheads had either blue or green eyes. But how do we report this relationship? If we said, 'Most of the persons with brown or black hair also had brown eyes', this would also be true of the first table. It would be possible to imagine a situation in which virtually every single brown-haired person also had brown eyes. In this case, the relationship between the variables would be even stronger. Obviously there is some sort of a continuum between what we would expect purely by chance and a perfect relationship, and we need some sort of measure to indicate where along such a continuum the table with which we are concerned falls.

It is possible, of course, that there is really no relationship between hair colour and eye colour despite the apparent relationship we observe in

Table XI. 8. We might have chosen a bad sample where, just by chance, there were a lot of redheads with blue or green eyes and a lot of brown-haired persons with brown eyes. The first major category of statistical test, a *test of association*, measures how likely it is that the distributions we observe is due merely to chance.

Suppose that I had a coin with a 'head' side and a 'tail' side, and I wondered whether it was a 'fair' coin or perhaps was minted improperly such that one side was heavier than the other. If I flipped the coin once, and it came up 'heads', I would not think my suspicions were true, since there is a 50-50 or 50 per cent probability that this would happen just by chance. If I then flipped the coin again and got another head, I would perhaps begin to suspect something. There is still a 25 per cent probability, however, that this would occur by chance. There is a 12.5 per cent chance of three consecutive heads, and a 6 per cent chance of four, a 3 per cent chance of five, a 2 per cent chance of six, etc. By the time seven or eight consecutive heads had come up, either a very unlikely event had occurred or else my suspicion about the coin was correct.

Naturally, different researchers would become convinced at different points in the above test. Some people would be convinced after five or six heads, others would wait for ten heads to become convinced, etc. Statisticians have set certain standard *levels of significance* or probability levels at which one might become convinced. The lowest of such levels is usually 0.05 or 5 per cent. This means that the observed distribution might come up 5 out of 100 times purely by chance. Stated differently, there is a 5 per cent chance that the distribution occurred randomly. The next level is 0.01, where the distribution only has a 1 per cent probability of occurring by chance. The last commonly-used level of significance is 0.001 or only one chance out of 1,000 of the distribution occurring randomly.

Which level of significance should you use? That is up to you. What are you willing to accept? If you accept the 5 per cent level, there is a good chance that 5 per cent of the relationships that you report will be due to chance. Unfortunately, the type of data that social scientists use are often 'sloppy'. No matter how careful you have tried to be, at least some of your data will be inaccurate. Informants sometimes lie or are mistaken. Sometimes you make mistakes yourself. For this reason, we often accept the 0.05 level.

Returning to the table of hair colour and eye colour, how do we obtain such probability using a statistical test of association? There are many such statistical tests, which usually take the same form. A statistic is computed which is associated with a probability level depending upon the size of the table. For nominal data, the appropriate statistic is called the chi-square, written x^2. Just to give you an idea of how such statistics are computed, we will look at how we would work out a chi-square by hand. Keep in mind that, just as we did not really want to do standard deviations by hand, we would rather have the computer figure our chi-squares for us.

First you need some basic vocabulary. Look again at Table XI. 8. You will see that eye colour forms two rows while hair colour has three columns. Contingency table sizes are named in an R X C format where R is the number of rows and C is the number of columns. Thus Table XI. 8 is a 2 X 3 contingency table. The totals in the margins of the table are called *marginals*. We see that 57 is the blue/green colour row total. The number in the lower right, in this case 141, is the grand total or total sample size.

The overall strategy in computing the chi-square is to figure out what we would expect, by chance, to occur in each box. Then we look at what actually occurs in each box. The bigger the difference between what is expected and what really occurs, the more convinced we are that there really is a relationship between the variables in question.

How do you figure out the *expected* value for each box? Consider the upper left hand box; red hair and blue or green eyes. How many persons would we expect to have this combination? There are about 10 people out of 141 who have red hair which represents about 7.1 per cent of our sample. If there is really no relationship between the variables, we would expect about 7.1 per cent of the persons with any given eye colour to be redheads. Thus, out of the 57 persons with blue or green eyes, we would expect about 7.1 per cent or about 4 persons also to be redheads. This is very different from the ten persons who were *observed* in this category.

A formula for figuring out the expected value in each box is as follows:

$$E_i = \frac{\text{Row total} \times \text{Column total}}{\text{grand total}}$$

Using this formula to calculate the expected value in the first box we would have:

$$\frac{57 \times 10}{141} = 4 \qquad \text{formula (rounded to the nearest whole number)}$$

just as we computed above. Once we know that 4 of the 10 redheads would be expected to have blue or green eyes, we know by simple subtraction that the remaining 6 redheads would be expected to have brown/other eyes. We could, of course, apply the above formula as follows

$$\frac{84 \times 10}{141} = 6 \qquad \text{formula (rounded to the nearest whole number)}$$

The purpose of this section is not so much to show you *how to compute a chi-square* as to give you some appreciation of how it is *computed*. The formula for the chi-square is as follows:

$$\chi^2 = \Sigma \frac{(O_i - E_i)^2}{E_i}$$

χ^2 is the chi-square statistic
S is the sum of
O_i is any given observed value
E_i is the expected value

Again, we read the formula 'from the inside out'. We compute the expected value for each box or *cell*. We then find the difference between the observed value in each cell and the associated expected value, square the difference, and divide by the expected. We do this for each cell, then add all these values.

If you have followed all this so far, you will realise that the bigger the difference between observed and expected values, the bigger the chi-square. That is, when the numbers in the contingency table are very different from what we would expect by chance, we would expect to find a very large chi-square value. Let us actually compute this chi-square. First we letter the boxes going across the rows so that the blue/green eye row has boxes a, b and c and the brown/other row has boxes d, e and f. We would compute the chi-square as follows:

Table XI. 9
COMPUTATIONS FOR CHI-SQUARE

Box	O^i	E^i	$(O^i - E^i)$	$(O^i - E^i)$	$(O^i - E^i)$
a	10	4.0	+ 6.0	35.5	8.8
b	33	22.6	+10.4	107.3	4.7
c	14	30.3	−16.3	266.3	8.8
d	0	6.0	− 6.0	35.5	6.0
e	23	33.4	−10.4	107.3	3.2
f	61	44.7	+16.3	266.3	6.0
					37.5

We still have not yet realised our ultimate goal, which is to translate the chi-square statistic into a probability. We do this by determining the *degrees of freedom*, which we calculate by the following formula:

$$d.f. = (R-1)(C-1)$$

Where
    d.f. is the degrees of freedom
    R is the number of rows in the contingency table
    C is the number of columns in the contingency table

The d.f. for this table is 1 x 2 = 2. We would then look at a chi-square table found in most statistics texts and see that the probability level associated with this particular table is 0.001. Thus there is less than 1 chance out of 1,000 ($p<0.001$) that the distribution is due to sampling error, and we can be reasonably sure that there really is a relationship between hair colour and eye colour.

At this point, you will perhaps be cheered to know that the chi-square is the only statistical test of association to be described in this chapter. Each such test takes basically the same form, and the final figure is a probability. Thus, even where you are unsure as to how the statistic is actually calculated (as some of you may still be unclear about the chi-square), so long as the statistic is appropriate, the results are not difficult to interpret; just the probability of the observed distribution occurring by chance or through sampling error.

Naturally, the smaller our sample size, the greater the probability that the distribution is due to chance. In other words, if you only had recorded the eye and hair colour for 20 or 30 persons, even though the proportions of types of persons might be exactly the same as reported in Table XI. 8, it is more likely that you might have selected an unusual sample. Since the numbers involved are smaller, the chi-square would be smaller, and the probability would be greater that the distribution was due to sampling error. This, in fact, is the reason why social scientists are so enamoured of large samples; observed relationships are probably not due to chance.

Because of this problem of sample size affecting probabilities, statisticians have devised another type of statistic: *measures of correlation*, which measure the *strength* of the association, regardless of sample size. For a 2 × 2 contingency table (one with two rows and two columns), the measure of correlation associated with the chi-square statistical test is called the *phi coefficient*. Phi is computed by dividing the chi-square by the sample size (thus controlling for sample size) and then taking the square root of this number. For tables other than 2 × 2, a related statistic called *Cramer's V* is computed.

Just like the statistical tests of association, the measures of correlation all take the same form. Thus, without knowing exactly how such indices are actually computed, you can successfully interpret them once you know a few basic principles. Measures of correlation generally range between -1 and $+1$. A *correlation coefficient* of zero means that there is absolutely no relationship between the variables. Positive measures of correlation indicate positive relationships. This means that as one variable increases, the other also increases. An example of such a relationship would be height and weight. Generally speaking, the taller a person is, the more she or he will weigh. Of course, the relationship is not perfect, because there are some short, stout persons and some tall, thin persons, but the relationship generally holds. If the relationship *was* perfect, the correlation coefficient would be one. The greater the measure of correlation, the stronger the relationship.

Sometimes variables may be related in a negative direction. An example might be income with number of trips per year using public transportation. As income increases, we might expect frequency of use of public transportation to decrease because of increasing reliance on private motor vehicles. In this case, we would expect a negative index of correlation, the 'more negative', the stronger the relationship. At this point, a little more vocabulary might be useful. The *absolute value* of a number is the size of a number if we ignore the sign (+ or −) of the number. We could then say that the greater the absolute value of the measure of correlation, the stronger the relationship between variables. The sign merely tells us whether the relationship is positive or negative.

To summarise the above discussion, for each bivariate relationship there are two classes of statistics which might be useful in evaluating the relationship: a *statistical test of association* which will ultimately be expressed as the probability of the relationship being due to chance (such as sampling error), and a *measure of* correlation between −1 and +1 which tells us about the strength of the relationship. We generally consider relationships which have less than a 5 per cent probability of occurring to chance ($p < 0.05$) as being 'significant'. We consider relationships with correlation coefficients having absolute values of about 0.7 or 0.8 as being fairly strong. In contrast, probabilities of about 0.3 (3 chances out of 10 of being randomly distributed) and correlation coefficients of 0.3 or 0.4 are not thought to show much relationship between the variables of interest.

Table XI. 10 summarises the types of data we have discussed together with the names of the tests of significance and measures of correlation most commonly used. You are referred to almost any introductory statistics text (such as those listed as the end of this chapter) for a further discussion of these tests and measures.

Table XI. 10
COMMON TESTS OF ASSOCIATION AND MEASURES OF CORRELATION

Type of Data	Statistical Tests of Association	Measures of Correlation
Nominal	Chi-square	Phi
	Fisher's exact test	Cramer's V
Ordinal	Wilcoxen U	Gamma
	(Mann-Whitney U)	Kendall's tau
		Spearman's r
Interval	Student's t	Pearson's r

One word of caution concerning Table XI. 10. This table is based on the assumption that we are comparing nominal data with nominal data or ordinal with ordinal. In some cases we might need to compare data of different levels: nominal with ordinal, for example. In this case, we must use the tests and measures of correlation associated with the data of the lower order. When we are comparing nominal with ordinal data, we must use the tests for nominal data. This is because ordinal tests are based on the order of the data; we want to know whether, as one variable increases, the other either increases or decreases. For nominal data, the order is meaningless, so we are only seeking to find out whether there is an association of any type between the variables in question.

If you use SPSS to analyse your bivariate data, there are three programmes which are particularly useful: *Crosstabs, T-Test,* and *Scattergram.* The *Crosstabs* programme is generally used for nominal or ordinal data, the other two are used when at least one variable is interval. The Crosstabs programme produces contingency tables together with associated statistics. Let us look at such a print-out for one of the relationships we might like to examine.

Some people might assume that persons of a lower socio-economic class might be more likely to commit violent offences. Suppose that, on the basis of your interviews with inmates of St Michael's, you did not feel that this assumption was true, and you wanted to support your statement quantitatively. You may have divided the inmates into ordinal categories (lower, middle and upper) based on socio-economic class. You have also divided them into categories according to increasing violence of offences (either non-violent or violent). You then request the computer to provide you with a cross-tabulation or contingency table comparing relative violence of offence with socio-economic class, and get a print-out resembling Table XI. 11.

Table XI. 11
VIOLENCE OF OFFENCE RELATED TO SOCIO-ECONOMIC CLASS

		Count Row % Col % Total %	Class Lower 1.	Middle 2.	Upper 3.	Row Total
	Non-Violent	1.	3 10.0 30.0 6.5	20 66.7 95.2 43.5	7 23.3 46.7 15.2	30 65.2
Offence	Violent	3.	7 43.8 70.0 15.2	1 6.3 4.8 2.2	8 50.0 53.3 17.4	16 34.8
	Column Total		10 21.7	21 45.7	15 32.6	46 100.0

Kendall's Tau c = −0.01701   Significance = 0.4555
Gamma = −0.02350

The first thing you probably notice is that there are a lot more numbers in the boxes than there were when we looked at similar contingency tables produced by hand (Tables XI. 7 and XI. 8). For the moment, focus your attention on only the top numbers in each box: these are the frequency counts, indicating 'how many' are in each box. If the other numbers are ignored, this contingency table is the same as the others we produced.

The rest of the numbers in the boxes are percentages to aid you in your descriptive discussions of the data. In the upper left-hand corner of the table is a guide to the numbers in each box or cell. First is the *count*, which we have already described. Next is the *row %*, or the percentage found in each box for that row. For example, the first row consists of the 30 persons who committed non-violent offences. The row % in the first box is 10.0 per cent indicating that 3 out of 30 or 10 per cent of the non-violent offences fall into that category. This indicates that only 10 per cent of non-violent offences were committed by persons of the lower class, which seems to support the position that lower class persons commit violent crimes. However, look now at the box in the lower right hand corner, and examine the third number down in the box, the *column %*. Here the column contains the 15 upper-class inmates who were interviewed. The column % tells us that 53.3% of the upper class inmates had committed violent crimes, tending to contradict the above position. The *total %* expresses the count in each box as a % of the total sample, rather than as a row or column %.

Benjamin Disraeli is credited with stating that there are three types of lies: lies, damn lies, and statistics. Judicious use of our percentages could appear to make a case for either position, indicating that Disraeli may have been correct. But, in fact, statistic measures have been devised to put more 'objectivity' into data analysis. For this reason, we need to examine the measures of correlation which accompany the table. Both the Kendall's tau and the Gamma coefficients have very small absolute values, indicating no real relationship between the variables. We have used ordinal measures here, since the categories of 'offence' could be considered either as nominal (different categories) or as ordinal (ranked according to severity). We have considered them to be the latter.

As we have stated previously, the computer is a slave to your instructions. We know by reference to Table XI. 10 that Pearson's r is inappropriate for ordinal data. It should be used for interval data only since the nature of the computations for Pearson's r require actual measurements of some sort. But the computer will compute Pearson's r for Table XI. 11 if you ask it to, again illustrating the principle of GIGO – 'garbage in, garbage out'. This would be rather like 'averaging' ten apples and ten oranges and getting 'apple-and-a-half'. For this reason, you should be careful to give the computer meaningful instructions, asking it to compute appropriate statistics.

For interval data, the Crosstabs programme is not as useful. There are generally so many categories for each interval variable (since nearly every measurement is slightly different) that we get an enormous contingency table that we cannot make any sense of. We need to turn to other types of analysis.

When we have an interval measurement as one variable (for example, test scores or IQ scores) and the other variable consists of a few categories (males and females, for example) we can use the *Student's t* test to examine whether there is a difference between any two categories. By comparing the mean or average scores of males and females, for example, we could see whether any difference we observe is significant.

For example, I recently gave an examination to the students in my quantitative methods class. The males in the class had an average score of 91, whereas females averaged 86. I could use the t-test to find out what the probability would be of this difference being due to sampling error or chance. If I arrived at a final probability of 0.02 I would know that there would only be a 2 per cent chance of sampling error and might assume that there really was a difference between males and females. On the other hand, if the t-test indicated a probability of 0.8, I would know that the observed distribution had an 80 per cent chance of being random. This would mean that if I had tested two groups of similar sample size in which each group consisted entirely of males, I would find a similar difference in test scores about 80 per cent of the time. In this case, I would not conclude that there was any important difference between males and females on the test. SPSS has a programme called *T-Test* to compute the t-test for you; all you have to do is know how to read the resulting probability (explained in the SPSS manual listed at the end of this chapter).

You should realise by now that the type of data you have determines the type of bivariate analysis you will undertake. In the Crosstabs example (Table XI. 11), we used a contingency table because the variable 'socio-economic class' was an ordered (ordinal) variable. Suppose we had wanted to examine non-violent and violent offences as a function of family income instead of class. Here, income (measured in exact amounts as reported for tax purposes) is an interval level variable. We could use the t-test to compare the mean incomes for the two groups (those who had committed non-violent offenses and those who had committed violent ones).

At times you might want to examine or report the strength of relationship between two interval variables: height and weight, age and income, family size and distance migrated and so forth. SPSS has a programme called *Pearson Corr* which computes Pearson's r, the appropriate measure of correlation, for you. Another useful programme, *Scattergram,* not only computes Pearson's r but also provides a plot of the two variables. An example of such a plot is illustrated in *Figure XI. 3.*

Figure XI. 3 plots the distribution of two interval level variables in a study of housing in the city of Pittsburgh, Pennsylvania, USA. It is meant to illustrate the relationship that, as the acreage or amount of the land which a house is located increases, the value of the house also increases. Each * on the table represents a data point or house. You will notice that a line extends from the lower left across the figure to the upper right. This line would not be plotted on the print-out, but has been added for illustrative purposes. This line, which best approximates the *linear* or straight-line relationship between the two variables is called a *regression* line. Pearson's r is computed by measuring how far the data points are from this 'ideal' line. Here, the

STUDY OF HOUSING IN A NEIGHBOURHOOD OF PITTSBURG

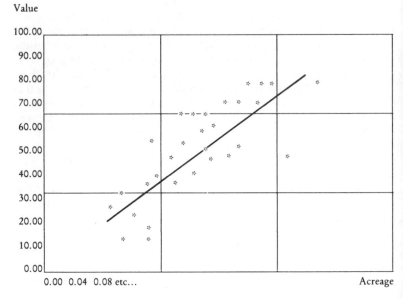

Figure XI. 3
SIMPLE SCATTERGRAM

Statistics:

Correlation (R)	0.75095	R squared	0.56393	Significance	0.00000
Std err of est	12.40473	Intercept (a)	7.43996	Slope (b)	241.01621
Plotted values	32	Excluded values	0	Missing values	1

Pearson's r is 0.75095, indicating a fairly strong positive correlation. The other values provide additional information about the relationship. The *intercept*, for example, indicates the point at which the regression line crosses the vertical axis; the *slope*, logically enough, represents the slope of the regression line. The other indices need not concern us here.

A word of caution concerning 'linear regression' analysis. This type of analysis, together with Pearson's r and associated statistics, is only meant to test or examine variables that are associated in a simple straight-line fashion. Such relationships could be roughly expressed in the form, 'the more of A, the more (or less) of B'. But interval variables could be related in other ways; for example, where the plot looked like a curve which increased and then decreased. Such a relationship might be described as, 'the more of A, the more of B *up to a point*, after which the less of B'. There are quantitative techniques for describing such relationships, of course, but they become rather complicated and are beyond the scope of this discussion. In basic descriptive social research, we are interested in illustrating straight-forward relationships. If for some reason, a complex bivariate relationship between interval variables became critical to your discussion, you could simply show the Scattergram plot to allow the reader to examine the relationship visually.

We are now at a logical point to conclude our discussion of how data analysis can help you provide support for your descriptive research. We have indicated that the first step is to look at the distribution of each important variable to understand the make-up of your study population. You probably will have an intuitive 'feel' for how many persons or things are in each category of each variable just from having done the study. The data analysis merely helps to confirm what you already know. You may choose to include a few frequency distributions or descriptive statistics from your univariate analysis in your write-up to clarify the nature of your population. This helps you to be more precise and convincing in your description.

In doing descriptive research, social researchers generally also have a 'feel' for bivariate relationships. If, indeed, violent crimes are associated with persons in the lowest socio-economic class, and this is the general topic of the research, the researcher is likely to know or at least suspect that this is true. Again, bivariate analysis helps to confirm what you already suspect is true. Inclusion of contingency tables and statistical tests in your write-up helps to convince the reader that you are being objective and 'have nothing to hide'. I am always suspicious when I read a descriptive report in which I am simply 'told' that there is a particular relationship. I am also very suspicious of mere percentages, since, as we have seen, these can be very misleading without reference to all the data. I feel much more comfortable when I can scan a contingency table for myself. Finally, I tend to be suspicious of overly complex quantitative treatments, where simple tables and statistics would suffice. These are often used to mask the absence of straightforward relationships between variables.

In this chapter, I have discussed what, for the most part, is called *descriptive analysis*. As more variables become involved, they begin to affect one another in complex ways, and the researcher loses the 'feel' for the data which was present in univariate and bivariate analysis. *Multivariate analysis* is used to explore the relationships among a number of variables. Such analyses are generally called *exploratory statistics*. The researcher is less interested in confirming relationships already suspected than in revealing relationships obscured by the complex interaction of variables. While such analyses can be of use in descriptive research, they take us somewhat beyond the bounds of basic social research and are beyond the scope of this treatment.

A final word of caution: just because two variables are associated, do not assume that one 'causes' the other. Correlation makes no statement about causality. Consider the following contingency table:

Table XI. 12
RELATIONSHIP BETWEEN FIRE ENGINES AND FIRES

		Fires	
		present	absent
Fire	present	20	2
engines	absent	0	30

This might be based on a number of observations in a small town. The fire department is apparently efficient: whenever there were fires, the fire engine was on the scene. If you were not careful, you might conclude that the fires were *caused* by the fire engines. Obviously, this is stupid, but researchers who ignore the fact that correlation is not causality often form equally stupid conclusions!

You should also keep in mind the idea that you are never *proving* that any relationship exists, you are only showing that it is more or less likely. If someone flips a coin which comes up heads one hundred or one thousand straight times, we would be inclined to suspect that something is 'wrong' with the coin. But the laws of probability tell us that it is *possible* although extremely unlikely to get one hundred straight heads just by chance. For this reason you should avoid statements such as, 'This *proves* that. . . ' or even, 'this *shows* that. . .' You *can* say something like, 'This *suggests* that. . .' or 'This supports the idea that. . .'

Lastly I should add that the hope that the material in this section has not increased the anxieties of readers who are not quantitatively-orientated. Remember data analysis is a tool to help you be more convincing and to make your work easier. You can make use of data analysis at a variety of levels. If you just have a few variables that you want to describe, or want to show how strong one or two relationships are, you might consider doing a few simple statistical tests by hand. Basic statistics texts will help you to do this. You may actually save time by not computerising your data. But if you plan to look at a relatively large number of variables, consider computer analysis. It really isn't difficult. There are so many 'canned' or packaged programmes that it is really only a matter of defining your variables and requesting the appropriate statistics. SPSS, which we have described in this chapter, is available at most computer facilities. You need only to put aside your fears, tabulate some of your data, and use it to make your final report that much more precise and convincing!

Some texts which will help you to select and apply appropriate statistical techniques, and to make decisions about computer use and packages are —

Andrews, F. M.; Kelm, L.; Davidson, T. N.; O'Malley, P. M.; and Rodgers, W. L., *A Guide for Selecting Statistical Techniques for Analysing Social Science Data.* Ann Arbor, Mich: Survey Research Center, University of Michigan, 1974.

Armour, David J. and Crouch, Arthur S., *DATA-TEXT Primer.* New York: Free Press; London: Collier-Macmillan, 1972.

Babbie, Earl R., *Theory Construction and Data Analysis in the Behavioural Sciences*. San Francisco: Jossey-Bass Publishers, 1978.

Behlins, John H., *Research Methods, Statistical Concepts, and Research Practicum*. Millburn, New Jersey: RF Publishers, 1976.

Berkowitz, Stephen D., *The Computer as Master or Servant*. Toronto: Institute for Policy Analysis, University of Toronto, 1978.

Blalock, Hubert M. (Jr.), *Social Statistics*. 2nd ed. New York: McGraw-Hill Book Co., 1972.

Coxon, A. P. M., 'Recent Developments in Social Science Software', in *Social Science Research Council Newsletter* 33 (March 1977): 6-9.

Herbert, Frank, with Max Bernard, *Without Me You're Nothing: The Essential Guide to Home Computers*. New York: Simon and Schuster, 1980.

Irvine, John; Miles, Ian; and Evans, Jeff, eds., *Demystifying Social Statistics*. London: Pluto Press, 1976.

Klecka, William R.; Nie, Norman H.; and Hull, C. Hadlai, *SPSS Primer: Statistical Package for the Social Sciences Primer*. New York: McGraw-Hill Book Co., 1975.

Marks, Ronald G., *Analysing Research Data*. Belmont, Calif.: Lifetime Learning Publications, 1982.

Nie, Norman H. *et al.*, *SPSS: Statistical Package for the Social Sciences*. 2nd ed. New York: McGraw-Hill Book Co., 1975.

Nie, Norman H., *SPSS: A Users' Guide to the SPSS Conversational System*. New York: McGraw-Hill Book Co., 1980.

Rowe, Beverley Charles, and Scheer, Marianne, *Computer Software for Social Science Data*. London: Social Science Research Council, 1976.

Thomas, David Hurst, *Figuring Anthropology: First Principles of Probability and Statistics*. New York: Holt, Rinehart and Winston, 1976.

Vasu, Ellen, Storey, *An Introduction to Researach and the Computer*, Chapel Hill, North Carolina: University of North Carolina, 1980.

Wright, Sonia R., *Quantitative Methods and Statistics*. Beverly Hills: Sage Publications, 1979.

XII. Writing the Research Paper

THE TECHNIQUES referred to in this book can be used to prepare material for anything from a pamphlet to a university thesis. Here is a checklist for writing up your results, whatever the form.

A. Clarity

Many people believe that a study, to be scientific or impressive, must be nearly unintelligible. Unintelligibility does not confer accuracy. The form, language and style of your writing will depend upon your audience. Each of the professional and academic disciplines has a shared vocabulary and conventions for presentation of material. You can learn these, if you wish, by consultng the journals and professional literature of the field. If you are writing a thesis, universities fequently have their own requirements ('style sheets') for preparing a manuscript. Your thesis supervisor should be able to tell you if you are expected to adhere to a particular style and form. A wide variety of manuals for various subjects and presentations is available. Consult the listings at the end of this chapter.

If your audience is your local residents' association, parents' group or club, you probably know their 'language' as well as anyone. Most people today are too busy to waste time wading through jargon. On the other hand, forced informality or heavy-handed chattiness can be equally annoying. Do not write 'down' and do not try to get the approval of your audience by using their in-group dialect or slang if you are not a member of the group. Older people who try to use teenagers 'in-words', for example, can look foolish and alienate their audience. Clear, concise, understandable writing should be your aim.

B. Honesty and Accuracy

A report for a neighbourhood association deserves the same meticulousness, careful statement of fact and presentation of argument as does a university thesis. Be honest. Write exactly what you found. Do not try to dramatise it or slant your findings to make them appear more significant or supportive of a particular position. Do not present conclusions you cannot back up by research. If you tried your best and can find no sense or pattern to some (or even all) of your results, say so. It may be that there is no sense or pattern, and you have made a contribution to the world by discovering that. Or it may be that your research techniques or sample size or selection of respondents was inappropriate. If you think that is the reason, say so. Describe what you did; it will help the next person to develop a better project. Science advances by explaining what went wrong as well as what went right. It is nothing to be ashamed of; the only thing to be ashamed of is manipulating your findings to give them a meaning they do not have.

Many research reports or studies are so self-important and inflated that honesty is not only a good moral principle, it is also disarmingly attractive. People like to read short, clear, modest, truthful reports. They do not often get all four in one.

C. Length

This might seem a silly point, except to those hundreds of students who ask their instructors, 'How long should my paper be?' That, to my mind, is like asking, 'How long is a piece of string?' Your paper should be long enough to cover your material, no more and no less. In 1905, Albert Einstein's Ph.D. thesis was rejected by his professor as being too short. 'Einstein promptly resubmitted it with a single sentence added and it was accepted' (Hoffman 1972: 55).

Your Research Outline is a good guide to what you have to cover. Some research can be beautifully described in three pages. Having said that, I should add that if you are a student in a class where the instructor does not take such an enlightened (others may say devil-may-care) attitude, you will find that most university-level student papers are expected to be between 3,000 and 6,000 words. In that case, you can plan your work accordingly; the introduction will probably take up about one-tenth of the total number of pages, including the conclusion. You may then find that you can divide the rest of the paper roughly equally among the main points in your Research Outline, although this, like all arbitrary limits, could make your divisions very artificial.

D. Organising the Parts of the Paper

Your intended audience is the main guide to the type of organisation you use. Every paper, no matter how simple, has to have form and organisation. The academic disciplines, professions and business have developed conventions for organising presentation. But if your audience falls outside these areas, there is no reason why you should use these particular standardised forms if something else makes sense and is useful. Whatever form you use, if you have used any direct quotations from other works, or any ideas which are not your own, you *must* use a footnoting system, such as the ones described on pp. 000-000.

Every type of paper has 1. a title and 2. a text. Beyond that, however, a paper *may* have any of the following —
Preliminary material
1. Title
2. Abstract
3. Preface (in a book, the Preface may appear *after List of Illustrations*)
4. Table of Contents
5. List of Tables
6. List of Illustrations (pictures, charts, diagrams, graphs, maps)

Main body
    7. Introduction
    8. Methodology
    9. (The Paper Proper)
    10. Conclusions
    11. Suggestions for Future Researach
Reference materials
    12. Appendix
    13. Footnotes
    14. Glossary
    15. Bibliography or References Cited
    16. Index

Various standards are used to organise papers —

1.   *Academic Works:* long papers, reports and theses, often having all the parts listed under points 1-15; short papers and reports might have the following points–1 (title page), 2, 7, 8, 9, 10, 11, 12, 13 & 15; articles might have points 1, 2, 7, 8, 9, 10, 11, 13 & 15.

2.   *Business and Technical Reports:* these tend to contain divisions similar to those of academic works of the same size and complexity, with three differences: first, a summary, giving the methods, findings and conclusions of the report or paper frequently appears at the beginning of the paper, preceding the main body. Secondly, sections of the paper are numbered, and major paragraphs within the sections may have sub-numbering:

    5.1 Reports from all managers indicated that they preferred the new
           method of invoicing. However. . .

The numbers prefacing this paragraph indicate that it occurs in section five of the paper, and is the first paragraph or set of related paragraphs in section five. If one wishes to make sub-sections of this paragraph, they can be numbered 5.1.1; 5.1.2, and so on. The next new paragraph or group of paragraphs is numbered 5.2.; and its sub-sections, if any, will be 5.2.1; 5.2.2, and so on.

Finally, Recommendations may follow the Conclusions. Two possible layouts, one for a business paper or technical report, and the other for the scientific paper are:

Report (Mitchell, 1974: 42): 1 (title page), plus points 2, 4, 5, 6, 7, 8, 9, 10, (Recommendations), 12, 13, 14 & 16 *(illustrations).*

Scientific Paper (Barrass, 1978: 132): 1 (title page), plus points 2, (Abstract or Summary), 4, 5, 6, 7, (Theory and/or Experimental Procedures and Results), (Discussion), (Conclusions), (Acknowledgements), 13, 12 (includes points 15 and 14) & 16.

1. Title

Although many people use their research statement as their title, you can call your study anything you like. Some research statements are simply too cumbersome to be titles.

For articles, the title is placed two or three inches from the top of the page on which the paper begins. For term papers, reports and books to be published, a separate title page is usual. A university may have its preferred style, but otherwise the title page for non-published works can range from the simplest information (title of the work; the author; the course or class for which it is being prepared, and the date (see p. 180) to the more standardised form required for Master's and Ph.D. theses (see p. 181).

The title page of a business or technical report page often contains the basic information of author and title plus a variety of pieces of information related to its circulation, classification and sponsorship (see p. 182). International agencies such as UNESCO and government bodies prepare style guides for work to be published by them, such as the United States Government Printing Office *Style Manual* (rev. ed., Washington, D.C., 1967).

If you are writing a book for publication, consult a guide such as the University of Chicago *Manual of Style*, or a style sheet provided by your publisher. Many people reading this book, however, are not writing for institutions or business; if your title page does not have to conform to any particular layout, you can choose any form you like.

2. Abstract

Some journals require an abstract or condensation of certain major points in your article. Even if you are not writing for a journal or preparing a university thesis, an abstract is still useful to the reader who is scanning a number of reports and articles, looking for research which is of interest to him. An abstract is usually about ten lines or less, and tells —

1. the subject of the research
2. the research methods used
3. the findings (and recommendations, especially in business and technical papers)

For example:

This paper examines changes in selected characteristics – age, sex, education, social class and type of offence – of juvenile delinquents aged 13-18 years in St Michael's Correctional Institution, Dublin, between 1945-50 and 1975-80. Analysis of records of 380 youths indicated that average age of male offenders dropped by 2.8 years; number of female offenders increased by 40 per cent; level of education remained constant, and offences against property declined. Findings on class were inconclusive.

3. Preface

The preface is normally found only in long papers and theses. It is a personal statement, telling, for example, what interests and reasons brought you to the subject; problems you had with the material, sources, and techniques; and acknowledgements of people, institutions and organisations who helped you. If you have nothing to place in this section except acknowledgements, simply call the section 'Acknowledgements'.

A CROSS-CULTURAL ANALYSIS
OF THE ROLES OF WOMEN
AS RELIGIOUS LEADERS

BY
VIRGINIA LANG

Anthropology 201
August 25, 1980

ANALYSIS OF THE
USE OF TEXTILES
IN EARLY IRISH ART

BY

MARGARET VERONICA LITTLE

College of Hard Knocks
Hard Knocks, Pennsylvania

Submitted to the Faculty of the Graduate School of
College of Hard Knocks
in partial fulfillment of the requirements
for the degree of

DOCTOR OF PHILOSOPHY

December 12, 1980

JMT2/EAK   12 December 1980

(reference number)   (date)

SECRET

(classification)

ASSESSMENT GUIDELINES
FOR PROJECT TR-2

(title)

OLIVER MCKIMMONS

(author)

Lake Anchor Company
28 O'Connell Avenue
Dublin, Ireland

(address of organisation)

PREPARED FOR THE

WATER RESOURCES ASSOCIATION

(sponsorship, if any)

Under Contract No. M(22-11)–1600

DISTRIBUTION

Director
Deputy Director
File
(circulation)

4. Table of Contents, or Contents

The table of contents, or simply 'contents', can be presented as follows, unless you are working from a particular style sheet. Note the use of upper- and lower-case letters (adapted from Turabian 1955: 99):

CONTENTS

5. List of Tables

Tables are numbered with Arabic numbers and titles, and the format is similar to that of 'Contents', but is placed on a separate sheet.

LIST OF TABLES

Table		Page
1.	Title	4
2.	Title	27

6. List of Illustrations

The same format is used, on a separate sheet.

LIST OF ILLUSTRATIONS

Figure		Page
1.	Title	17

7. Introduction

The paper opens with two sections, the introduction and the explanation of methodology. In a short paper, you need not give these two sections their own headings or titles. Begin the main body of the paper, use the first paragraph or paragraphs as the introduction, and the next paragraph or paragraphs for your explanation of methodology. However, in a long paper (thirty typed pages or more, for example) you may want to break up the main body with a numbered heading, followed by a numbered 'Method-ology'. Whether you call these 'Chapter' depends on whether the remaining parts of your paper are divided into chapters, or simply into numbered sections.

In the longest works, such as books, the Introduction is often placed with the preliminary material, before the main body. (See sample Table of Contents)

The introduction can have a number of functions, depending upon the type of study:

a.   It may explain the theoretical background or experiences which prompted the study. For example —

> The background to the present work springs from a wide experience of intergroup conflict and a sociological and social pyschological interest in exploring the causes and consequences of social prejudice (MacGreil 1977: xx).

or

> People seeking free legal aid freqently complain that their choice of lawyers is restricted and that their cases receive less attention than do those of paying clients. . .

b.   It may provide a brief review of the relevant literature on the subject:

> Although the most notable early anthropological research in Ireland was that of Browne and Haddon, published between 1891 and 1902, their lead was not followed in succeeding years. . . The most widely-cited piece of anthropological research in Ireland, and the next to occur chronologically, is that of Arensberg (1937) and Arensberg and Kimball (1940). (Kane, 1977).

c.   It *does* explain what your study is about. Give the full research statement and an explanation of any definitions or limitations of your research statement. If you have any hypotheses, give them here.

d.   For technical or business reports, it can give —
   (1) terms of reference;
   (2) a short history of the case or subject;
   (3) reasons for writing the report or for conducting the investigation;
   (4) who called for the report;
   (5) the scope of the subject;
   (6) the limitations of the report;
   (7) the way the subject is to be treated;
   (8) any special considerations that apply to it (Mitchell, 1974: 48).

8. Methodology

Explain what research techniques you used, the numbers or categories of people involved, and any problems which you had in carrying out the study.

9. (The Paper Proper)

Do not, as one of my students once did, title this section, 'The Paper Proper'. Begin with a chapter number in Roman numerals and the title of the chapter, all in upper-case letters; or, for shorter papers, just Roman numerals and the title of the section; or for shortest papers, nothing; just begin.

In this section of your paper, you will present your research material. Since this may involve a number of pages, you should work out a plan of organisation. Your Research Outline is intended as a guide to the information you have to collect, but frequently it can also be used as the outline for your paper. If your Research Statement is *Educational Levels* (I) and *Work Productivity* (II) among *Industrial Employees* (III) in the *Belfast Shipyards* (IV), and you broke it up into main points as shown above in order to make a Research Outline, you can probably now re-order the points in the following way, and thus have an outline for writing your paper:

   I.   *Belfast Shipyards*
  II.   *Industrial Employees*
 III.   *Work Productivity*
 IV.   *Educational Level*

You can also look at the *sub-points* under each main point and see whether you can re-order and use them as guides to the planning of each main point section.

In the example given above, you open your paper by describing the general background of the shipyard, then the characteristics of the workers, and then move to the two main points you want to relate; work productivity and educational levels.

If your research is *Professional Interaction* (I) between *Nurses* (II) and *Doctors* (III) in a *Private Mental Hospital* (IV), you can re-order the points now to get —

   I.   *Private Mental Hospital*
  II.   *Nurses*
 III.   *Doctors*
 IV.   *Professional Interaction*

because it makes sense to start your paper by describing the general setting (the hospital), then the research subjects involved (the nurses and the doctors) and finally, your main concern, their professional interaction.

You cannot re-organise all Research Outlines into paper outlines, and you should never confuse the two. A Research Outline is a guide to the information you have to collect. The paper outline is a plan for laying out your paper. You must have both, but if you are lucky, the Research Outline, with a little re-organisation, can be made into a paper outline.

In the main body of your paper, you present a discussion of your research findings, and any analysis you have made. (If your study is purely descriptive, your paper might contain only the facts, without any analysis or conclusion on your part.) You can organise this in a number of ways: you might give all your material first, and then the analysis. In a very long paper, however, you might give the analysis at the close of each chapter or section, and then, to remind the reader, and to assemble all the analysis in one place, re-present it briefly in a summary at the close of the paper. There is no single way to present research and your own material will often suggest a particular presentation.

Here are a few points to remember in the presentation:

a.   Most research papers are presented impersonally, in the passive rather than the active form: 'This material was collected in the autumn of 1979' rather than 'I collected this material in the autumn of 1979'. This is merely a convention and unless you are preparing your work for a publication which prefers this form, you can cast your presentation any way you like. Once you decide on a form, however, do not switch. For example, do not refer to yourself as 'the author' in one sentence and as 'I' in another.

b.   Keep judgemental adjectives out of your presentation as much as possible, just as you tried to keep them out of your recording and analysing process. For example, 'The prison sits in nice surroundings' is unnecessarily judgemental. Just describe the surroundings and let the reader decide if they are nice. Of course, if your study informants use judgemental adjectives ('This is a nice prison'), you can report them.

c.   Use charts, tables, diagrams, maps and illustrations whenever they simplify the presentation. If an understanding of the physical layout of a place is important, a floor plan, drawn to scale if necessary, will complement or even replace a written description. Tables reduce the need for reciting strings of numbers and percentages. Give each table, diagram, etc., a number and a caption. For example:

TABLE 1
EDUCATIONAL LEVELS OF WORKERS BY TYPE OF JOB
(or)
MAP 1
BALLYGLASS TOWNLAND, 1907

If you have a small number of each of many types of illustrations – perhaps a map, a few charts, several diagrams – you may want to refer to all of them as 'Figures' and number them consecutively, instead of numbering them in separate categories. If you use maps, charts, and such like, from other sources, you must footnote them as you would any information borrowed from another author.

10. Conclusions

In some purely descriptive studies, the paper has no conclusions. It may have, instead, a brief summary of the main ideas or facts in the paper. In any other kind of study, you will use this section to make analyses and draw inferences *or* to summarise; if the paper is very long, and analyses and inferences have been made at the end of each section the Conclusion can be used to review them and tie them together.

Do not present conclusions which you cannot support, and do not omit conclusions which are contrary to what you had expected or desired.

11. Suggestions for Future Research

Your paper need not have this section, but often you can provide useful suggestions to other researchers who may wish to use your work as a basis for planning new research. Perhaps after completing your study you concluded that your topic was not sufficiently defined, that another research technique would have been better, that an all-female interview team would have had better rapport with the research subjects, or that the wording of your questionnaire was too technical. It may be useful to future researchers to know that.

On the other hand, in doing your research you may have come across something worth exploring which, for one reason or another, you did not pursue. Or, in preparing your conclusions you formed some hunches for which you do not have enough supporting evidence. Someone might be sufficiently interested in your suggestion and take up where you left off.

12. Appendix

An appendix is the place where you put any material which is relevant to the study but which is too long, detailed or is in some form which would interrupt the flow of the paper. If you used a questionnaire, interview form or special test form you should include a copy of it in an appendix. Examples of other items which might appear in an appendix are detailed case examples or case histories, excerpts from historical documents, testimonies, and extensive tables and charts.

If you have several unrelated items, you may put them into separate appendices, lettered 'Appendix A. School Children's Questionnaire' and 'Appendix B. Extracts from Minutes of Board of Governors, St Michael's Correctional Institution'.

You may not have an appendix, particularly if your paper is short. The appendix is *not* meant to be a catch-all for everything you collected but could not find a place for in your paper.

13. Footnotes

There are two kinds of footnotes, reference or documentary footnotes, and content footnotes.

a. *Reference Footnotes*

These are necessary in your paper whenever you use ideas or facts which are not your own, i.e. material borrowed from another person or source, whether published or unpublished. If you take information word-for-word from another source,[1] you *must* use quotation marks (inverted commas) and give the material a footnote.

---

[1] Generally, one is not permitted to take ten or more consecutive lines of direct quotation from a written work without permission from the author or publisher. However, if you

Although women did not have a high standing in medieval life, 'women's status in the 14th century had one explicit female exponent in Christine de Pisan, the only medieval woman, as far as is known, to have earned a living by her pen.'

These words, taken directly from Barbara W. Tuchman's book *A Distant Mirror: The Calamitous 14th Century*, page 217, must be attributed to her, using one of the two reference footnoting methods explained in this section.

You may also be required to footnote verbal sources, for example, in quoting from a speech which was only presented orally. You do not have to footnote material which is common knowledge; when referring to George Washington as the first president of the United States, for example, or when giving the freezing point of water.

If you simply paraphrase or summarise the material, or take the substance of it, you do not use quotation marks but you *still* must footnote the material.

Although women did not have a high standing in medieval life, one 14th century woman, Christine de Pisan, appears to have supported herself by writing.

All of these examples require footnotes, for two reasons: first, to give credit to the person or persons from whom you are taking the information; and, second, to enable your readers to consult the original source if they wish.

There are several methods for presenting reference footnotes. Two general types are widely accepted, one which I shall call a traditional method, and the other, a shorter method. I prefer the second, and if you are not required by a university or publisher to use the traditional method, you, too, might find it easier. Each method requires a particular form of footnote, accompanied by a particular form of bibliographic reference. Whichever of the many forms you choose, be consistent. Please note that we cannot, in a work of this focus and size, cover any but the most common kinds of footnote and bibliographic problems which you may encounter. For a comprehensive guide to footnoting and bibliographic form, consult the books listed at the end of this chapter.

(1) Traditional Method

(a) first reference to a work:

The traditional method involves inserting a number in the text, immediately after the sentence or paragraph containing the quotation or extract, and then repeating the number at the bottom of the page, or in a list at the end of the paper, followed by the information necessary to identify the work. This information should read as follows —

are preparing your work for publication, you may find that your publisher suggests that you get permission for any quotation longer than four printed lines, or about forty to fifty words. Sometimes a publisher may advise you to get permission before publishing *any* excerpt from someone else's work. Such a practice will spare you from accusations of plagiarism or even from being sued for copyright infringement. (This, incidentally, is an example of a *content* footnote.)

Books:

1. the name of the author, or authors, first name first; comma (if the work has more than three authors, you may give the name of the first author followed by 'et al.', an abbreviation for 'and others'.)
2. the title of the work, underlined; comma (omit comma here if there is no number 3, 4 or 5)
3. name of translator, compiler, or editor, if there is one; comma
4. number of the edition, if it is not the first edition, comma
5. total number of volumes, if there are two or more
6. parenthesis
7. place of publication; colon
8. name of publisher; comma
9. date of publication
10. parenthesis
11. comma
12. number of this particular volume, if the book is in volumes; colon; name of volume; comma
13. page number or numbers material is taken from; period.

For example, this note could appear at the bottom of your page (or at the end of your paper):

[1]J. Gatto and E. T. Vimmerstedt, *Industrialisation in Poland*, trans. Ralph T. Kane, 2nd ed., 3 vols. (New York: Nathan Press, 1979), vol. 1: Labour Conditions, pp. 40-43.

Most of your footnotes will probably be much simpler, however:

[1]Mona McCormack, *The New York Times Guide to Reference Materials* (New York: Popular Library, 1971), pp. 31-35.

[1]T. P. O'Neill, *British Parliamentary Papers: A Monograph on Blue Books* (Shannon: Irish University Press, 1968), p. 24.

[1]Julius Gould and W. L. Kolb, eds., *A Dictionary of the Social Sciences* (New York: Free Press, 1964), p. 88.

Articles:

There is a slight variation between the form for recording articles in popular magazines and in scholarly journals. Popular magazines first:

1. the name of the author, first name first; comma
2. the title of the article, in quotation marks; comma inside the second quotation mark
3. the name of the magazine or journal, underlined; comma
4. date of publication; if day and/or month is included, no comma between day, month and year; comma at end of date
5. page number or numbers material is taken from; period.

For example:

[1]Meg Greenfield, 'The Hostage of the Convention,' *Newsweek*, 25 August 1980, p. 80.

For scholarly journals, the procedure is the same, except
1. a volume number, if given, appears immediately after the name of the journal, with no punctuation between or following; and
2. the date appears in parenthesis, followed by a colon.
For example:

[1]Conrad M. Arensberg, 'The Community Study Method,' *American Journal of Sociology* 60 (1954): pp. 112-113.

In addition to books and articles, there are several other types of published sources:

Newspapers:

[1]*Youngstown Vindicator,* 16 May 1940, p. 3.
[1]"Courtroom Slap Propels Middle-Aged Lawyers into Ring,' *Washington Post,* 20 August 1980, sec. A, p. 14.

Public documents and reports:

[1]U.S., Congress, House, Comittee on Education and Labor, *Equal Opportunity and Full Employment: Hearing,* 94th Cong., 1st sess., 1975, p. 3.
[1]U.S., Federal Energy Administration, *Project Independence Report,* (Washington, D.C.: U.S. Government Printing Office, November, 1974), p. 3.
[1]Great Britain, *Parliamentary Papers,* 'Bill to Prohibit the Passing of the Sentence of Death Upon Expectant Mothers,' p. 20, 1930/31 (89), iv, 337. (Numbers cited are page used/session date/paper/volume/manuscript page. Some papers are presented by command; the command number appears in square brackets before the date. All references are made to the House of Commons bound set unless the paper [Bill, Report, or Accounts and Papers] is in the House of Lords set only, in which case 'H.L.' follows the command number, if any, and precedes the session date. [Ford and Ford 1955: 45-47]. Irish parliamentary papers are cited thus: title of paper; page used; ministry or department; year of publication; paper number; house, and command number, if any [Shearman 1944: 33-37].)

Unpublished sources:

Interviews:

[1]Interview with Richard Arthur, Hall Construction Co., Masonville, 1 May 1980.

Letters:

[1]Michael Morris, personal letter, 1 May 1980.
[1]Letter to St Michael's Detention Centre Board of Trustees, from William Brown. London, 15 April 1958.

Theses:

[1]Maurice Everett Nathan, 'Concepts and Values of Future Industrial Leaders: A Spencerian Approach to the Survival of American Capitalism' (Master's thesis, Wharton School, University of Pennsylvania, 1957), p. 7.

Some common problems in footnoting:
An association or group as author:
  [1]Energy Project of the Ford Foundation, *A Time to Choose: America's Energy Future* (Cambridge, Mass.: Ballinger Publishing Co., 1974), p. 10.
  [1]Committee for Economic Development, *Fighting Inflation and Promoting Growth* (New York: Committee for Economic Development, 1976), p. 4.
Note in the last example that the author is also the publisher.
No author given:
  [1]*A History of Poland, Ohio* (Cleveland: Stanton & Co., 1977), p. 3.
Editor's name given, no other author listed:
  [1]Theodore Citron, ed., *It's Not Ordinary: Unusual Mechanical Inventions* (Belfast: Windsor Press, 1980), p. 61.
Privately printed work:
  [1]William B. Nolan, *Sources for Local Studies* (Dublin: By the Author, Carysfort College, n.d.), pp. 18-19.
No date given:
See previous example. If no date is given on the copyright page but you can ascertain the date from another source, such as a library catalogue card, give the date, in brackets [ ] in the usual place.
No place or publisher given:
  [1]Hugh Kearney, *My Life and Times* (n.p.), p. 22.
Article as a part of a collection in a book:
  [1]Judith Merril, 'Survival Ship', in *Anthropology Through Science Fiction*, eds. Carol Mason, Martin Harry Greenberg and Patricia Warrick (New York: St Martin's Press, 1974), p. 194.

(b) footnote references after the first reference
    If you find a useful source and draw upon it many times, you can imagine how annoying it would be to have to repeat the full footnote reference each time you drew upon that source.
    After you have given the full information in a footnote, each time you refer to the same work again, give a shortened footnote. If the reference appears in the footnote immediately after the original footnote, this form is acceptable:
  [1]Mona McCormack, *The New York Times Guide to Reference Materials* (New York: Popular Library, 1971), pp. 31-35.
  [2]McCormack.
If the reference is to a different page,
  [3]McCormack, p. 62.
If references to other authors have occurred between this new reference and the original, you have to give some reference to the title of the book:
  [4]T. P. O'Neill, *British Parliamentary Papers: A Monograph on Blue Books* (Shannon: Irish University Press, 1968), p. 24.
  [5]McCormack, *Guide*, p. 62.

(c) typing the footnotes

Traditional footnotes can be typed at the bottom of the page on which the source material is presented, or at the end of the paper on a separate sheet. If you type them at the bottom of each page, you start with '1' on each page, or you can start with '1' and continue to number consecutively all through the paper. If you are putting your footnotes at the bottom of the page, every footnote number in the text *must* have a corresponding footnote at the bottom of the same page.

At the bottom of your typed page, skip one line and then type a line either eight spaces long, or the full width of the paper. Skip another two lines, indent eight spaces, type a raised number, and begin the footnote. Single space the note itself, and double space in between notes:

---

[1]Kate L. Turabian, *Student's Guide for Writing College Papers*, 3rd ed. (Chicago: University of Chicago Press, 1976), pp. 73-75.

Finally, if you use the traditional method of footnoting, you should pair it with the traditional form of bibliography (see p. 00).

(2) Shorter Method

Now that you have seen the traditional method, you will appreciate the beauty and brevity of the shorter method, or 'author-date' method of putting the citation right in the text, as I have done in the other chapters of this book. Variations on this method are most commonly used in the sciences, but unless you are required by a university or publisher to use the traditional method, you might find that a shorter method suits you.

At the close of each quotation or extract, put *right in the text,*
1. parenthesis
2. the author or authors' last names
3. the year of publication
4. a colon
5. the page or pages from which the material comes (if referring to a page)
6. parenthesis.

Thus: 'In one major study of prejudice in Ireland, the author concluded that 'the prejudice against the "ancient enemy", England, is relatively low, without weakening the desire for National Unity' (MacGréil 1977: 531). Others, however, state. . .'

If your book has more than one author, but fewer than four, list them all:
(Gottschalk, Kluckhohn and Angell 1945: 80)

However, if the work has more than three authors, you may give the name of the first author, followed by 'et al.':
(Naroll et al., 1970: 235-248)

If you have two or more authors with the same last name, give not only the last name but the first name or initial as well to distinguish which author you mean:

(Kaplan, J. 1967: 13)

(Kaplan, M. 1973: 28)

If you are using more than one source written by an author in the same year, distinguish the sources by giving each date a letter:

(Michael 1968a: 117)

(Michael 1968b: 57)

If you have summarised material from two or more consecutive pages, list the first and last pages of the extracted material:

(Cottle 1974: 119-203)

If you have taken material from non-consecutive pages, list the pages:

(Grahame 1969: 41, 97, 176-77, 215)

Do this for each quotation or paraphrasing or summary which you use. You may have a number of reference footnotes on one page, and perhaps none on the next. If you do not use any material from other sources, you will probably have no footnotes at all.

This system of footnoting satisfies the two requirements listed For example, the reader can track down MacGréil and read his work in the original from the information given in the footnote and then look up the 'List of References' or 'Literature Cited' or 'Bibliography' at the end of your paper, where all the details of each publication are given. If you use this shorter method of footnoting, you should also use the 'shorter' form of bibliographic reference

b. *Content Footnotes*

These present material which you think is useful and relevant but which, for one reason or another, would interrupt the text. You can also use content footnotes to acknowledge assistance in your research. For example:

* I am indebted to Professor Alexander Spoehr for suggesting this theoretical distinction between …….. and ………

Content footnotes can be typed at the bottom of each page, as traditional reference footnotes are, or at the end of each paper. If you put them at the bottom of the page with your reference footnotes, number them, as they appear in the text, in along with the reference footnotes. If you put them at the end of the paper, put them on a sheet separate from your 'Bibliography' or 'References Cited', and call them 'Notes'; preface them with symbols, rather than numbers, in this order: *, †, ‡, §, ‖, #, doubling them if additional symbols are needed.

14. Glossary

This is a dictionary of special terms, such as scientific, technical or professional terms, or of foreign words, used in your text. A glossary would be unusual and pretentious in most papers, because any unfamiliar term which you use in the text should be defined immediately after using the term. However, if you have a number of such words, and if they are used in several places in the text, you will save the reader considerable frustration by providing a glossary, in alphabetical form.

15. Bibliography or List of References

A 'List of References' or 'Literature Cited' is an alphabetical listing of works mentioned in the paper. A 'Bibliography', 'Selected Bibliography' or 'Annotated Bibliography' is more extensive, and includes all the useful and relevant works which were examined in the course of the study and not simply those in the paper. An 'Annotated Bibliography' is a bibliography in which the entries are followed by any or all of these items:

a. an indication of the contents of the work
b. a short summary of the work or its relevant parts
c. an assessment of the work's usefulness to the reader.

If you have traditional or shorter method footnotes in your paper, or have consulted any written sources, or want to recommend any related books or articles, you will have this section in your paper.

For short articles in journals, a 'List of References' or 'References Cited' is more usual; in most other cases, it is up to you to decide between this and a 'Bibliography'. Having decided that, the procedures are the same in both cases. All entries are listed in alphabetical order by the author's last name. Below are examples of the forms for the types of sources which you are most likely to use:

a. Traditional Method

If you are using the traditional method for footnoting, this is the form you should use for your bibliography:

Books:

1. author's name, last name first. Two authors' names are separated by a comma and 'and'; three authors by semicolons and 'and' before the final author; period
2. title of book, underlined; period
3. name of editor or translator, if there is one; period
4. number of this edition, if it is not the first edition; period.
5. total number of volumes if there are two or more; period
6. place of publication; colon
7. name of publisher; comma
8. date; period
9. number of this particular volume, if the book is in volumes; colon; title of this particular volume, if the books is in volumes; period.

For example:

> Gatto, J., and Vimmerstedt, E. T. *Industrialisation in Poland.* Translated by Ralph Kane. 2nd ed. 3 vols. New York: Nathan Press, 1979. Vol. 1: Labour Conditions.

Some simpler references:

> Committee for Economic Development. *Fighting Inflation and Promoting Growth.* New York: Committee for Economic Development, 1976.

Energy Project for the Ford Foundation. *A Time to Choose: America's Energy Future.* Cambridge, Mass.: Ballinger Publishing Co., 1974.

Gould, Julius and Kolb, W. L., eds. *A Dictionary of the Social Sciences.* New York: The Free Press, 1964.

McCormack, Mona. *The New York Times Guide to Reference Materials.* New York: Popular Library, 1971.

O'Neill, T. P. *British Parliamentary Papers: A Monograph on Blue Books.* Shannon: Irish University Press, 1968.

Articles:

Once again, a distinction between popular magazines and scholarly journals. For popular magazines:

1. author's name, last name first. Two authors' names are separated by a comma and 'and'; three authors by semicolons and 'and' before the final author; period.
2. title of the article, in quotation marks; period inside final quotation mark
3. the name of the journal, underlined; comma
4. date of publication; if day and/or month is included, no comma between day, month, and year; period.

For example:

Greenfield, Meg. 'The Hostage at the Convention.' *Newsweek,* 25 August 1980.

For scholarly journals, the procedure is the same except

1. a volume number, if given, appears immediately after the name of the journal, with no punctuation between the name and number, or following the number
2. the date appears in parentheses, followed by a colon
3. the inclusive page numbers (first and last pages of the article) are given, without 'p.' or 'pp.'; period.

For example:

Arensberg, Conrad M. 'The Community Study Method.' *American Journal of Sociology* 60 (1954): 109-124.

Other sources:

Newspapers:

Youngstown Vindicator, 16 May 1940.

'Courtroom Slap Propels Middle-Aged Lawyers into Ring.' *Washington Post,* 20 August 1980, sec. A, p. 14. (however, page numbers are often omitted because they vary by edition.)

Public documents and reports:

U.S., Congress, House. Committee on Education and Labor. *Equal Opportunity and Full Employment: Hearing,* 94th Cong., 1st sess., 1975.

U.S., Federal Energy Administration. *Project Independence Report.* Washington, D.C.: U.S. Government Printing Office.

Great Britain. *Parliamentary Papers.* 'Bill to Prohibit the Passing of the Sentence of Death Upon Expectant Mothers.' 1930/31 (89), iv, 337.

Unpublished sources:

Interviews:

Arthur, Richard. Hall Construction Co., Masonville. Interview, 1 May 1980.

Letters:

Morris, Michael. Personal letter, 1 May 1980.

Brown, William. Letter to St Michael's Detention Centre Board of Directors. London, 15 April 1958.

Theses:

Nathan, Maurice Everett. 'Concepts and Values of Future Industrial Leaders: a Spencerian Approach to the Survival of American Capitalism.' Master's thesis, Wharton School, University of Pennsylvania, 1957.

For additional examples, I have used the traditional method for the references in Chapter IX, 'Written Sources' and for the references at the ends of chapters.

b. Shorter Method

If you are using the shorter method for footnoting, this is the form you use for your Bibliography or References Cited.

Books:

1. author's name, last name first: if there are second and third authors, forenames before surnames, separate names with semicolon;
2. date of publication
3. title of book, no underlining; period
4. name of editor or translator, if there is one; period
5. number of this edition, if it is not the first edition; period.
6. total number of volumes if there are two or more; period
7. place of publication; colon
8. name of publisher; period
9. number of this particular volume, if the book is in volumes; colon; title of this particular volume, if the books is in volumes; period.

Example (note the difference in typing form between this and the traditional method):

Gatto, J.; and E. T. Vimmerstedt
1979   Industrialisation in Poland. Trans. by Ralph Kane.
2nd ed. 3 vols. New York: Nathan Press, 1979. Vol. 1:
Labour Conditions.

Usually, however, your references will be much simpler:

Committee for Economic Development
1976   Fighting Inflation and Promoting Growth. New
York: Committee for Economic Development.

Energy Project of the Ford Foundation
    1974   A Time to Choose: America's Energy Future. Cambridge, Mass.: Ballinger Publishing Co.
Gould, Julius, and W. L. Kolb, eds.
    1964   A Dictionary of the Social Sciences. New York: The Free Press.
McCormack, Mona
    1971   The New York Times Guide to Reference Materials. New York: Popular Library.
O'Neill, T. P.
    1968   British Parliamentary Papers: A Monograph on Blue Books. Shannon: Irish University Press.

Articles:
1. author's name, last name first; succeeding authors forenames first
2. the date
3. title of the article, no quotation marks; period
4. the title of the journal, no underlining
5. volume number, if any; colon
6. the inclusive page numbers (first and last pages of the article) with 'p.' or 'pp.'; period.

For example:
    Arensberg, Conrad M.
        1954   The Community Study Method. American Journal of Sociology 60: 109-24.
    Brown, William M. and Herman Kahn
        14 July   Why OPEC is Vulnerable. Fortune 66-69.
        1980.

Other sources:
Newspapers:
    Youngstown Vindicator
        16 May
        1940.

Public documents and reports:
    U.S., Congress, House. Committee on Education and Labor
        1975   Equal Opportunity and Full Employment: Hearing, 94th Cong., 1st sess.
    U.S., Federal Energy Administration
        November   Project Independence Report. Washington,
        1974   D.C.: U.S. Government Printing Office.
    Great Britain, Parliamentary Papers.
        1930/31   Bill to Prohibit the Passing of the Sentence of Death Upon Expectant Mothers.' (89), iv, 337.

Unpublished sources:

Interviews:

Arthur, Richard

1 May   Hall Construction Co., Masonville. Interview
1980.

Letters:

Morris, Michael

1 May   Personal letter.
1980.

Brown, William

15 April   Letter to St Michael's Detention Centre Board of
1958   Trustees. London.

Theses:

Nathan, Maurice Everett

1957   Concepts and Values of Future Industrial Leaders: a
Spencerian Approach to the Survival of American Capitalism.
Master's thesis, Wharton School, University of Pennsylvania.

For additional examples, I have used the shorter form in the 'References Cited' at the end of the book.

c. Typing the Bibliography

Head the first page listing your sources with 'Bibliography' or 'References Cited' or 'List of References'. List every source used in your paper, in alphabetical order. For works which have no author, list under the first major word of the title (ignore 'A', 'An', 'The').

Traditional form:

Begin reference at the left hand margin. If reference continues beyond first line, indent second and subsequent lines three spaces.

'Shorter' form:

Begin reference at left hand margin. Type author's name on a separate line. One line below author's name, indent two spaces and type date.

Allow two spaces, and begin title of work, on same line as date.

16. Index

An index is usually found only in large works. You have probably noticed them in scholarly texts, such as history books, and in technical studies. The index is an alphabetical list of the items covered in a book, including subjects, people's and place names, together with the page numbers on which the items appear. Sometimes all items are placed in one list. In other cases, you may find them listed separately; for example, a 'Subject Index' or 'Topic Index'; and an 'Author Index'.

The index is made after the paper is typed in final form, or in the case of a work which is to be published, when you get back the page proofs from the printer. Using a carbon of your paper, or your duplicate set of page proofs, underline each important item on the page, and make an index card containing each item on the page (or pages, if the particular item runs over more than one page). The most important word comes first — so instead of 'use of drugs', you have 'Drugs, use of'. You may have sub-entries, as well —

    Detention centres, 90-100
        admission rates to, 94, 98
        recidivism rates in, 93
        recreation in, 97

If your work is being published, your publisher may provide a guide to the construction of your index.

E. Finishing the Paper

The care that you put into your research should also be reflected in the way you present it. You are responsible for the contents of your study. Proof-read it. Get someone else to do your proof-reading if your spelling is so poor that you do not even know how to look up the words in the dictionary.

If your paper is going to a printer and you need to make corrections on your typed copy, use proof-reader's symbols to do so. You can find a list of these in many dictionaries, or can get a list from your printer or publisher.

Type your paper or have it typed, and proof-read it again for typing errors. Unless you are attempting a special type of presentation, follow some standardised form for typing. Use white, sixteen to twenty pound bond paper of standard size. Allow a margin of 1½ inches on the left side of the page and one inch on the other three sides. Double space the material, except for the Abstract, which is single-spaced with the entire contents indented about eight spaces on each side. Single space and indent any long quotations taken from other sources. When starting a new section of the text (such as the first page of the main body, or the first page of a chapter, begin one-third of the way down the page, two spaces below the heading.

Articles for publication are numbered differently from the other types of papers. Articles have no separate title page — the title is simply placed on the first page, two or three inches from the top. Then triple space, and begin the text. All pages are numbered, either at the top right or top centre, with Arabic numbers (1, 2, 3, etc.).

For all other papers, give each page, except the title page (which is separate) a number. The 'Preliminary' sections are numbered with small Roman numerals at the bottom of the pages; start with (ii) since the title page, although not numbered, is (i). Number the rest of the paper with Arabic numbers, at the top centre, except for the first page of the main body, and the first page of each chapter — the Arabic numbers for those go at the bottom centre of the page.

Most people do not intend to publish their studies, but if you are sending your study to a publisher, send the original (keep a copy) loose and flat; do not bind it or put it in a folder. Photographs should be rolled and sent in in a cardboard tube. If your study is unsolicited (the publisher did not ask you to submit it), enclose sufficient postage stamps, unattached, for return if necessary. If you are sending it to a publisher abroad, use International Reply Coupons, available at a post office.

Send the study by first class post or express. Insure it for the amount it would take to have the copy re-typed from your carbon, and the cost of re-placing additional material like illustrations, photographs. You may include a brief letter identifying yourself and providing any necessary information. Both the letter and the parcel should contain your return address.

For more specific help on writing specialised kinds of papers, and reports, consult the following:

American Psychological Association. *Publication Manual of the American Psychological Association.* 2nd ed. [Washington, D.C.: 1974.]

Bart, P., and Frankel, L. *The Student Sociologist's Handbook.* Cambridge, Mass.: Schenkman Publishing Co., 1971.

Barzun, Jacques and Graff, Henry F. *The Modern Researcher.* 3rd ed. New York: Harcourt, Brace, Jovanovich, 1977.

Butcher, Judith. *Copy-editing: the Cambridge Handbook.* [London]: Cambridge University Press, [1975.]

Davis, Gordon B. and Parker, Clyde A. *Writing the Doctoral Dissertation.* Woodbury, New York: Barron's Educational Series, 1979.

Harris, John S. and Blake, Reed H. *Technical Writing for Social Scientists.* Chicago: Nelson-Hall, 1976.

Janis, Jack Harold. *The Business Research Paper: a Manual of Standards. . .* New York: Hobbs, Dorman, [1967.]

Lester, J. D. *Writing Research Papers: A Complete Guide.* Rev. ed. Glenview, Ill.: Scott, Foresman & Co., 1971.

Linton, M. *A Simplified Style Manual: For the Preparation of Journal Articles in Psychology, Social Sciences, Education and Literature.* New York: Appleton-Century-Crofts, 1972.

Mitchell, John. *How to Write Reports.* Glasgow: Fontana/Collins, 1974.

Modern Language Association of America. *MLA Handbook for Writers of Research Papers, Theses, and Dissertations.* New York: Modern Language Association, 1977.

Mullins, Carolyn J. *A Guide to Writing and Publishing in the Social and Behavioural Sciences.* New York: John Wiley & Sons, 1977.

O'Connor, M., and Woodford, F. P. *Writing Scientific Papers in English: An ELSE-Ciba Foundation Guide for Authors.* The Hague: Elsevier, 1975.

Standing Committee on Publications of the British Psychological Society. *Suggestions to Authors.* Rev. ed. London: Cambridge University Press, 1971.

Woodford, F. P., ed. *Scientific Writing for Graduate Students: A Manual on the Teaching of Scientific Writing.* New York: Rockefeller University Press, 1968.

PART FOUR

Counting the Costs

XIII. Getting a Grant

IN PLANNING your research, you should consider whether there might be a public or private body or organisation which will support all or part of your project. Research does not necessarily have to be expensive, but if you have to include costs like travel, use of assistants, stationery, postage, computer time, printing and typing, the total may well exceed the limits of your own resources. By preparing a research project budget (see pp. 000 for an example) you can decide whether you need financial help.

Competition for grants increases each year. Many of the more traditional bodies prefer applicants with advanced degrees and research experience, but an awareness is developing that for some kinds of projects, well-prepared people and groups in the community can do the job as well as 'professionals'.

A. Types of Funding Bodies.

1. Government Agencies.

In most western countries, government agencies are the largest sources of grant money. Most are legally obliged to, or prefer to, make grants to institutions rather than to individuals.

2. Foundations

Foundations also prefer to award to institutions, but often an individual can qualify by arranging that an institution administer the grant on his or her behalf. USA foundations are legally limited to awards to charitable, educational, religious, scientific and cultural organisations; almost all successful applicants are non-profit corporations with tax-exempt status.

Hillman and Abarbanel (1977: 90-93) group foundations into the following categories:

a.   General purpose – large 'independent' foundations such as the Ford Foundation and the Carnegie Corporation;

b.   Company-sponsored – legally independent, but in practice closely associated with the originating company. Such foundations tend to award grants, usually in the area of education, to causes related to the company's financial interests ('pet' causes of major clients, for example) and to employees' interests;

c.   Community foundations – foundations which receive and channel money from a variety of sources to various local causes;

d.   'Family' foundations – many were originally established by wealthy individuals to distribute money to selected charities;

e.   Special-purpose foundations – funded to further one specific cause or locality. (It should be noted that very few foundations are international in scope; over ninety per cent are local.) (Hillman and Abarbanel 1977: 95).

3. Business and Industry

Corporations will often award grants out of current revenue to individuals as well as to institutions; some, in fact, resent the 'indirect costs' or over-head payment which would be required should an institution administer the grant for an individual. Generally, western European corporations have been more receptive to funding research, cultural and community projects than American businesses have.

4. 'Interest' Associations

This is a catch-all which includes labour unions, fraternal societies and fund-raising interest groups.

In addition to these standard granting agencies, there are some 'unorthodox sources'; these include commercial and voluntary groups which have no connection with research but which may consider sponsoring your project if it meets one or both of these criteria:

- the subject matter relates to their areas of interest; for example, a prisoners' rights organisation might be prepared to contribute financially to a project which examined the range of training opportunities in detention centres for juvenile offenders; an adoption society might sponsor research on anomalies in the adoption laws.

- subsidising the research may create good will, improve public relations or enhance the image of the organisation. A cigarette company, for example, might sponsor research into the improvement of local recreational facilities; a baking company which is the biggest local employer might help on a study of how best to upgrade local vocational educational training. The subject matter does not have to be related to the activities of the company; in fact, a cigarette company will hardly sponsor your research if it focusses on the deleterious physical and social aspects of smoking.

How do you find out about these funding sources?

B. Guides

For US government assistance, the best source is the *Catalog of Federal Domestic Assistance;* for Britain *Government Research and Development: A Guide to Sources* gives addresses of bodies such as the Social Science Research Council; for Canada, get the publications of the Social Science and Humanities Research Council; for Ireland, Whelan's *Funding Sources for Research Ireland,* which covers government and other sources.

For USA foundations, a major source is the Foundation Center and its publications. The Foundation Center is a national source of funding information on 22,000 foundations, and is supported mainly by foundations. It maintains a nation-wide library network, which also extends to Mexico and Canada, plus two national libraries in New York and Washington. The Foundation Center provides a wide variety of free and subscription information services, and a number of guides, including the *Foundation Directory* to nearly 5,500 foundations; *Foundation Grants to Individuals,* and the *Foundation Grants Index.* Unfortunately, telephone information, even for the most basic inquiries, is limited to subscribers.

The *Annual Register of Grant Support* covers both public and private fundings sources for a wide number of topic and geographic areas (almost exclusively in the USA).

For Britain, there is the *Directory of Grant-Making Trusts,* covering approximately 2,000 foundations, and for Europe, the *Guide to European Foundations.* Canadian grants, in addition to being listed by the Foundation Center, are covered in the *Canadian Universities Guide to Foundations and Granting Agencies;* and in *Awards for Graduate Study and Research.* Details on all of these are given at the end of this chapter. For established business and industrial grants, write to the Office of the President of each to inquire about their funding practice; for possible 'unorthodox' sources such a simple inquiry will usually bring the reply, 'We don't fund', so send instead a letter giving a brief, clear explanation of what you wish to do, how long it will take, what relevant experience or credentials you have, and why you think the organisation might be interested. Give an estimate of what it will cost to do the research, and indicate any other sources of funding which you already have. If the body is willing to fund all or part of your research, you should then supply a proper research proposal, if requested, and work out a contractual agreement. (See below for both.)

C. Subscription Information Services

In addition to membership of the Associates Program of the Foundation Center, one may subscribe to various commercial or non-profit organisations whose services range from basic information to individual consulting. Some hold training seminars, produce publications, do specialised computer searches, evaluate proposals, and advise on fund-raising. In the case of the USA membership organisations, fees can run to several hundred dollars; one gets access to the information of the other organisations by subscribing to their publications. Some subscripton services are listed at the end of this chapter.

D. Applying for a Grant

How do you apply for a grant? The process depends partly upon whether you apply as a non-profit corporation or through an institution; or whether you apply simply as an individual with no institutional connection. In the latter case, step 5 in the following list is omitted:

1.   Decide what you want to do. Work out a Research Statement, and from that, a complete Research Outline, so that you have a command of all aspects of the study. Be able to summarise your project in a paragraph or two.

2.   Find appropriate funding sources. Get information for the various types of government, foundation, business and 'interest' funding through sources such as those listed at the end of this chapter. Rule out any from which you are obviously disqualified. Granting bodies do not deviate from their terms of reference; if a foundation's purpose is to fund research into lengthening the life span of the house fly, and elderly house flies are not your aim, that is it, no matter how worthy your idea. Find out, through a source such as the *Foundation Grants Index*, or through a computer search service, what kinds of projects the body has funded in the past. Determine if you need a special legal or tax status to qualify, and arrange to get it. Take note of the application deadline.

3.   Get application forms and any other relevant literature.

4.   Now select the funding bodies which seem most relevant, and whose criteria you can meet. The application process requires great care and preparation; firing off dozens or even hundreds of vague, all-purpose applications usually yields nothing.

5.   If you are operating through an institution, discuss your plans with its officials: what are their requirements for administering a grant? Will the institution be prepared, if necessary, to match funds and/or make necessary facilities and services available? Who owns equipment acquired during the project? How will the funds be administered? What kind of reporting and accounting is required?

6.   Arrange an appointment by telephone or letter with the granting body. Your Research Statement and prepared paragraph or two will help you to make a *brief* project description on the phone; if you send a letter, state, in addition to the purpose of the project, its length, its costs, why you think the organisation would be interested, and a *curriculum vitae* or résumé, which is a summary, listing point by point your education, work and experience. Give the schools and dates attended, major subjects studied, degrees and academic awards, if appropriate; your occupational experience from the present, in reverse order, with dates; any other relevant experience, such as research or major volunteer or committee work; any grants which you may have received in the past, together with title and amount; and any relevant publications. The names, positions and addresses of at least three references are often included at the end; select people whose pro-

fessional specialisations would have some meaning to the agency's evaluators rather than character or financial references. A professionally-done *curriculum vitae* has a certain appearance; consult a source such as one of those listed at the end of this chapter, or ask to see those of people who have had to prepare them, such as business executives or university faculty members.

Finally, if you represent an organisation, describe its appropriateness to this project. Ask for an appointment to discuss your plan. Your letter should usually be no longer than two standard pages. For some ideas, see the sample letters in Urgo, listed at the end of this chapter.

7.   Write a draft proposal.[1] Your Research Design will be very useful in helping you to describe the project and estimate time and costs. If you have a complete draft prepared before your first meeting with the funding body, you are more likely to be well-prepared for any questions.

Remember the purpose of the proposal: 'To convince those who control the distribution of funds and judge the worth of a project that —

• a proposed activity is within the scope of the established objectives of the funding agency's programme or stated purposes.

• the action to be taken is valuable because it will solve an immediate problem or elicit fundamental information, or because it will extend existing knowledge and assist in the eventual solution of a problem.

• the proposer is well acquainted with the 'state-of-the-art'; that he knows what has already been done, is qualified to perform the desired activity, and has access to the necessary facilities.

• the importance of the anticipated results sufficiently justifies the time to be spent on it and the money it will cost (White 1975: 230).

The proposal itself will tell what is to be done, why it needs to be done, how and by whom it will be done, how long it will take and how much it will cost. Get professional writing assistance if necessary, but be wary of 'consultants' and organisations which guarantee the success of a proposal drafted by them. Ask colleagues to show you successful proposals, and study the examples presented in White, Hillman *et al.*, Urgo, or Brodsky.

Most government agencies and some foundations require you to apply on a set form; if not, your application should be about the equivalent of four single-spaced letter sized sheets (Hillman and Abarbanel 1977: 55) although some proposals, because of necessary enclosures such as examples of questionnaires, legal documents, or background material, may run to hundreds of pages.Generally, however, shorter is better.

If the agency provides a standard application form, make a copy for your first draft, and include the following information, as requested. When no

---

[1]Inexperienced researchers have been known to jump the gun by writing the research proposal before/instead of preparing the Research Design and Outline, and if the application is successful, they try to carry out their researach with the proposal as a guide. This does not work, and the researcher usually does not discover it until the research project has taken three times longer than it should, and ultimately covers, rather vaguely, something other than what he or she had intended.

form is provided, you can use these categories as a guide:

a. a cover page, stating to whom the submission is being made; the title of the project; its starting and closing dates; the amount requested, the applicant's name, address and institution, if relevant; and the date submitted. Many agencies and foundations supply their own standard cover page or 'face- sheet' which may request additional information.

b. an introduction or abstract, about 200 words, written *after* the proposal is completed. It contains a sentence or sentences explaining the following:

— what is being proposed and how much is being asked (indicate if you have funds from other sources; funding bodies tend to react favourably to this);

• how it will be done;

• why the idea or project is needed, and by whom;

• why it should interest the agency or foundation

• how it fits its goals;

— what your own and/or your institution's qualifications are.

Needless to say, the abstract should be written with extreme care; in some cases, it may be the only part of your proposal which is read.

For certain projects, especially 'action' projects such as the setting up of a day-care centre, it is useful to add two main sections here after the abstract and before going on to the description of the project – one describing the need for what you plan to do, and another describing what you hope to achieve.

c. a description of the project: Proposals differ widely, but most will include the following sections:

• introduction: This will restate the project's purpose and set it in its practical and theoretical context by explaining background and current thinking in the field; a well-chosen review of relevant literature and/or similar undertakings to show that you are familiar with related developments and are not reinventing the wheel. In research grants, specialists in the field usually serve as reviewers, and they must be satisfied that you are not attempting something which has been outdated by other research. Some of the references listed in Chapter IX should help to make you aware of recent research in your field. Remember, however, that this is not a license to summarise everything you've ever read; nor is it the place for disparaging the research of others.

• the description itself: your Research Outline will provide the basis. Avoid jargon and attempts to dress up the project. If you have a hypothesis, show how it is to be tested.

• the objectives or significance – the practical or theoretical contributions

d. the methods to be used: This is one of the most important parts of the proposal. 'Talk is cheap' but the real test of your project will be whether you have any plan of how to proceed when you are finally let loose on that first day. Like most members of university faculties, I am occasionally asked to evaluate a research proposal for a foundation or agency, and have learned from experience to issue a flat 'No' to proposals which waffle on this point and reduce the entire methodology to 'I intend to spend a year in the community doing participant observation' or something equally vague. Writers of such proposals are somehow able to come up with a budget which itemises expenses down to the last typewriter ribbon; I want to know, in similar detail, what they are actually going to *do*. The plan may have to be altered later in the course of the research, but at least the person has shown himself/herself capable of relating action to ideas. Your Research Design, under the headings 'Techniques' and 'Sources' will be of considerable help to you in planning this section. If necessary, establish that you have the appropriate technical skills to collect the data.

e. the evaluation: In some projects, you may be expected to monitor and evaluate your progress, particularly if yours is an 'action' project, for example, trying to get a vocational training plan for young offenders. In such a case, you may need to develop a system for determining how the project is working, by establishing goals and inviting an independent evaluator, an individual or institution, to gauge the results.

f. the schedule: Work out a realistic timetable for your project, allowing for unexpected hitches. Give a step-by-step allocation of time.

g. the budget: To figure out your budget, see Chapter III. Some funding bodies will cover only certain kinds of expenses (salaries may be excluded, for example) or may expect their funds to be matched. A standard budget form may be provided; if not, here are some categories which will probably be represented in your budget. Summarise the budget at the beginning of this section. Then present in detail:

- personnel: salaries, wages, fringe benefits; costs of external personnel, such as accountants, consultants, etc.;
- equipment (purchasing, renting);
- supplies, often described as expendable or disposable, such as office supplies, films, tapes, etc.;
- rent and utilities, if appropriate;
- travel, including mileage costs for private car; local, internal and foreign travel; and *per diem* costs. The funding body may exclude categories or may stipulate limits;
- miscellaneous: postage, informants' fees, books, computer time, bank charges, maintenance and repair of equipment; for foreign travel, shipping, innoculations, visas, currency exchange;
- indirect costs: a fixed rate percentage of the total budget or of salaries, which goes to the administering institution (if any) to defray costs of operation and services in relation to the project. These costs are decided upon by the institution and the granting body.

If all of the budget items are not obviously justified, conclude with a 'Budget Justification'.

Do not underestimate your costs in the hope of enhancing your chances

of funding. Funding bodies are well-versed in project costs and will conclude that you are badly prepared and/or that you will try to hit them later
on for the shortfall.

   h. professional qualifications – your *curriculum vitae* and those of your
research staff; and the credentials of the institution, if appropriate.

   i. approval of the institution, if you are applying through one.

8.   Attend meeting with the officials of the granting agency. Ask for
suggestions for improving your proposal, and take them, unless they would
distort your research idea. Discuss the legal and administrative requirements of their grants. If appropriate, go back and explain these to the
institution which will be administering the grant.

9.   Write your final proposal, incorporating changes suggested by the
funding body. Edit it several times. Is it brief, clear, confident, honest? Is it
written to a human reader, rather than to an institution? Is there any
background or supporting material in the body which might be put into an
appendix instead? (Note, however, that some funding bodies will not
include unsolicited appended material in their review process). Have you
attached any necessary tax or legal documents? Does it look professional –
well-typed and double-spaced on good paper, unostentatiously bound if
necessary?

10.   Send your application, or see that your institution sends it, well ahead
of the deadline. If there is no deadline, aim to submit it at least six months
prior to the time when you will need the funds. Attach a cover letter summarising what you are asking, what you want to do, how it relates to the
body's interests, and your own qualifications.

11.   Revise, if requested, and re-submit your application. If you are
rejected, try to find out why. It will help you in re-applying, and in your
next project.

   If accepted, your research proposal may become a legally-binding contract, covering your responsibilities. Be sure you are also clear about what
the funding body's rights and obligations are — can they exert any control
over the research process or the publication of findings? In your euphoria at
getting an organisation to carry the financial burden for you, you could also
overlook the unlikely but possible prospect that you will be a pseudo-
scientific 'front man' for the group's vested interests. In the case of granting
bodies which do not have a standardised or acceptable contract, get a
written agreement which will outline your rights and the rights of the sponsoring group. These should cover the following points:
• the subject matter of the research
• the general research methods to be used
• the direction and control of the research project
• the costs which will be covered, and the duration of the study
• the control of the final material, including publication rights.

   The meanings of each of the major words above should be clearly
specified in the agreement. For a discussion of the ethical rights and responsibilities of both researcher and sponsoring agency, see Chapter XIV.

Guides to Grants:
Annual Register of Grant Support. Los Angeles: Academic Media, 1969– (USA).
Association of Universities and Colleges of Canada. *The Canadian Directory to Foundations and Granting Agencies.* Ottawa: 1978–.
Canada. Bureau of Statistics. *Awards for Graduate Study and Research.* Ottawa: Queen's Printer, 1951– (awards open to Canadians; published irregularly).
Charities Aid Foundation. *Director of Grant-Making Trusts.* Tonbridge, Kent: The Foundation, 1978.
Coleman, William Emmet. *Grants in the Humanities.* New York: Neal-Schuman Publishers, 1980.
Foundation Directory. 7th ed. Comp. by the Foundation Center. New York: distributed by Columbia University Press, 1979 (*Supplement* published quarterly).
Foundation Grants Index, 1970/1–; *A Cumulative Listing of Foundation Grants.* Comp. by the Foundation Center. New York: distributed by Columbia University Press, 1972– (annually).
Foundation Research Service. *Foundation Research Service Index.* Washington: 1972–.
Great Britain. Cabinet Office. *Government Research and Development: A Guide to Sources of Information.* London: HMSO, 1974.
Grants Register, 1969/70–; *Postgraduate Awards in the English Speaking World.* Chicago: St James Press, 1969– (every two years).
Guide to European Foundations, 1973–. Milan: Franco Agnelli, 1973–.
Guide to Grants, Loans and Other Types of Government Assistance Available to Students and Educational Institutions. Washington: Public Affairs Press, 1967.
The International Foundation Directory. Consultant ed. H. V. Hodson. Detroit: Gale Research Co.; London: Europa Publishers, [1974].
McClellan, Georgia. *Fellowship Guide for Western Europe.* 2nd ed. Pittsburg: Council for European Studies, 1971 (includes research grants).
Margolin, Judith B. *About Foundations.* New York: Foundation Center, 1977.
Reif-Lehrer, Liane. *Writing a Successful Grant Application.* Boston: Science Books International, 1982.
United Nations Educational, Scientific and Cultural Organisations. Social Science Clearing House. *International Organisations in the Social Sciences: a Summary Description of the Structure and Activities of Non-governmental Organisations Specialised in the Social Sciences and in Consultative Relationship with UNESCO.* 3rd rev. ed., Paris: UNESCO, 1964.
United States Office of Management and Budget. *Catalog of Federal Domestic Assistance.* 1965–. Washington, D.C.: Government Printing Office.
Watson, W. M. R. and Winter, Ross M., comps. *Canadian Universities Guide to Foundations and Similar Grant-Giving Agencies.* Ottawa: Association of Universities and Colleges of Canada. Research and Information Service, 1966.
Whelan, Sara. *Funding Sources for Research in Ireland.* Dublin: National Board for Science and Technology, [1981].
World Index of Social Science Institutions; Research; Advanced Training; Documentation and Professional Bodies. Répertoire mondial des institutions

de sciences sociales. . . Paris: UNESCO, 1970 (updated by *International Social Science Journal*).

Preparing a Curriculum Vitae or Résumé:

Angel, Juvenal L. *Specialised Résumés for Executives and Professionals.* New York: Regents Publishing Co., 1967.

McDaniels, Carl. *Developing a Professional Vita or Résumé.* Garrett Park, Md.: Garrett Park Press, 1978.

Résumé Service. *Résumés that Get Jobs: How to Write Your Best Résumé.* Edited by Jean Reed. New York: Arco Publishing, 1976.

Smith, Michael Holley. *The Résumé Writer's Handbook: A Manual for Writing Résumés.* [New York]: Smith, 1978.

Subscription Services:

(This is a brief selection from the many services available)

Foundation Center Associates Program. 888 Seventh Ave, New York, New York, 10106; 1001 Connecticut Avenue, N.W. Suite 938, Washington, D.C. 20036 (access to computer searches of Foundation Grants Data Bank).

Grantsmanship Center. 1031 South Grand Avenue, Los Angeles, Calif., 90015 (publications, workshops).

Taft Information System. 1000 Vermont Ave, N.W., Washington, D.C. 20005 (publications).

Grant Information System (database of the online bibliographic retrieval system ORBIT).

ORYX Press Grant Information System. 5024 N. 45th Place, Phoenix 85018 (publications).

Writing Proposals:

Brodsky, Jean, ed. *The Proposal Writer's Swipe File.* Washington, D.C.: Taft Products, 1973.

Denham, Woodrow W. 'Research Design and Research Proposal Checklists.' *Anthropology Newsletter* 20 (April 1979): 9-11.

Hillman, Howard and Abarbanel, Karin. *The Art of Winning Foundation Grants.* New York: Vanguard Press, [1975].

Hillman, Howard and Natale, Kathryn. *The Art of Winning Government Grants.* New York: Vanguard Press, [1977].

MacIntyre, Michael. *How to Write a Proposal.* Washington, D.C.: Education. Training and Research Sciences Corporation, 1971.

White, Virginia P. *Grants: How to Find Out About Them and What to Do Next.* New York: Plenum Press, 1975.

Urgo, Louis A. *Models for Money: Obtaining Government and Foundation Grants and Assistance.* 2nd ed. Boston: Suffolk University Management Education Center, 1978.

XIV. Ethical Considerations

YOU ARE trying to discover what situations precipitate child-beating. A good way would be to observe and listen to members of a self-help group of child-beaters, but you would have to join the group and represent yourself as having engaged in child-abuse.

A sociologist studying drug addiction in the local school system had so much harassment and obstruction from school officials that he could not complete his research. You think the research was a good idea and would like to try it yourself, but think that if you said you were studying leisure and recreation preferences, the officials might be more co-operative.

An organisation has offered to give you badly-needed research money for your study in a community in which many of the members are recipients of public assistance funds. You suspect the organisation is associated with a group which disseminates racist propaganda and which might be able to use some of your data out of context. You are considering taking the money, however, because otherwise the research will not get done.

You are commissioned to do a study to see whether a new system of decision-sharing has improved workers' attitudes towards the factory they work in. It has not, but you think the system is more democratic and just. To recommend the new system, you do not have to change any data; all you have to do is leave out a few findings. The factory will be a more humane place to work.

You are studying how practically people act in emergencies. You tell people in a shopping centre that a bomb has exploded in one of the shops, seriously injuring many inside. The information you get will be useful for training people to meet real emergencies.

Are you justified in doing any of the above?

Many ethical principles for operating in your own society are based upon a combination of sensitivity, courtesy and horse sense. Some are embodied in law; others are simply convention, but equally important. Ethical responsibilities fall into several categories:

1. Responsibility to those studied

There are some specific ethical points to observe, but basically, one important way to protect everyone's rights is to develop the right attitude. Put yourself in the other person's situation whenever possible. Do not think of those you study as 'subjects'; they are people with dignity, feelings and rights. This is easier to understand when the people studied are similar to you in culture, class, religion, sex and so forth. It is more difficult to appreciate the finer concerns of people who are very unlike you and who perhaps have standards and viewpoints which you do not share.

As a researcher, your first responsibility is to the individuals you study, and your research must not interfere with their physical, social or mental welfare. The people you study have a right to remain anonymous, unless (a) you have reached an agreement to the contrary; and (b) they understand the consequences of not remaining anonymous, as well as such consequences can be predicted. This means insuring that in your final paper individuals cannot be identified. Simply changing their names does not necessarily satisfy this requirement. Describing a person as a 'priest' when he is the only priest in the community does not, either. On the other hand, it may change the whole meaning of what you are trying to convey if, in your effort to protect his identity, you give him a new occupation – 'a leading businessman', for example. It is your responsibility to figure out how to convey the sense of your information while simultaneously respecting the individual's right to privacy. This responsibility for respecting the privacy of people extends to photographs, tape recordings and any other techniques you may use.

The aims of the research should be explained to the person being studied, and the more he or she is to be involved, the more essential it is that the person understand what you intend to do. Similarly, any repercussions or consequences of the research which you can reasonably anticipate should be made known to the people who are likely to be affected. This requirement does not imply that you must be a seer — the level of predictability in the social sciences, for example, is rather low in many cases, and you also cannot be expected to anticipate freakish consequences. If your project is intended or is likely to lead to change in the lives of individuals or the community, you should involve those who will receive the change, not only because it is ethically desirable, but also because voluntary change programmes rarely work if they do not have the co-operation and participation of the recipients. The aims and needs of the affected people or group must be taken into account. Sometimes they can participate actively in planning the research, and be involved at various other stages of the work.

A person has the right to be informed of any considerations which might reasonably be expected to affect his or her decision to participate in your study, and to choose not to be involved at any time. In some situations, this means that you cannot conduct the study; in others, if the omission does not distort the results, you can simply leave the person out.

Sometimes, particularly when you are doing participant observation, people may not even know that they are involved; in such cases, you must act as if they had chosen not to be involved, and take every precaution to protect their privacy.

You must be particularly careful if your research involves people less privileged or powerful than yourself, as much social science research does. Prisoners, the mentally retarded, poor people, children and members of some minority groups, for example, often provide easy research situations because someone else, usually a middle-class person who has power over them, makes the decision as to whether they should participate. The people you are actually studying may have had no part in the decision-making and no understanding of what the consequences of the research will be. It is your responsibility to see to it that they can make as informed a choice as possible.

Finally, the results of your study should be available not only to the sponsors of your research, if you have sponsors, but also to the public, and especially, where possible, to those involved in the study. Ideally, your raw data should be available to the scientific community for examination and further analysis. However, you have no professional obligation to share with *anyone* raw data which allows individuals to be identified, and these data, in fact, should probably be destroyed when they are no longer needed. Legally, however, your notes can be subpoenaed by courts, and if you intend to make your raw data available to other researchers, participant observation material and interviews should be recorded with this consideration in mind. Some might argue that you should be able to trust other researchers. You should be, but in the last analysis, you are responsible for protecting the people you study.

In addition to sharing the results of your study, you should also give appropriate compensation to the people you study. This may simply mean providing company or an opportunity to give their opinions. Making your research skills available for small projects, or teaching people how to track down information for themselves is often appreciated. In some cases, people may have to be compensated financially for their time or expertise, especially if a person is losing paid time at his or her job by helping you.

2. Responsibility to science

You are responsible for carrying out and presenting your research truthfully, without distortion or suppression of relevant material. You must clarify any distortion of your results by sponsors or others. No scientist can be completely objective; he or she can, however, report methods and data as completely and accurately as possible, and let readers make their own analysis.

Faking and dishonesty in research do occur; not only are they a considerable disservice to the growth of human knowledge, but they can also reflect upon the discipline you represent, if you are professionally trained; and they can also throw your subject into disrepute so that other people are reluctant to do research or to provide funds for research.

3. Responsibility to sponsors

If an agency or organisation sponsors your research, it has certain rights, in addition to the results of the research. These include an assumption that you have correctly represented yourself, your credentials, and the aims, methods, projected costs and completion date of your research. You, on the other hand, can reject sponsorship by a particular body if you disagree with their aims or orientation, or mistrust the use to which they may put the research.

Except in special cases, such as for reasons of national security, and certain industrial research, a sponsor should not restrict the publication or circulation of the research information. The sponsor does *not* have a right to your raw data or any material which would destroy the anonymity of those studied. If you publish your research, you should acknowledge the financial support or assistance of the sponsor.

If, after reading this chapter, you think the answer to any of the questions posed at the beginning of this chapter is 'yes' here are some more detailed discussions of the issues:

Boruch, Robert F. *Assuring the Confidentiality of Social Data.* Philadelphia: University of Pennsylvania Press, 1979.

Bower, Robert T. *Ethics in Social Research.* New York: Praeger Publishers, 1978.

Diner, Edward, and Crandall, Rick. *Ethics in Social and Behavioural Research.* London: University of Chicago Press, 1978.

Reynolds, Paul Davidson. *Ethical Dilemmas and Social Science Research.* San Francisco: Jossey-Bass Publishers, 1979.

References Cited

Armor, David J., and Arthur S. Crouch
  1972   DATA-TEXT Primer. New York: Free Press.
Akeroyd J., and A. Foster
  1979   Online Information Services in U.K. Academic Libraries.
          Online Review 3: 195-204.
Arensberg, Conrad M., and Solon T. Kimball
  1965   Culture and Community. New York: Harcourt, Brace and World.
Babbie, Earl
  1973   Survey Research Methods. Belmont, Calif.: Wadsworth Publishing Co.
  1979   The Practice of Social Research. Belmont, Calif.: Wadsworth Pub. Co.
Bailey, Kenneth D.
  1978   Methods of Social Research. New York: Free Press.
Bales, Robert F.
  1952   Some Uniformities of Behaviour in Small Social Systems.
          In Reading in Social Psychology. Rev. ed. Guy E. Swanson, et al., eds.
          New York: Holt, Rinehart and Winston.
Barass, Robert
  1978   Scientists Must Write: A Guide to Better Writing for Scientists,
          Engineers and Students. New York: John Wiley & Sons.
Benedict, Ruth F.
  1946   The Chrysanthemum and the Sword: Patterns of Japanese Culture.
          Boston: Houghton Mifflin Co.
Birdwhistell, Ray L.
  1970   Kinesics and Context: Essays on Body Motion Communication.
          Philadelphia: University of Pennsylvania Press.
Bradburn, Norman M., and Seymour Sudman
  1979   Improving Interview Method and Questionnaire Design: Response
          Effects to Threatening Questions in Survey Research. San Franciso:
          Jossey-Bass Publishers, 1979.
Denzin, Norman K.
  1978 Triangulation: A Case for Methodological Evaluation and Combination.
          In Sociological Methods: A Sourcebook. Norman K. Denzin, ed.
          pp. 339-342. New York: McGraw-Hill Book Company.
Ford, Percy, and Grace Ford
  1955   A Guide to Parliamentary Papers: What They Are: How to Find
          Them: How to Use Them. Oxford: Basil Blackwell.
Hillman, Howard, and Karin Abarbanel
  [1975] The Art of Winning Foundation Grants. New York: Vanguard Press.
Hoffman, Banesh
  1972   Albert Einstein. Creator and Rebel. New York: New American
          Library, 1972.
Hoinville, Gerald, and Roger Jowell, et al.
  1978   Survey Research Practice. London: Heineman Educational Books.

Kane, Eileen
  1977   The Last Place God Made: Traditional Economy and New Industry in
          Rural Ireland. New Haven, Conn.: Human Relations Area Files Press.

Mac Gréil, Mícheál
  1977   Prejudice and Tolerance in Ireland. Dublin: Research Section,
          College of Industrial Relations.

Mitchell, John
  1974   How to Write Reports. Glasgow: Fontana/Collins.

Moore, Sharon
  1980   A Comparison of the Three Major Distributors of Online Bibliographic
          Services. Mimeographed: College Park, Maryland, College of Library
          and Information Sciences, University of Maryland.

Moser, Claus Adolf, and G. Kalton
  1971   Survey Methods in Social Investigation. 2nd ed. New York: Basic
          Books.

Murphy, Catriona
  1982   Personal communication.

National Board for Science and Technology
  1980   Science Budget. Dublin: The Board.

Parten, Mildred
  1950   Surveys, Polls and Samples: Practical Procedures. New York: Harper
          and Row Publishers.

Pelto, Pertti J.
  1970   Anthropological Research: The Structure of Inquiry. New York:
          Harper and Row Publishers.

Royal Anthropological Institute
  1951   Notes and Queries on Anthropology. 6th ed. London: Routledge
          and Kegan Paul.

Shearman, Hugh
  1944   The Citation of British and Irish Parliamentary Papers of the Nine-
          teenth and Twentieth Centuries. Irish Historical Studies 4:33-37.

Solomon, R. L.
  1949   Extension of Control Group Design. Psychological Bulletin
          46: 137-150.

Spradley, James P.
  1979   The Ethnographic Interview. New York: Holt, Rinehart and Winston.

Spradley, James P., and David W. McCurdy
  1972   The Cultural Experience. Chicago: Science Research Associates.

Tomberg, Alex
  1979   The Development of Commercially Available Databases in Europe.
          Online Review 3: 343-353.

Townsend, Peter
  1957   The Family Life of Old People: An Inquiry in East London.
          Free Press.

Tuchman, Barbara
  1978   A Distant Mirror: The Calamitous 14th Century. New York:
          Ballantine Books.

Turabian, Kate L.
  1955 A Manual for Writers of Term Papers, Theses and Dissertations.
        Chicago: University of Chicago Press.
University of Michigan
  1976 Interviewer's Manual. Ann Arbor, Mich.: Survey Research Center,
        Institute for Social Research.
Webb, Eugene J.; Donald T. Campbell; Richard Schwartz; and Lee Sechrest
  1966 Unobstrusive Measures: Nonreactive Research in the Social Sciences.
        Chicago: Rand McNally & Co.
White, Virginia P.
  1975 Grants: How to Find Out About Them and What to Do Next.
        New York: Plenum Press, 1975.
Williams, Martha E.
  1980 Data Bases. *In* Guide to Reference Books, 9th ed. Supplement.
        Eugene P. Sheehy, ed. pp. 240-246. Chicago: American Library
        Association.

Subject Index